IMAGES
of America

AROUND BALLENTINE

ON THE COVER: The 1964–1965 fifth-grade class of Martha Ballentine attended the original Dutch Fork Elementary School, located near the district office on Highway 76. The present Dutch Fork Elementary is still located on Highway 76 but is several miles away, closer to Irmo. (Courtesy of Mike Bull.)

IMAGES
of America

AROUND BALLENTINE

Marilyn Bull

ARCADIA
PUBLISHING

ISBN 978-0-7385-6828-7

Published by Arcadia Publishing
Charleston SC, Chicago IL, Portsmouth NH, San Francisco CA

Printed in the United States of America

Library of Congress Control Number: 2008937170

For all general information contact Arcadia Publishing at:
Telephone 843-853-2070
Fax 843-853-0044
E-mail sales@arcadiapublishing.com
For customer service and orders:
Toll-Free 1-888-313-2665

Visit us on the Internet at www.arcadiapublishing.com

To my husband, Jim, whose love, strength, and constant optimism have always strengthened me. And to my daughters, Jenny and Melissa, of whom I am very proud.

Contents

ACKNOWLEDGMENTS

There are so many people I would like to thank for sharing their pictures, stories, and time. Without some of the personal stories, this book would not have been possible.

First I would like to thank my editor, Maggie Bullwinkel, for her assistance, encouragement, and prodding. If not for that, this book might not been written.

I would like to thank the South Carolina Department of Archives and History, Guy Cruse and Bethel Lutheran Church for *A History of Bethel Evangelical Lutheran Church*, Bryson Lowman for "60 Years of Memories" and his hand-drawn map of Ballentine in 1935, Lexington School District 5 for the use of their copy of *Irmo and the Dutch Fork Legacy*, and Carol Black for her "Ballentine Family History."

If not for my mother-in-law, Myrtle Bull, and Bonnie Stevenson, this book would never been written. They were the inspiration for the book and provided some of the pictures. Pictures not designating a source were provided by Myrtle Bull.

I would also like to thank the following people and businesses for providing the photographs, oral history, or both, even if an image was not used: Bryson Lowman, Myrtle Bull, Tom Rhodes, Marvie Quattlebaum, William Sheely, Ballentine and Dutch Fork Civic Association, Agnew Lake Service/Norman Agnew, Barbara Porter, Pat Derrick, Lucy Lindler, John Bouknight, Ann Cameron, Dot Prater, Kay Shealy, Jonnie Mae Sites, Barbara Thomas, Alice Ruth Ballentine, Jim Bull, Furman Younginer, Eugene Brantley, Mike Bull, Caroll Jacob Lorick, Robert F. Lorick, Laura Bull, Fred Riddle Jr., Lake Murray Marina, Christine Chitwood, Buster Rhame, Jacob Dean and Quentin Meetze.

Last but not least, I would like to thank my husband, Jim, who is a constant inspiration, and my daughters, Jenny and Melissa, for their assistance especially when I accidentally deleted one-third of my book! My daughters were able to retrieve some of the information. I also want to thank my son-in-law Jacob for his photographic assistance. The love and support of my family has helped me when this project seemed overwhelming.

INTRODUCTION

Nestled between Lake Murray and I-26 and along Highway 26 are White Rock and Ballentine. These rural communities were once surrounded by hundreds of acres of farmland but are now considered a suburban community. It is also a part of a bigger area called the Dutch Fork area of South Carolina. Originally the Dutch Fork area included all of the land that lay between the Saluda and Broad Rivers from Columbia to Newberry. Now much of the land is covered by the waters of Lake Murray. The area was originally settled mainly by the German, Swiss, and Dutch. They were described as devoutly religious and hardworking.

Around 1750, a German colony from the Palatinate arrived in South Carolina. A short time after their arrival, a large portion of the settlers moved to the fork of the Saluda and Broad Rivers. They established their homes along the Saluda and the creeks that emptied into the Saluda. One of these creeks was High Hill Creek. In 1762, a date that has been agreed upon since there were no records available to verify the date, the Bethel Congregation at High Hill Creek was formed. In the late 1920s, Bethel and Mount Vernon merged their congregations because of the building of the dam. This meant that Bethel Church at High Hill would be covered by water. The last service was held on September 15, 1929. A number of the graves were not moved because of the rapidly rising water, and a monument was erected listing the names of those whose graves are still beneath the waters of Lake Murray. This marker is in the Bethel Lutheran Church Cemetery in White Rock. The land for the new church was obtained from the Lowman Home.

According to a member of the Ballentine family, Alan Ballentine moved his family to the community in the 1850s. Various members of the Ballentine family operated a gristmill, sawmill, a cotton gin, and later a general store in the following years. They also farmed, like the majority of the landowners around.

The railroad was built in the early 1890s and ran near the Ballentine mill. There was a mail depot and a flagman station located there. There was a device by the railroad track on which mail bags were suspended. The mail car of the train had a metal arm that swung out from the car and scooped up the mail without the train having to stop. The stop became known as Ballentine Mill and later just Ballentine.

The first Ballentine School was built around 1900 and was named after Alan Ballentine. It consisted of three classrooms and a small auditorium and was located where the Food Lion Shopping Center now resides. The school served grades 1 through 10. In 1938, Ballentine closed its doors when a new school, Dutch Fork Elementary, at the fork of Highways 76 and 176 was built. The new Ballentine Elementary opened on August 15, 2002, with 37 homeroom classes.

The Dutch Fork area changed tremendously when construction for the dam was approved. A lot of folks had to sell land that in been in their families for generations to the power company. Some complained they were not paid a fair price for the land. Then they had to find new homes and move out. It was a difficult time; some people were still moving their belongings out as the water was rising. People were working day and night harvesting the crops, and they were even working on Sunday. That was unheard of at the time. Then came the Great Depression. It was a hard time for a lot of families. Many lost their savings when the banks failed. Losing a home had to be rough but then to lose your money on top of that had to have been traumatic. But they carried on, rebuilding their lives. These German descendants have always prided themselves on their hard work ethic.

Around 1929, Eusebius ("Sebe") Ballentine opened the E. A. Ballentine General Store. According to older residents, the store sold a little bit of everything, even Poll-Parrot shoes. There were three stores within 2 miles of each other. John Riddle and Milford Ballentine also had a general store. In the 1950s, Sebe donated space in his store for the post office. Bonnie Stevenson became postmistress and held that position until 1987. Bull Oil Company also worked out of the store from the late 1950s until 2002. The building also housed Farm House Antiques from 1996 to 2006. Farm House Antiques was operated by Dr. Carlos Gibbons. Dr. Gibbons is a retired educator and professor and was executive director of SCEA (South Carolina Education Association). Now the building is home to High Noon, a gift shop, and also houses a frame shop in the back room.

The Ballentine/White Rock area is also home to two large marinas on Lake Murray. Lighthouse Marina is near White Rock, and Lake Murray Marina and Yacht Club is in Ballentine. Both of the marinas have a restaurant and bar on the premises that offer live entertainment in the summertime, usually on weekends. Both have boat slips, boat storage, boat rentals, gas pumps, and marine supplies. They also have public launch areas where people can launch their boats if they do not live on the lake or have a boat slip.

This area of the lake is a wonderful place to live. The interstate is within minutes, the lake is nearby, and it is a 10–15-minute drive to Harbison Boulevard, where there are a variety of retail stores and restaurants. The area still has the feel of a small community, but it is growing rapidly and changing even as I write this. Each generation has its stories. Some are interesting, some are funny, some are sad, and some are unbelievable.

When we think of history, we think maybe of the Civil War, George Washington, the first airplane flight of Wilbur and Orville Wright, the early Egyptians. We do not immediately think of our parents or grandparents in historical terms. This is what Images of America does by publishing these books. It is a way of preserving everyday life because if they are not preserved, the stories and pictures will be forever lost.

One

The Early Years

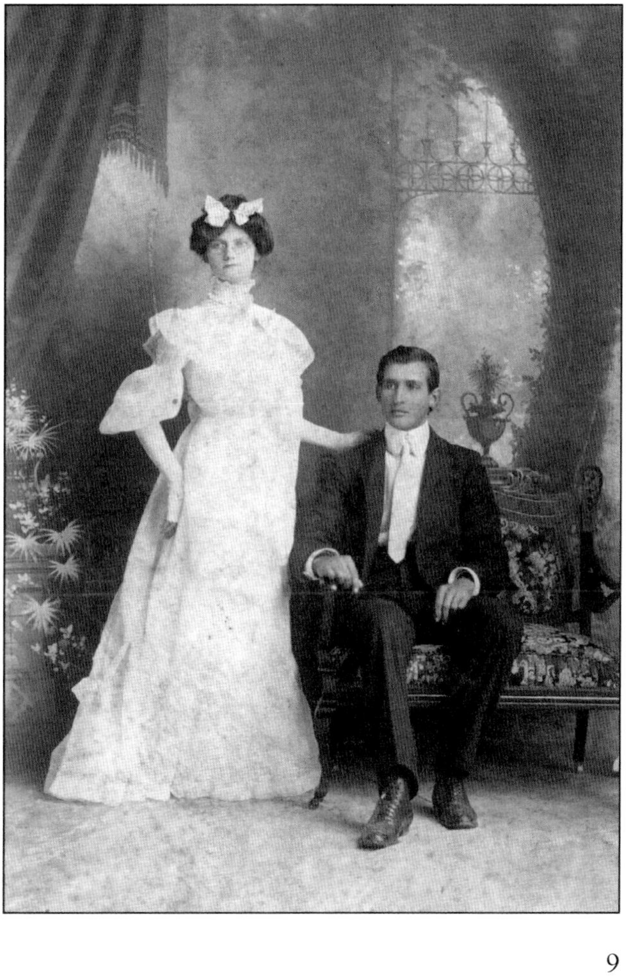

Jeanette Boozer and Eusebius Ballentine were married in 1903. This is the same year the Wright brothers had their first successful flight at Kitty Hawk and Dr. Ernest Pfenning of Chicago became the first owner of a Ford Model A. These two events were to have a tremendous impact on the way of life in the following years. Sebe and Jennie had six children. The first child, Verta, was born in December 1904 and their last child, Myrtle, was born in November 1923. The other children were Blanche, Rudolph, Eugene, and Bonnie.

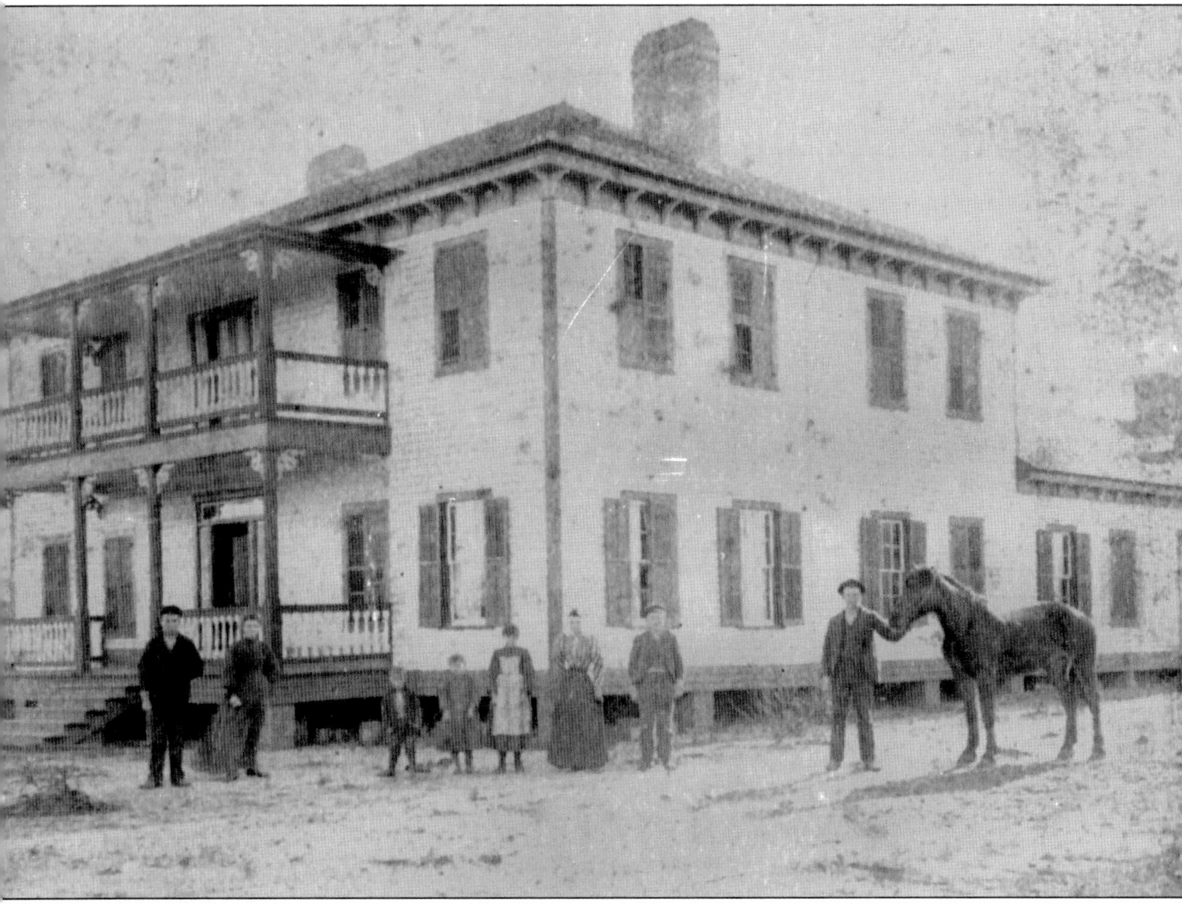

The Sheely House was the home of George Robert and Laura-Ann Elvira Sheely. George served in the Civil War and built this house after the war, sometime between 1865 and 1870, on the family land. The family originally acquired the land, over 400 acres, in 1752 through a land grant to John Shely (Sheely). The photograph was taken in 1895. In 1934, George Johnston Sheely bought the house from his sister, Bettie Lee Boozer. That same year, the house, a landmark in the community, was remodeled to add electricity and plumbing. The original house had eight 14-by-16-foot rooms, four downstairs and four upstairs, with a fireplace in each room. The kitchen was not attached to the main house when it was first built. At some point, a porch was added. In later years, the house was sold and became a teahouse, but not long after opening, the house burned and a landmark was lost. (Courtesy of Kay Sheely.)

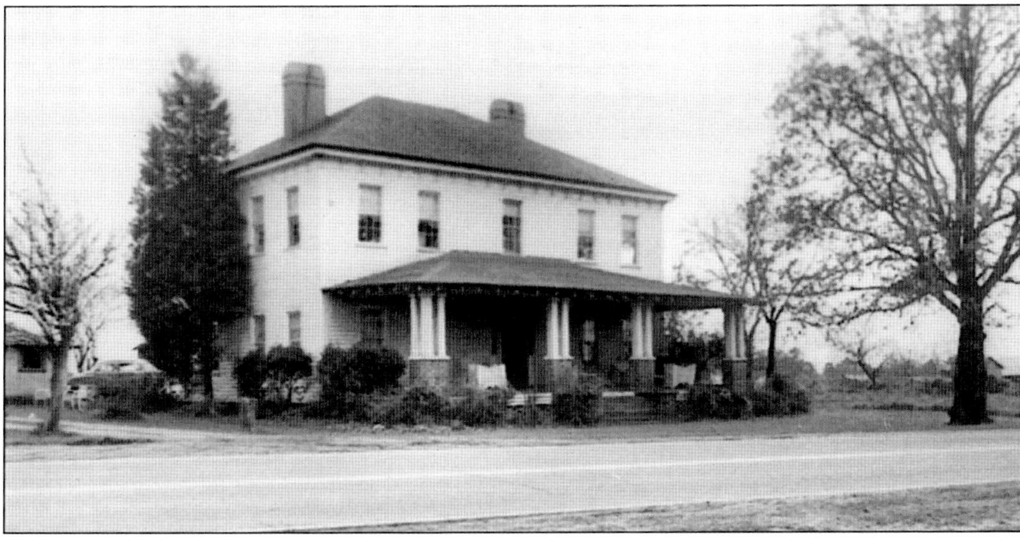

This is the Sheely House as many people remember it. It was originally white, but later it was painted pink and became known as the "Pink House" instead of the Sheely House. Ray Carter was the owner when the house burned, and the fire was attributed to a coffeemaker. (Courtesy of Kay Sheely.)

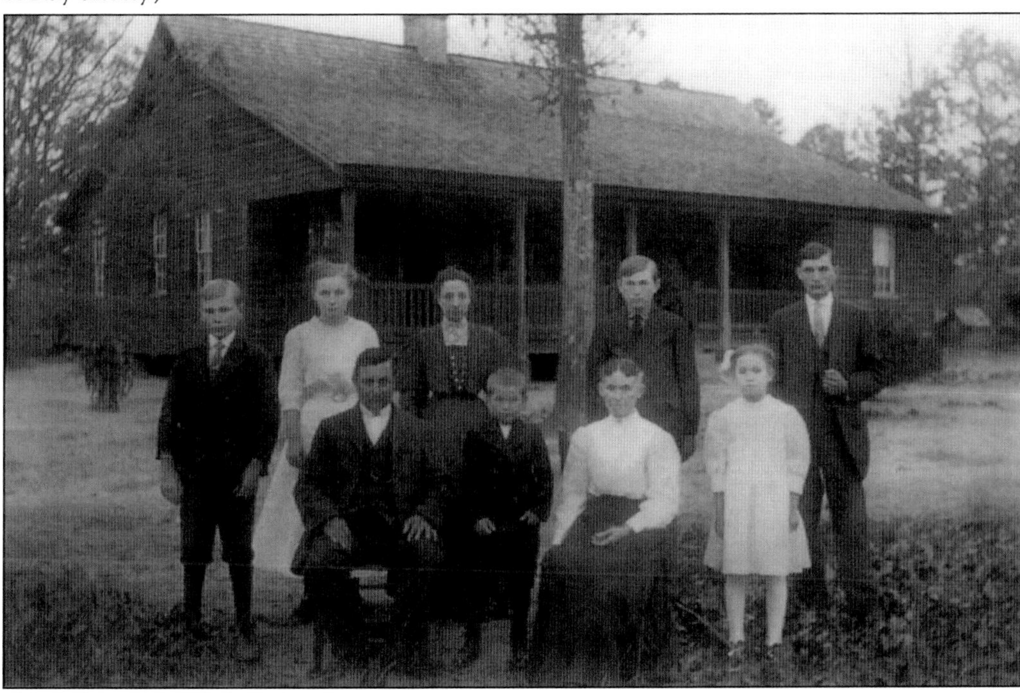

The Meetze family, of Irmo, can trace their ancestors back to Johann Yost Mutze (Meetze), who arrived in South Carolina in 1880 as a soldier in the Hessian Army (which had joined forces with the British in their war against the colonies). After the war, Mutze made his way to the German settlement in Lexington, South Carolina, where he married Anna Margaret Gross. Later descendants are shown posing in front of their home on Farming Creek Road not long after its completion. From left to right are (first row) Fletcher, Vem, Emma, and Annette; (second row) Oscar, Eva, Lizzie, Johnnie, and Gus Meetze. (Courtesy of Quentin Meetze.)

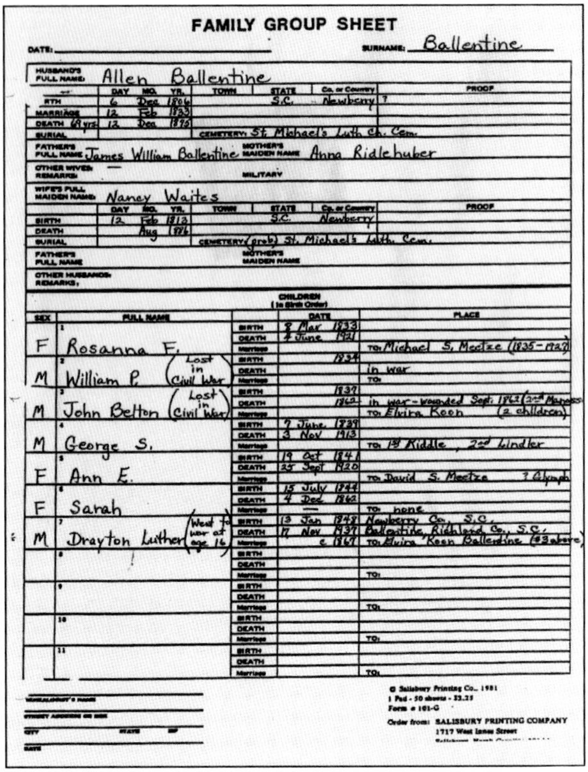

FAMILY GROUP SHEET

DATE: SURNAME: Ballentine

HUSBAND'S FULL NAME: Allen Ballentine

	DAY	MO.	YR.	TOWN	STATE	Co. or Country	PROOF
BIRTH	6	Dec	1806		S.C.	Newberry	?
MARRIAGE	12	Feb	1833				
DEATH 69 yrs	12	Dec	1875				

BURIAL CEMETERY: St. Michael's Luth. Ch. Cem.

FATHER'S FULL NAME: James William Ballentine MOTHER'S MAIDEN NAME: Anna Ridlehuber

OTHER WIVES: — REMARKS: MILITARY

WIFE'S FULL MAIDEN NAME: Nancy Waites

	DAY	MO.	YR.	TOWN	STATE	Co. or Country	PROOF
BIRTH	12	Feb	1813		S.C.	Newberry	
DEATH		Aug	1876				

BURIAL CEMETERY: (prob) St. Michael's Luth. Cem.

FATHER'S FULL NAME MOTHER'S MAIDEN NAME

OTHER HUSBANDS: REMARKS:

CHILDREN (In Birth Order)

SEX	FULL NAME		DATE	PLACE
F	1 Rosanna F.	BIRTH	8 Mar 1833	
		DEATH	4 June 1921	
		Marriage		TO: Michael S. Meetze (1835–1927)
M	2 William P. (Lost in Civil War)	BIRTH	1834	
		DEATH		in war
		Marriage		TO:
M	3 John Belton (Lost in Civil War)	BIRTH	1837	
		DEATH	1862	in war - wounded Sept. 1862 (2nd Manassas)
		Marriage		TO: Elvira Koon (2 children)
M	4 George S.	BIRTH	7 June 1839	
		DEATH	3 Nov 1913	
		Marriage		TO: 1st Kiddle, 2nd Lindler
F	5 Ann E.	BIRTH	19 Oct 1841	
		DEATH	25 Sept 1920	
		Marriage		TO: David S. Meetze ? Glymph
F	6 Sarah	BIRTH	15 July 1844	
		DEATH	4 Dec 1862	
		Marriage	—	TO: none
M	7 Drayton Luther (Went to war at age 16)	BIRTH	13 Jan 1848	Newberry Co., S.C.
		DEATH	17 Nov 1937	Ballentine, Richland Co., S.C.
		Marriage	c 1867	TO: Elvira Koon Ballentine (#3 above)
	8	BIRTH		
		DEATH		
		Marriage		TO:
	9	BIRTH		
		DEATH		
		Marriage		TO:
	10	BIRTH		
		DEATH		
		Marriage		TO:
	11	BIRTH		
		DEATH		
		Marriage		TO:

GENEALOGIST'S NAME

STREET ADDRESS OR BOX

CITY STATE ZIP

DATE

© Salisbury Printing Co., 1981
1 Pad - 50 sheets - $2.25
Form # 101-G
Order from: SALISBURY PRINTING COMPANY
1717 West Innes Street

This is a section of the family tree for the Ballentine family compiled by Carol Black in 1986. She had traced the family back to James William Ballentine, who was born in 1773 and was married to Anna Rosanna Ridlehuber Ballentine, his second wife and sister of his first wife, Mary. He had two children by his first wife and six by his second. It is believed that James was the son of William Ballentine, an immigrant who came to Charleston in 1767 aboard the *Earl of Denegal*, but this has not been proved or disproved. Allen was the first son of William and Anna (the family group shown at left), and Drayton was the youngest child of Allen and Nancy Waites Ballentine. (Courtesy of Carl Black.)

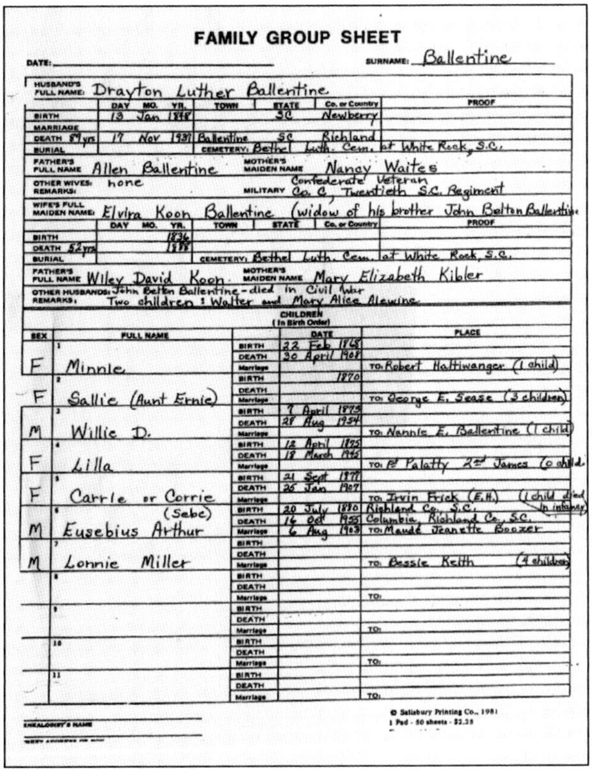

FAMILY GROUP SHEET

DATE: SURNAME: Ballentine

HUSBAND'S FULL NAME: Drayton Luther Ballentine

	DAY	MO.	YR.	TOWN	STATE	Co. or Country	PROOF
BIRTH	13	Jan	1848		SC	Newberry	
MARRIAGE							
DEATH 89 yrs	17	Nov	1937	Ballentine	SC	Richland	

BURIAL CEMETERY: Bethel Luth. Cem. at White Rock, S.C.

FATHER'S FULL NAME: Allen Ballentine MOTHER'S MAIDEN NAME: Nancy Waites

OTHER WIVES: none REMARKS: MILITARY: Confederate Veteran Co. C, Twentieth S.C. Regiment

WIFE'S FULL MAIDEN NAME: Elvira Koon Ballentine (widow of his brother John Belton Ballentine)

	DAY	MO.	YR.	TOWN	STATE	Co. or Country	PROOF
BIRTH			1836				
DEATH 52 yrs			1888				

BURIAL CEMETERY: Bethel Luth. Cem. at White Rock, S.C.

FATHER'S FULL NAME: Wiley David Koon MOTHER'S MAIDEN NAME: Mary Elizabeth Kibler

OTHER HUSBANDS: John Belton Ballentine - died in Civil War
REMARKS: Two children: Walter and Mary Alice Alewine

CHILDREN (In Birth Order)

SEX	FULL NAME		DATE	PLACE
F	1 Minnie	BIRTH	22 Feb 1868	
		DEATH	30 April 1908	
		Marriage		TO: Robert Haltiwanger (1 child)
F	2 Sallie (Aunt Ernie)	BIRTH	1870	
		DEATH		
		Marriage		TO: George E. Sease (3 children)
M	3 Willie D.	BIRTH	7 April 1873	
		DEATH	28 Aug 1954	
		Marriage		TO: Nannie E. Ballentine (1 child)
F	4 Lilla	BIRTH	12 April 1875	
		DEATH	18 March 1945	
		Marriage		TO: 1st Palatty 2nd James (6 child.)
F	5 Carrie or Corrie	BIRTH	21 Sept 1877	
		DEATH	26 Jan 1907	
		Marriage		TO: Irvin Frick (E.H.) (1 child died in infancy)
M	6 Eusebius Arthur (Sebe)	BIRTH	20 July 1880	Richland Co. S.C.
		DEATH	16 Oct 1955	Columbia, Richland Co. S.C.
		Marriage	6 Aug 1903	TO: Maude Jeanette Boozer
M	7 Lonnie Miller	BIRTH		
		DEATH		
		Marriage		TO: Bessie Keith (4 children)
	8	BIRTH		
		DEATH		
		Marriage		TO:
	9	BIRTH		
		DEATH		
		Marriage		TO:
	10	BIRTH		
		DEATH		
		Marriage		TO:
	11	BIRTH		
		DEATH		
		Marriage		TO:

GENEALOGIST'S NAME

STREET ADDRESS OR BOX

© Salisbury Printing Co., 1981
1 Pad - 50 sheets - $2.25

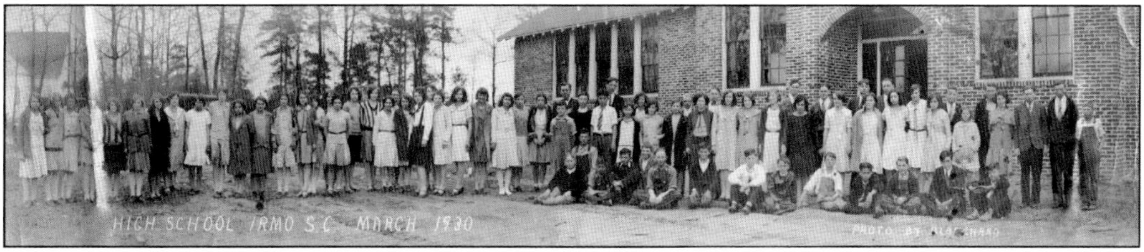

The panoramic picture above shows Irmo High School students in 1930. The photograph was taken in front of the school (now Irmo Elementary) by Blanchard, the name of the photographer listed on the image.

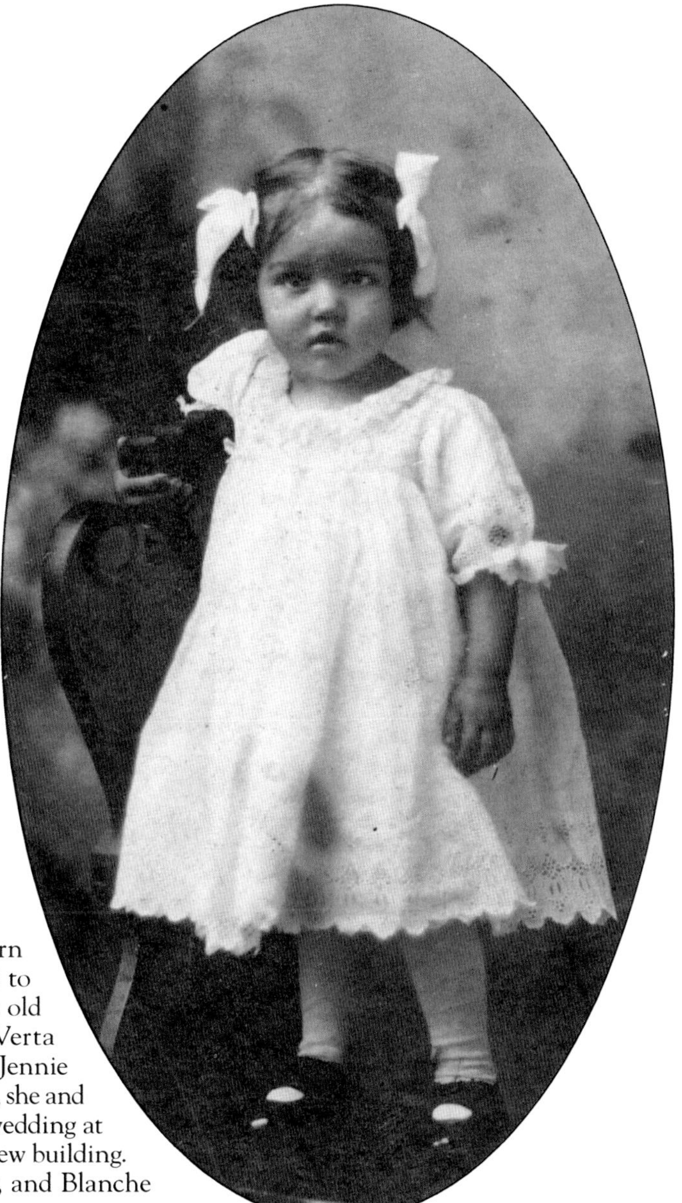

Verta Ballentine Sheely was born December 8, 1904, and she had to be between two and three years old when this picture was taken. Verta was the oldest child of Sebe and Jennie Ballentine. On December 24, 1931, she and her sister Blanche had a double wedding at Bethel, the first wedding at the new building. Verta married W. Curtis Sheely, and Blanche married John W. Derrick.

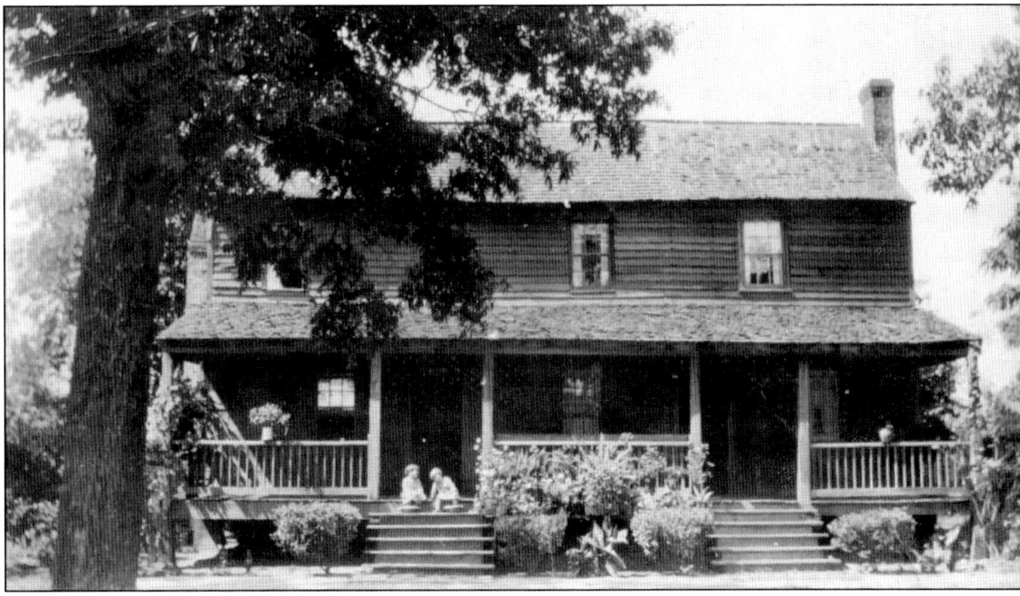

The old Lindler homestead is over 200 years old; years ago (more than anyone can remember), the house was moved from across the railroad tracks and Highway 76 to its present site on Highway 176, where it has stood for many years. It has been remodeled and added on through the years. Recently Wal-Mart bought the Lindler property and is developing it. Wal-Mart did agree with the historical society to save the house and donated land for the house. The house had to be moved again but only a few hundred feet. (Courtesy of Lucy Lindler.)

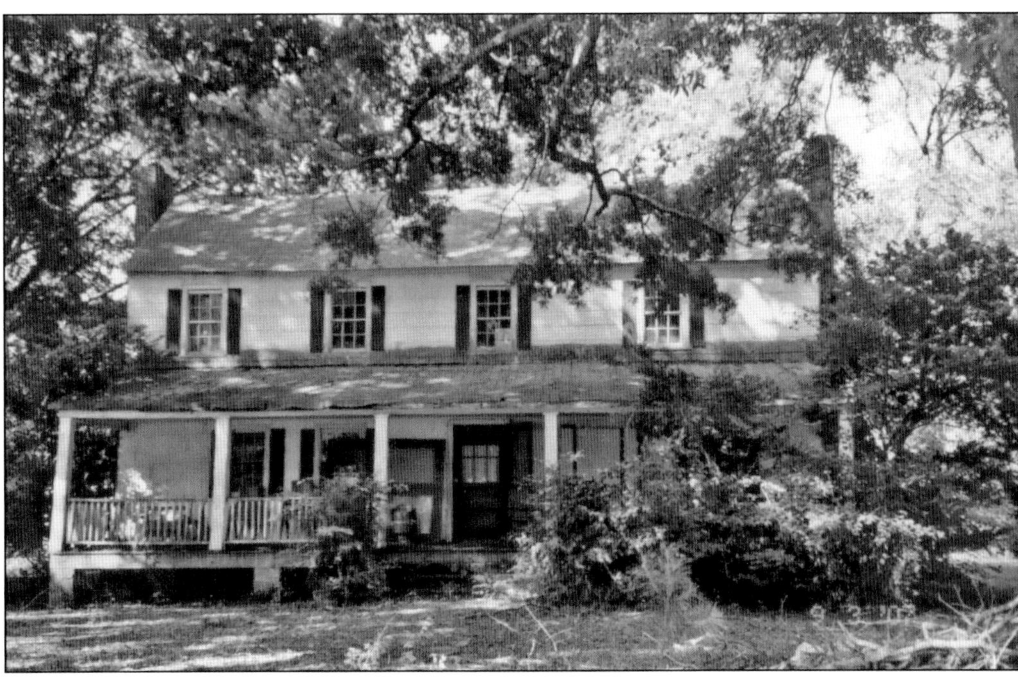

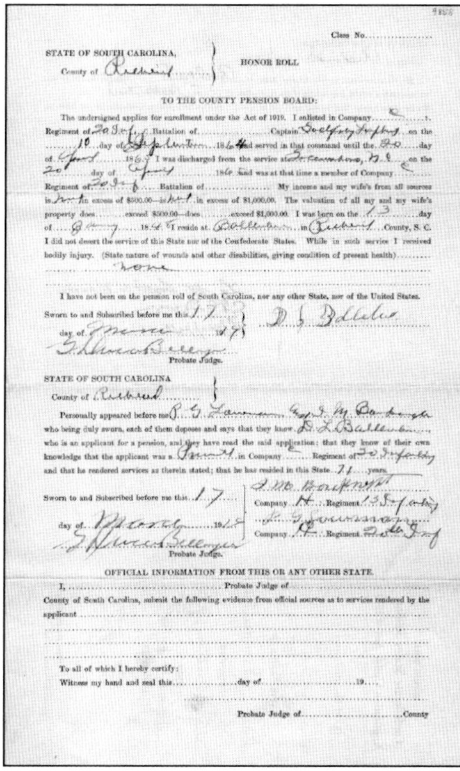
Class No.............

STATE OF SOUTH CAROLINA,
County of Richland

HONOR ROLL

TO THE COUNTY PENSION BOARD:

The undersigned applies for enrollment under the Act of 1919. I enlisted in Company....C....., Regiment of 20 Inf... Battalion of.......... Captain........ on the 10 day of September 1864 and served in that command until the 20 day of April 1865. I was discharged from the service at .... on the 20 day of April 1865 and was at that time a member of Company C, Regiment of 20 Inf, Battalion of........ My income and my wife's from all sources is not in excess of $500.00—is not in excess of $1,000.00. The valuation of all my and my wife's property does........exceed $500.00—does........exceed $1,000.00. I was born on the 13 day of May 1848. I reside at Ballentine in Richland County, S. C. I did not desert the service of this State nor of the Confederate States. While in such service I received bodily injury. (State nature of wounds and other disabilities, giving condition of present health)........ None

I have not been on the pension roll of South Carolina, nor any other State, nor of the United States.

Sworn to and Subscribed before me this 17 day of .... 19.... D. L. Ballentine

Probate Judge.

STATE OF SOUTH CAROLINA
County of Richland

Personally appeared before me .... who being duly sworn, each of them deposes and says that they know D. L. Ballentine, who is an applicant for a pension, and they have read the said application; that they know of their own knowledge that the applicant was a Private in Company........ Regiment of 20 Infantry and that he rendered services as therein stated; that he has resided in this State 71 years.

Sworn to and Subscribed before me this 17 day of .... 19....

Company H Regiment 13 Infantry

Company H Regiment 20 Inf

Probate Judge.

OFFICIAL INFORMATION FROM THIS OR ANY OTHER STATE.

I, ... Probate Judge of .... County of South Carolina, submit the following evidence from official sources as to services rendered by the applicant........................

To all of which I hereby certify:

Witness my hand and seal this............day of............19....

Probate Judge of............County

A state law enacted on December 24, 1887, permitted financially needy Confederate veterans and widows to apply for a pension. Generally, those who were indigent or disabled received a pension. From 1919 to 1925, South Carolina granted pensions to veterans and widows regardless of financial need. Pensions were granted by state of residence instead of the state of service. States had different pension programs: in Arkansas, they began granting pensions in 1891 to indigent Confederate soldiers, then in 1915 began allowing pensions for mothers and widows. (Courtesy of South Carolina Department of Archives and History.)

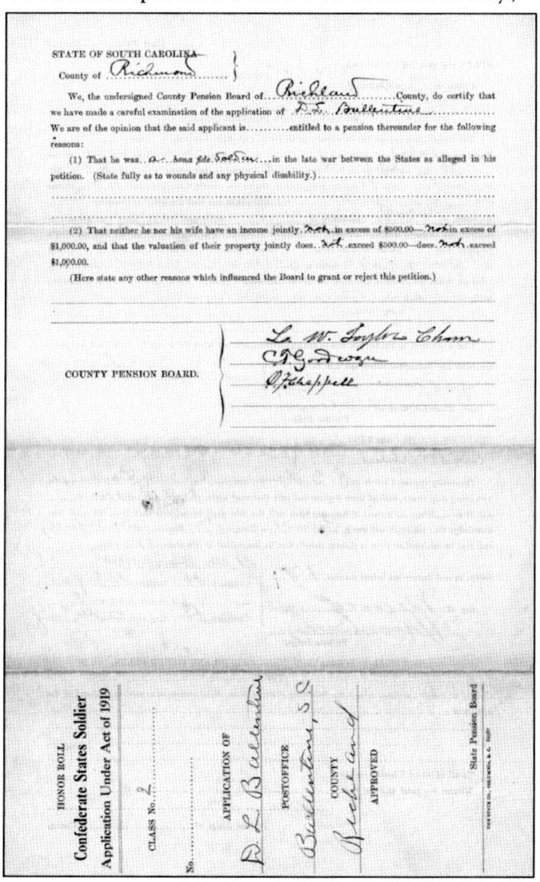
STATE OF SOUTH CAROLINA
County of Richmond

We, the undersigned County Pension Board of Richland County, do certify that we have made a careful examination of the application of D. L. Ballentine............

We are of the opinion that the said applicant is..........entitled to a pension thereunder for the following reasons:

(1) That he was a bona fide soldier in the late war between the States as alleged in his petition. (State fully as to wounds and any physical disability.)........................

(2) That neither he nor his wife have an income jointly not in excess of $500.00—not in excess of $1,000.00, and that the valuation of their property jointly does not exceed $500.00—does not exceed $1,000.00.

(Here state any other reasons which influenced the Board to grant or reject this petition.)

COUNTY PENSION BOARD.

L. W. Taylor Chm
C. N. Goodwyn
C. F. Chappell

HONOR ROLL
Confederate States Soldier
Application Under Act of 1919
CLASS No. 2
No.............
APPLICATION OF D. L. Ballentine
POSTOFFICE Ballentine, S.C.
COUNTY Richland
APPROVED
State Pension Board

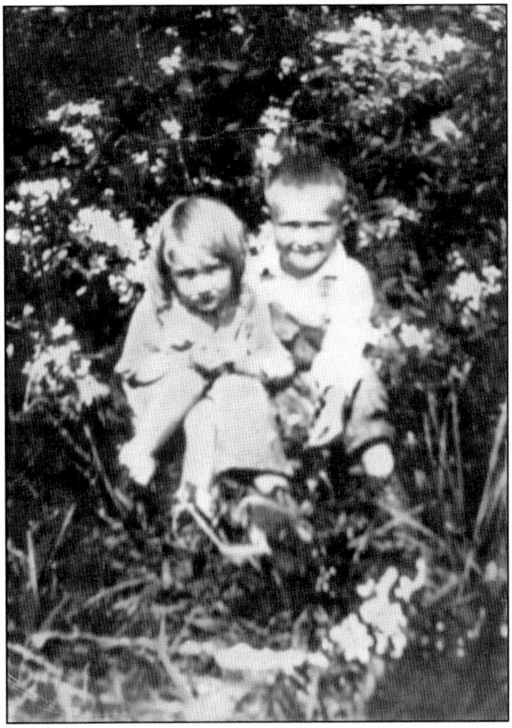

Lucy Lindler and her brother Tom Bailey are playing in their yard in Ballentine. Lucy's name is actually Lena Ruth. One day, her father was loading logs onto a boxcar, and when he opened the car there was a hobo there who said, "Man, me hungry." Her dad, Richard Bailey, took him home and fed him, fixed a place to stay in the barn (the Baileys had 12 children and the house was full), and gave him a job helping at the sawmill. His name was Koger and he began calling Lena Ruth "Lucy Locket" from a nursery rhyme. She was around three years old, and Ruth slowly became known as Lucy. (Courtesy of Lucy Lindler.)

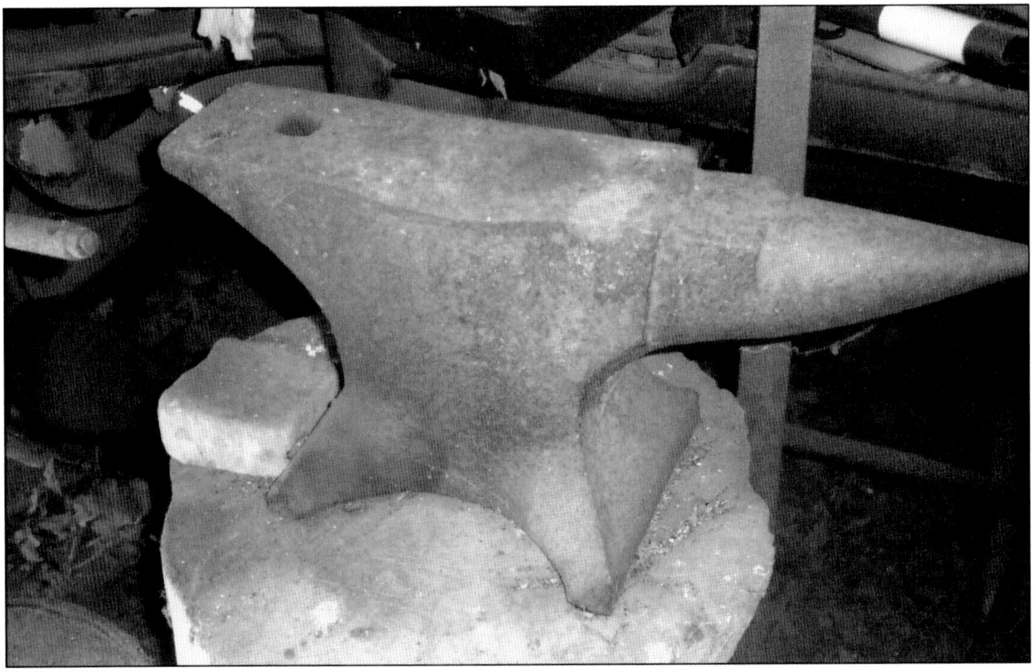

The anvil was used by a blacksmith to forge metal. The primary work surface was known as the face, and the horn of the anvil was used to form round shapes and was used mostly in bending operations. The pad or step of the anvil was used for cutting, and the square hole, called the hardy hole, was used to place specialized forming and cutting tools as well as for punching and bending operations. This anvil belongs to the Meetze family. (Courtesy of Quentin Meetze.)

Samuel F. Sheely was a rural mail carrier for the area. When he started delivering the mail, he rode on horseback; later he delivered the mail on his motorcycle. Besides delivering the mail, he was also a farmer.

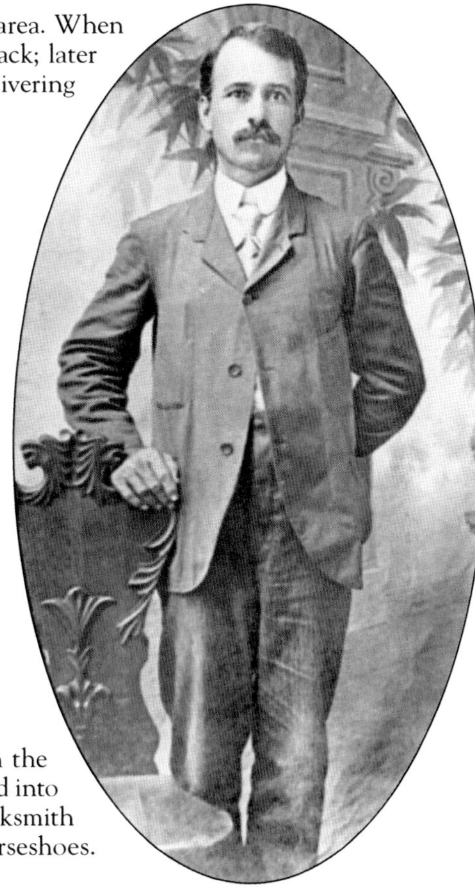

These bellows are still in the blacksmith shop on the Meetze property. The tip of the bellows was inserted into a hole in the side of the furnace, allowing the blacksmith to stoke the fire while making farm tools or horseshoes. (Courtesy of Quentin Meetze.)

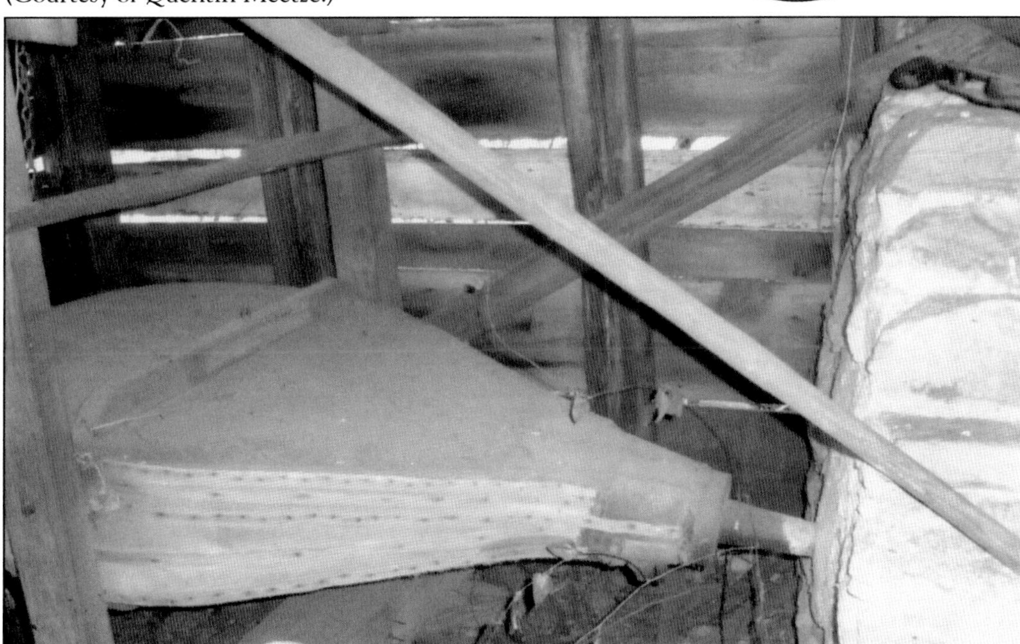

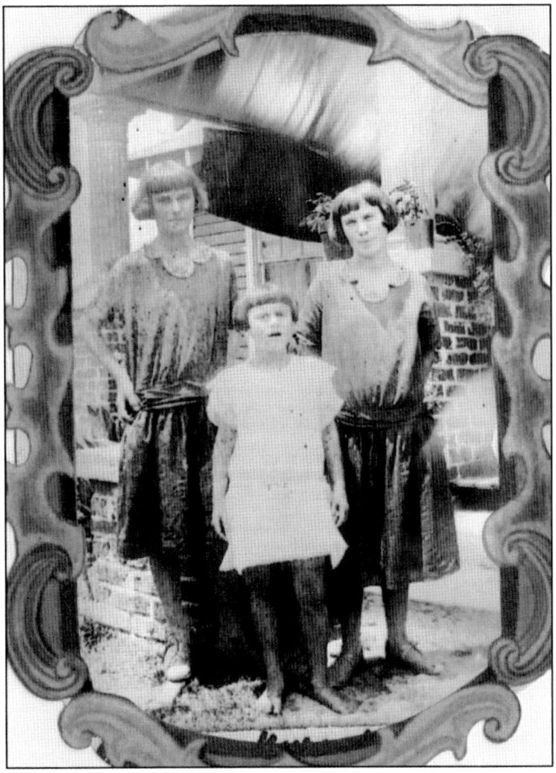

Ehrlene (left), Gurnelle (center), and Ruth Sheely (right) were all dressed up on a Sunday afternoon and had their picture taken at either their house or at a friend's house in the mid-1920s. All sisters would later become teachers, and Gurnelle would write a book on Ballentine called *Reflections of a Soon to be Forgotten Generation.* (Courtesy of Kay Shealy.)

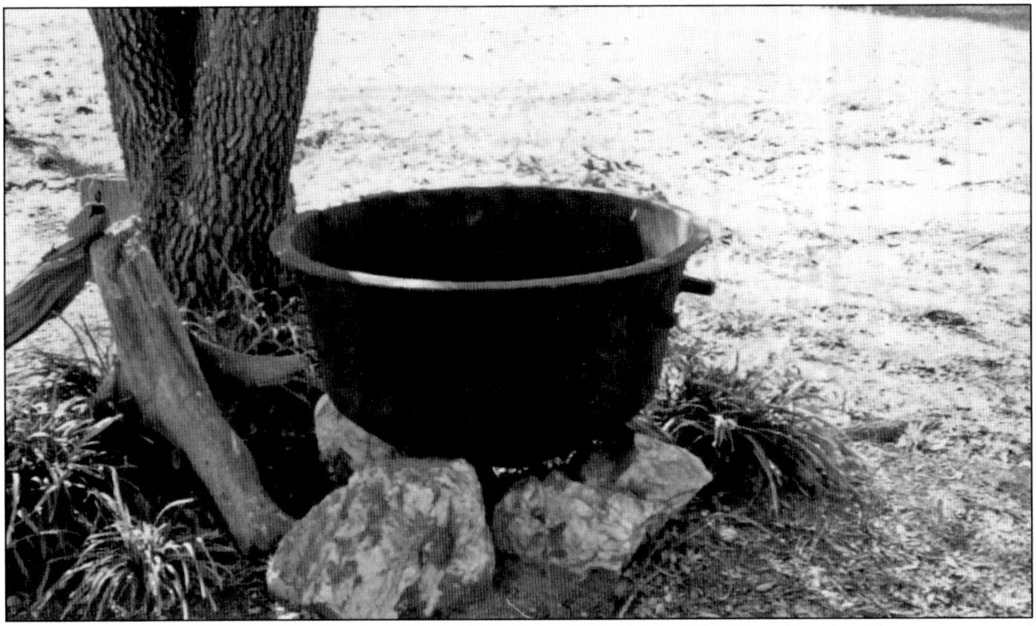

The old black pot, what is known as a syrup kettle, was used to cook juice that had been extracted from cane, usually sorghum, over an outside fire. When the syrup was ready, it was extracted from the kettle into 5-gallon jugs by an opening in the bottom of the kettle. This kettle belonged to Hamer Shealy, the great-grandfather of Jonnie Mae Sites. Jonnie was born in 1924, and this kettle is three generations older than her. (Courtesy of Jonnie Mae Sites.)

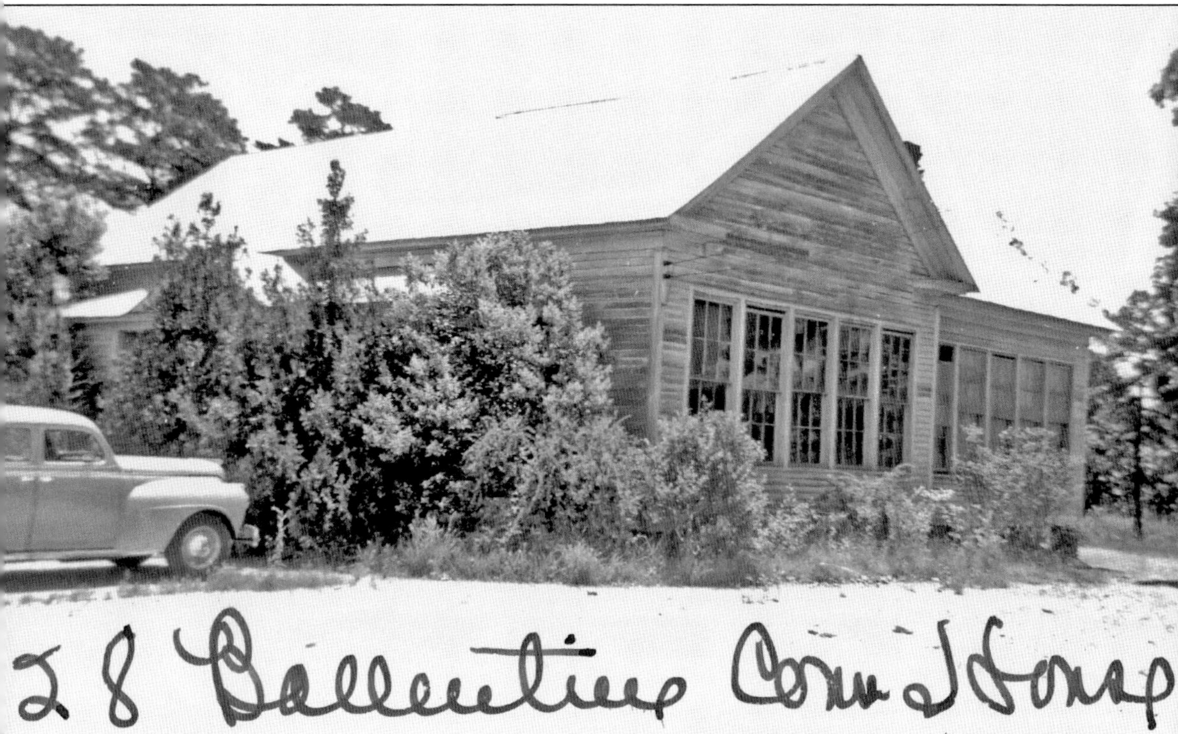

The original Ballentine School was built around 1900 and was named after Alan Ballentine. During the 19th and 20th centuries, the Dutch Fork area had many small community schools. This school was composed of three classrooms and a small auditorium and served grades 1 through 10 originally. Later Piedmont and Ballentine consolidated. Grades one through four went to Piedmont and grades five through seven went to Ballentine. According to Bryson Lowman, in the summer, the men of the community would spread used motor oil all over the floor. The purpose of this was to control the dust. The oil was obtained from Andrew Swygert, who owned a garage across the street. Lowman has wondered what the reaction of today's environmentalists would be, and apparently no one considered the fire hazard. The school closed in 1938 when the new Dutch Fork Elementary School opened. (Courtesy of South Carolina Department of Archives and History.)

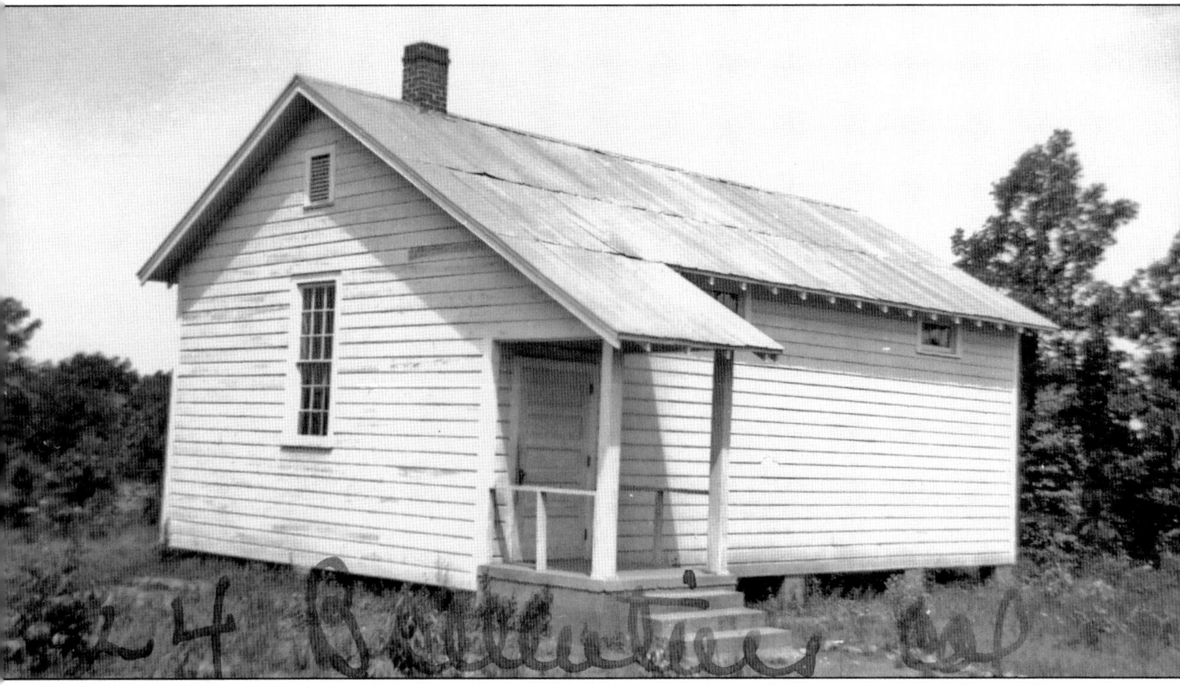

The original school for African American children in the Ballentine area was located between Highways 76 and 176. It later became the home of Jabo Corley, who lived there many years before he passed away. This photograph was taken sometime between 1935 and 1950. (Courtesy of South Carolina Department of Archives and History.)

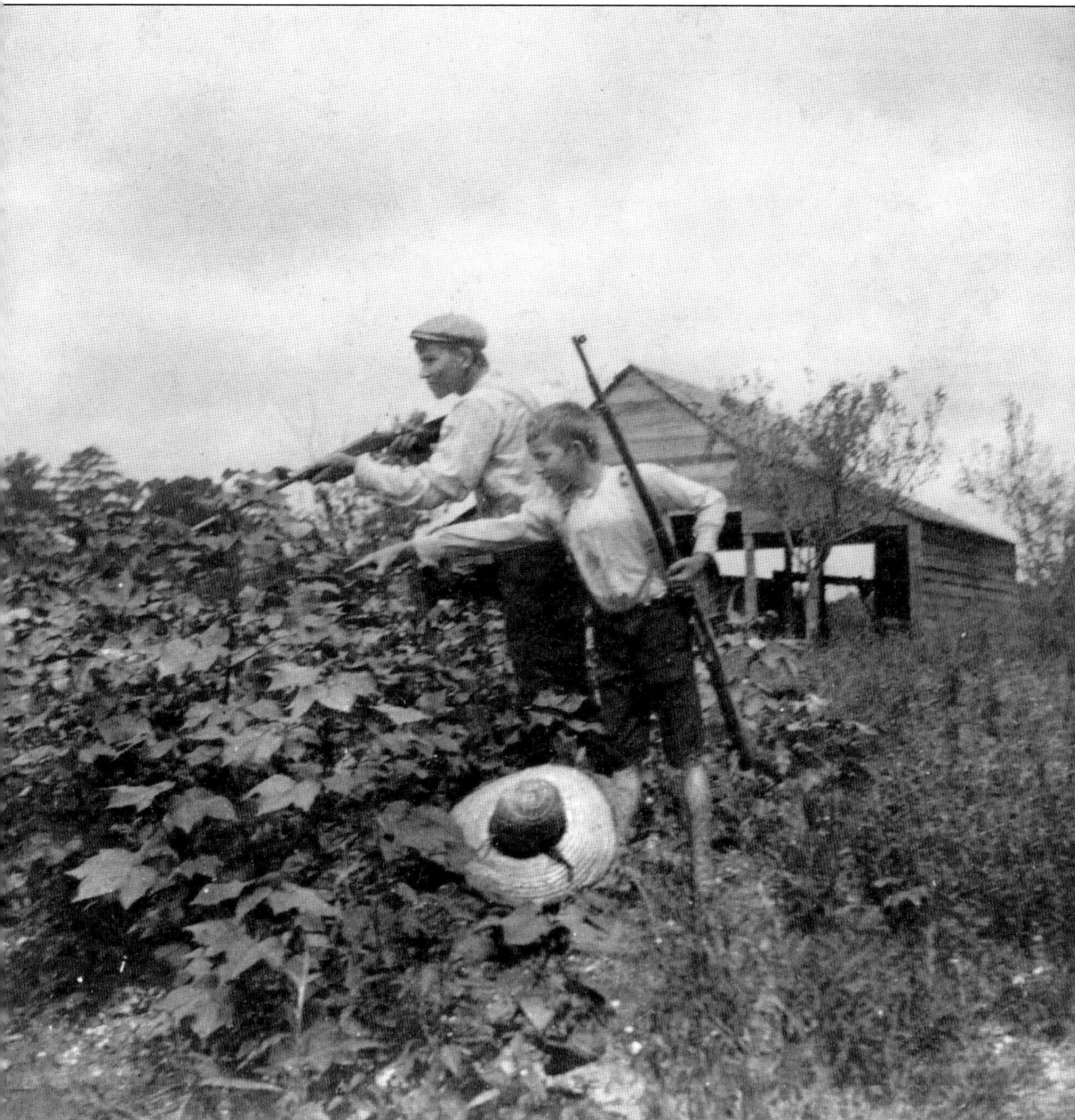

These boys, Ulysses and Madison, were hunting rabbits when this picture was taken. Rabbit hunting was a common sport, especially for young boys, and also kept the rabbits out of the vegetable gardens on the farm. (Courtesy of Ann Cameron.)

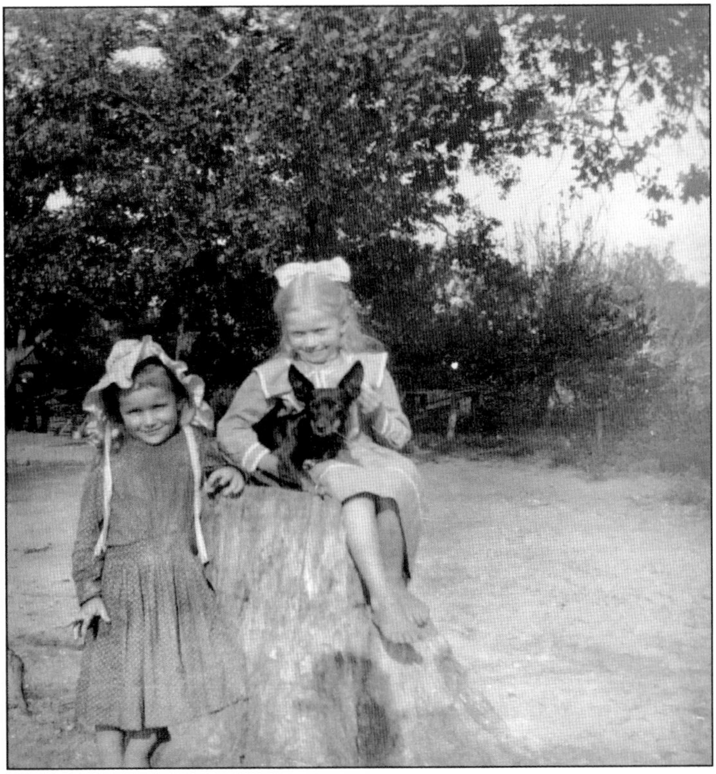

These unidentified girls seem to be enjoying the afternoon while posing with their pet dog. The picture was taken in the early 1900s, according to family members. (Courtesy of Ann Cameron.)

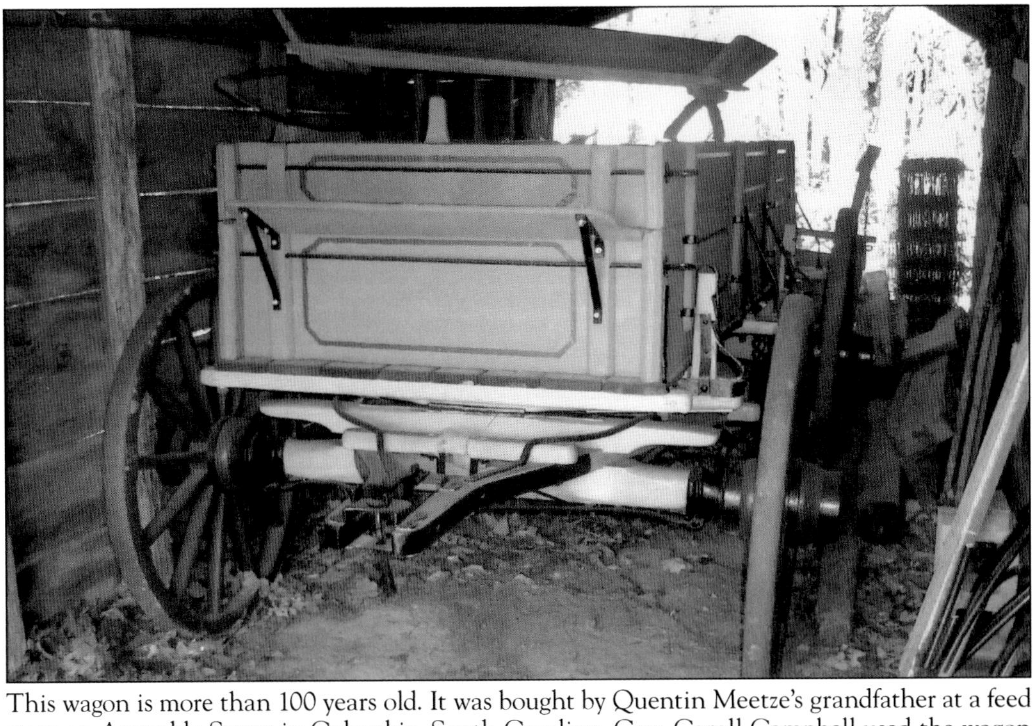

This wagon is more than 100 years old. It was bought by Quentin Meetze's grandfather at a feed store on Assembly Street in Columbia, South Carolina. Gov. Caroll Campbell used the wagon during his inauguration as governor. (Courtesy of Quentin Meetze.)

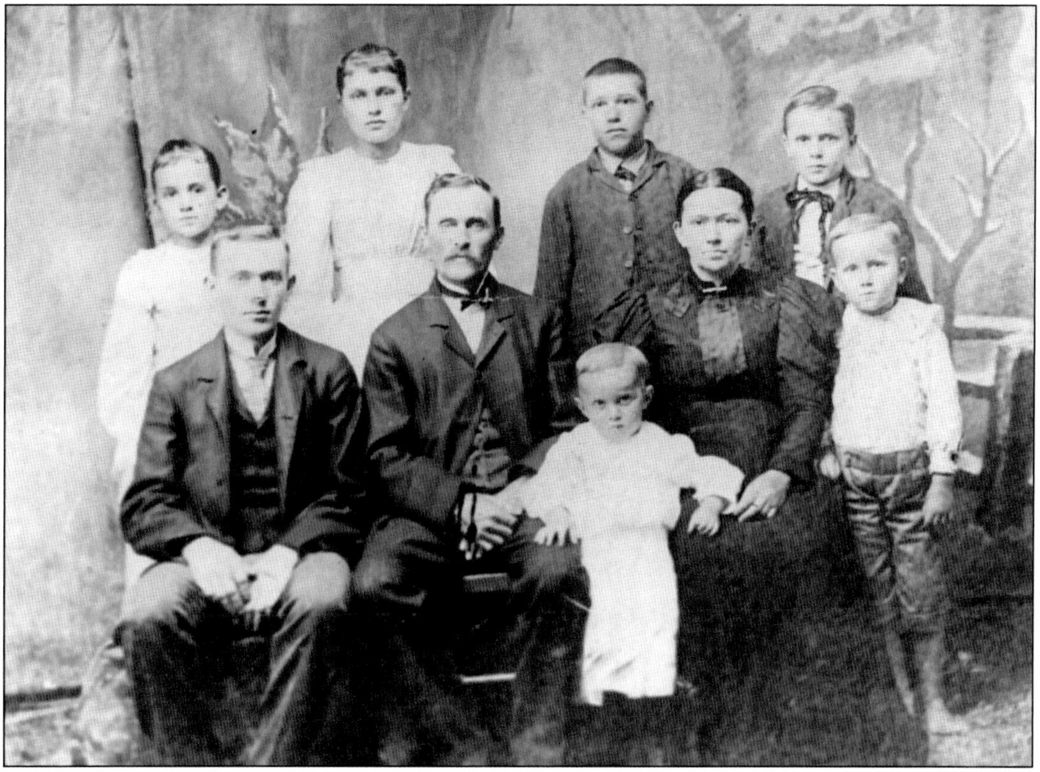

The Bauknight family lived in the Shady Grove area. This family photograph was taken about 1897. From left to right are (first row) Lucius Megnordie Bauknight, George Lucius Bauknight (grandpa), Mary Alice Bickley Bauknight (grandma), and William Emory; (second row) Minnie Mathilda, Lillie, David Lonnie, and Henry Madison. George and Mary Alice were the great-grandparents of Dick Cameron. (Courtesy of Ann Cameron.)

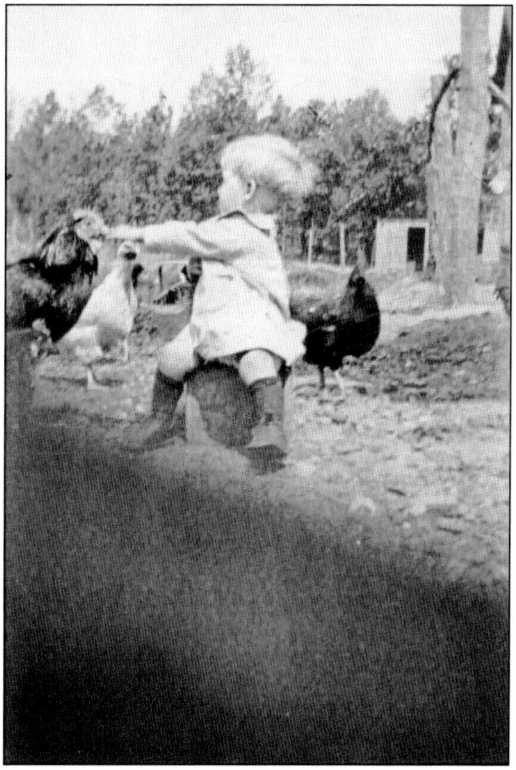

This unidentified child is feeding the chickens and does not appear to be afraid. The picture was taken in the mid-1920s.

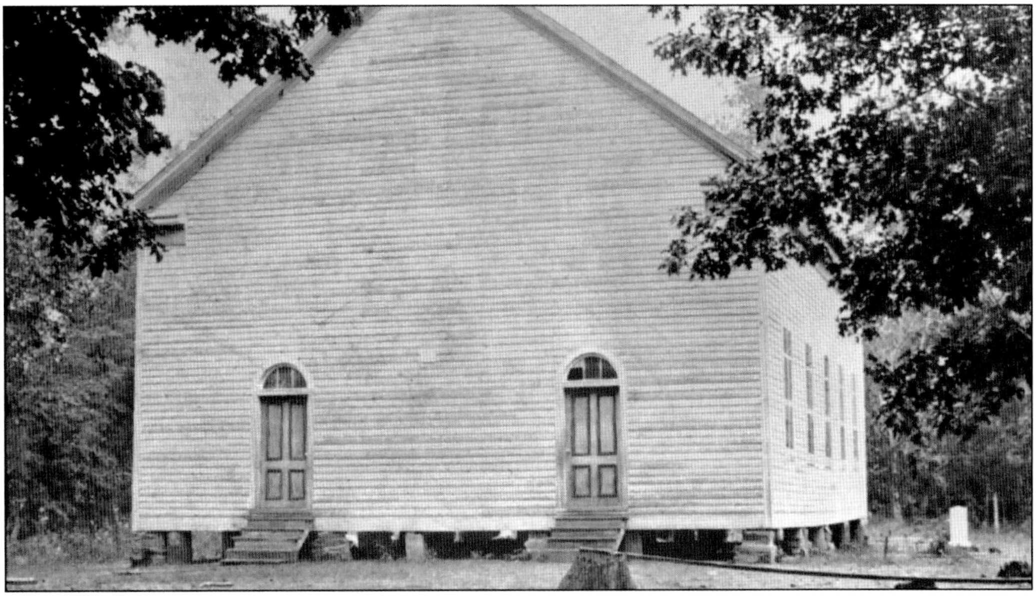

Bethel High Hill was the fourth frame church building and was built in 1881. The first building was a brush/log, the second a 1790s log building, and the third (pictured here) was a wooden frame structure built in 1843. Then Bethel had to move again because of the construction of the dam. The pastor in 1881 was Peter Miller, and he served from 1879 to 1884. According to Pastor Guy Cruse in his booklet, *A History of Bethel Evangelical Lutheran Church*, there was a reference made by a Mr. Schirmer in his own 1875 booklet that "the old church remained until it was destroyed by Sherman's army in 1865," but it is not clear which church building he was referencing. This could have been the first or second church. (Courtesy of Bethel Lutheran Church.)

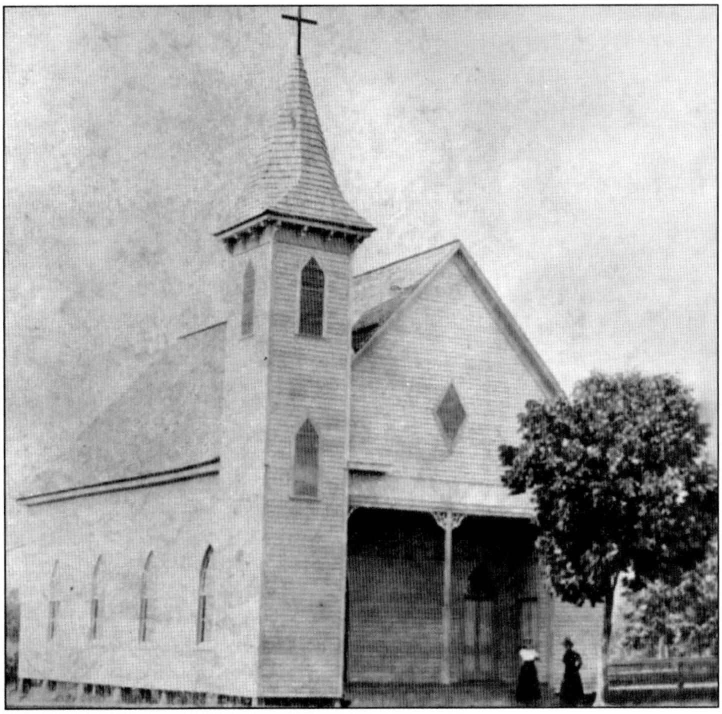

Mount Vernon Church was established in 1894 with most of the members coming from Mount Olivet Church in Spring Hill. The new congregation used the one-story schoolhouse at White Rock while the church was being built and was served primarily by seminary students. The Reverend S. C. Ballentine came as pastor in 1894 to the Bethel pastorate, which consisted of Bethel, Mount Vernon, and Mount Olivet. Here in 1895, Maggie Richardson (Shealy) and Orrie Shealy (Hiller) stand in front of the church. (Courtesy of Bethel Lutheran Church.)

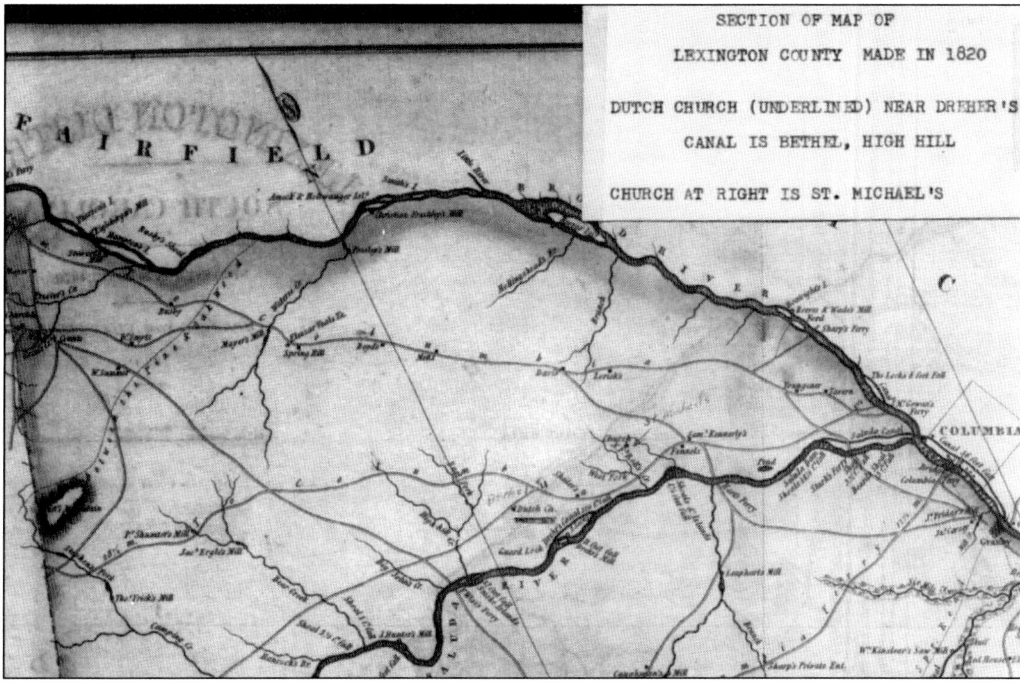

The Lexington County Map, made in 1820, is showing the northeast section of the county. "Dutch Church" (underlined on the map) near Dreher Canal is Bethel High Hill. The church to the right is St. Michaels. The county lines have changed since this map was made. (Courtesy of Bethel Lutheran Church.)

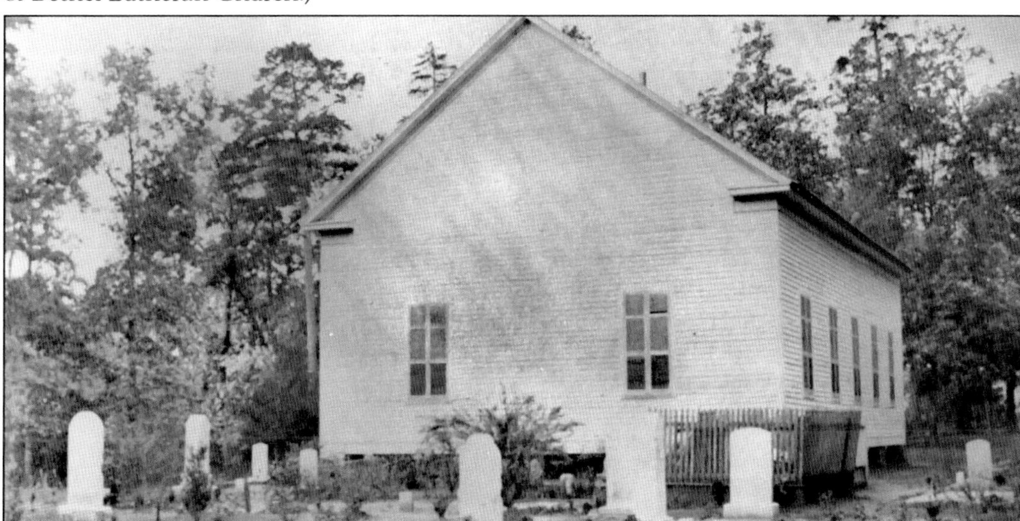

The rear view of Bethel High Hill shows the cemetery and church as they appeared before the dam was built. The first pastor of Bethel was John Nicholas Martin, who served from 1767 to 1774 at the first church site, a brush/log building near the mouth of High Hill Creek and what was called Pender Ridge. The settlement along the Saluda River did not have an easy time. There were constant Native American attacks, and the area had little spiritual leadership until Nicholas Martin, a self-taught man and layman ordained at Ebenezer, Georgia. (Courtesy of Bethel Lutheran Church.)

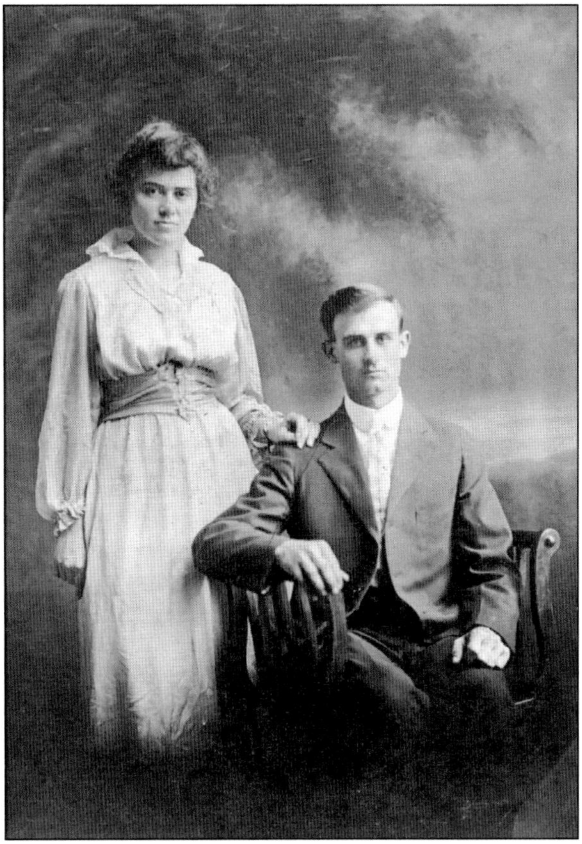

Minnie Mathilda Bauknight and Ernest Younginer were married and lived in Irmo, South Carolina. They were related to Dick Cameron. (Courtesy of Ann Cameron.)

This log cabin was the first home of Fletcher and Emma Riddle Meetze. The first three of their nine children were born here. The original shingle roof was replaced in the 1940s by a tin one. The family estimates the log cabin is more than 200 years old. (Courtesy of Quentin Meetze)

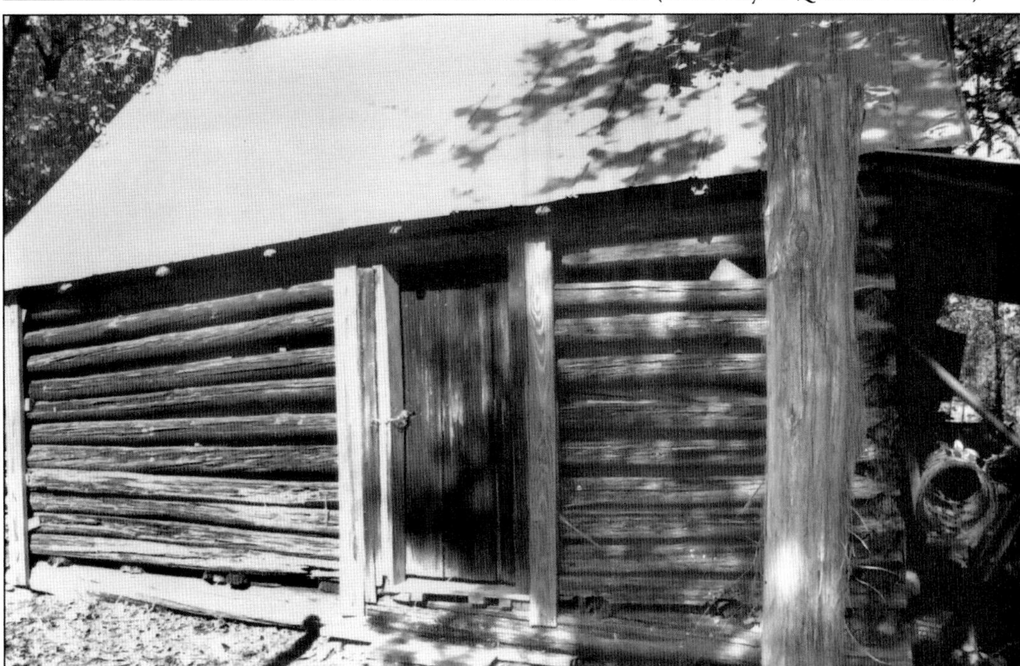

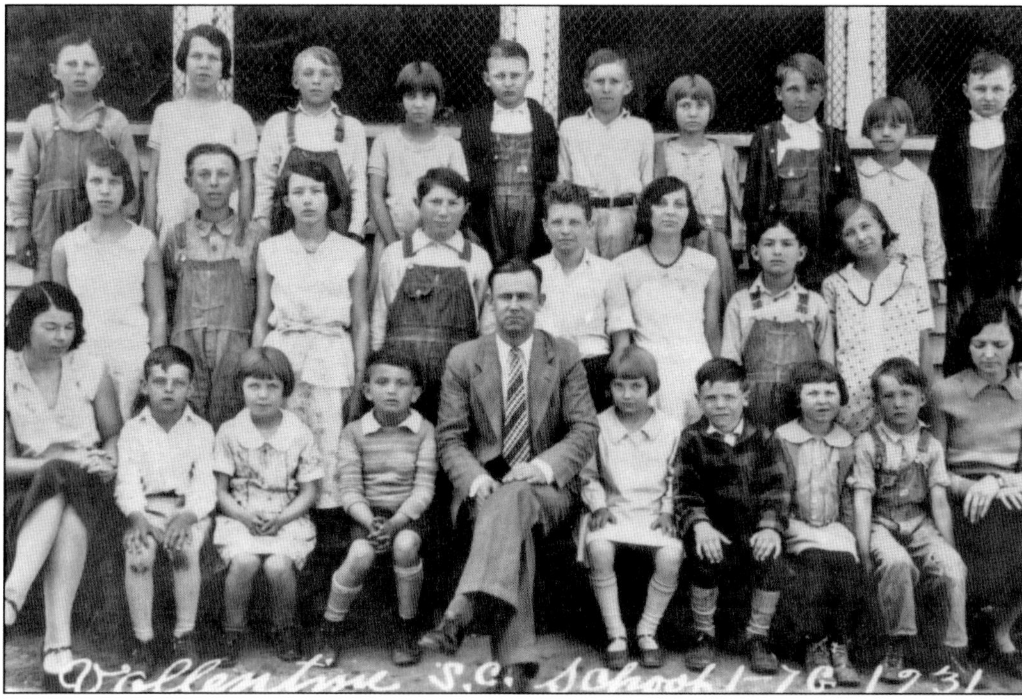

This is the 1931 class of the first Ballentine School, built around 1900. The school was located about where the Food Lion Shopping Center is now and consisted of three classrooms and a small auditorium. It housed grades 1 through 10 and was heated by one potbellied stove in the center of the building. Students took turns hauling in wood for the stove. The School Improvement Association, the forerunner of the PTA, planned fund-raising projects to provide the essentials to operate the school and also provided many extras, which could not be bought through state funds. The school closed in 1938 when Dutch Fork Elementary opened.

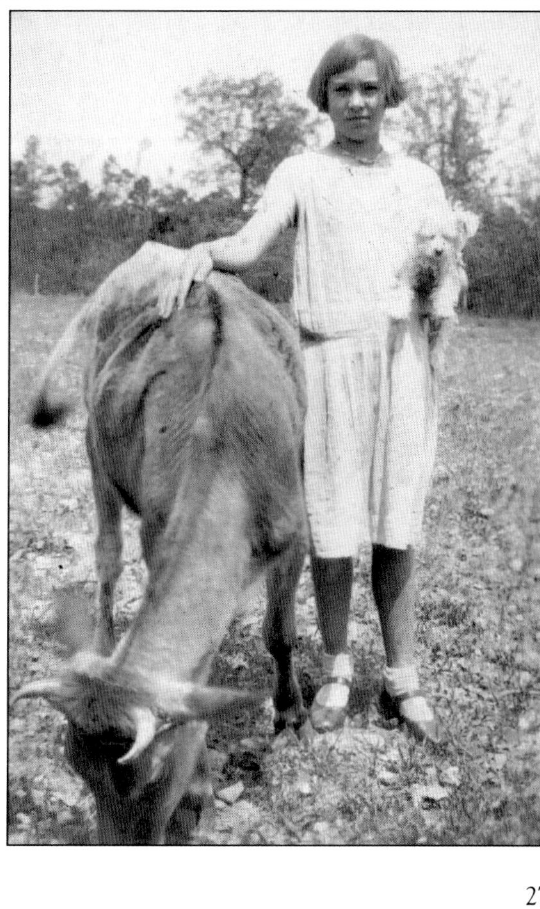

Juel Quick loved her animals. She is shown here with her cow, Billy, and her dog. This photograph was taken around 1932. (Courtesy of Ann Cameron.)

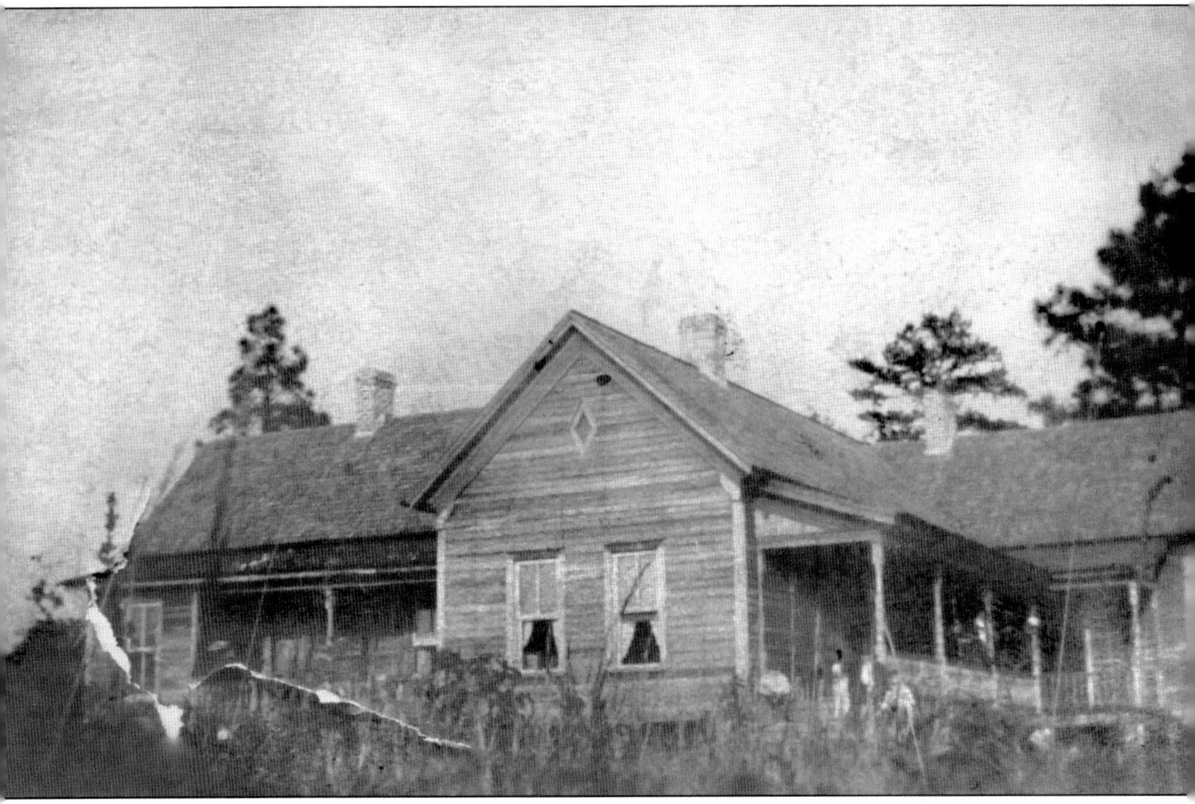

The original Ballentine house was built in 1917. It looks nothing like the house of today. The house was remodeled in the late 1920s, and a second story was added. Five generations, counting Drayton, of Ballentine descendants have lived in the house since its construction.

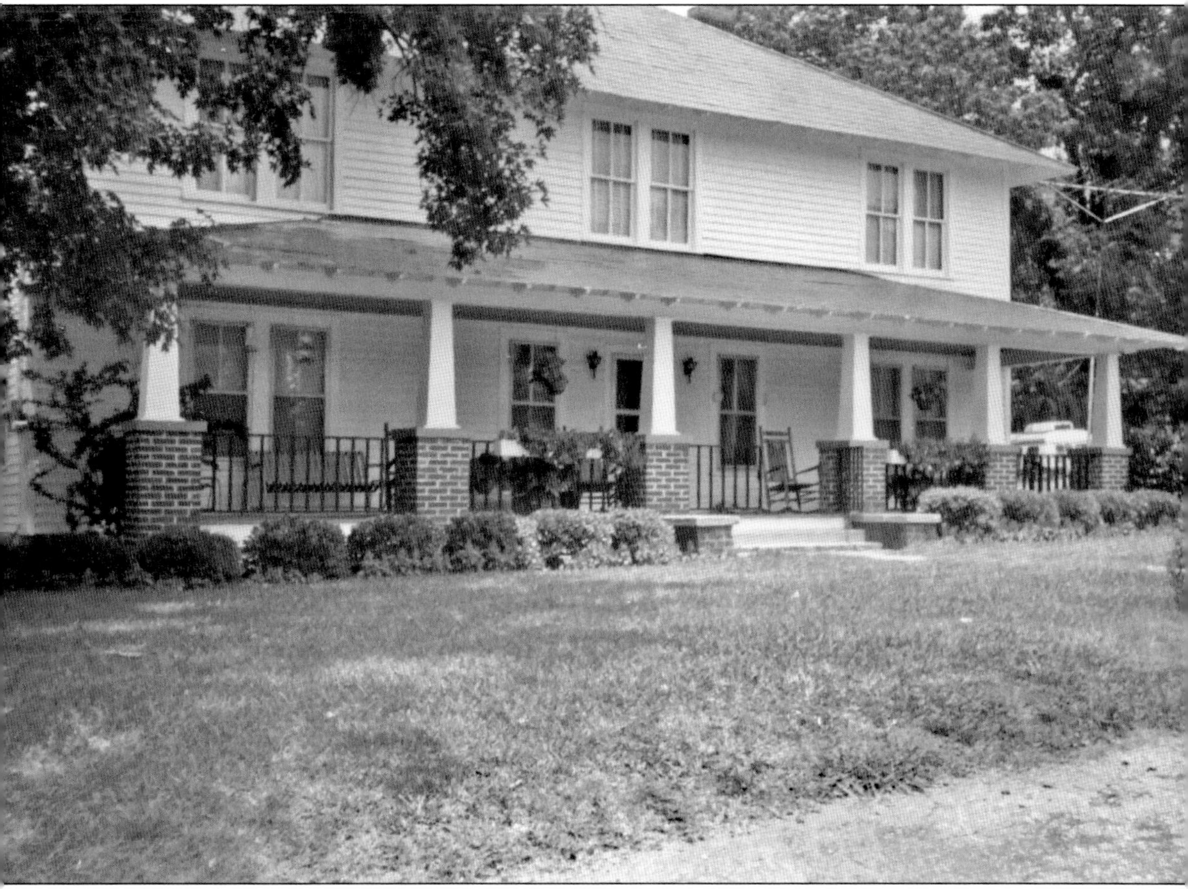

Members of the Ballentine family have lived in this house since 1917. The house has changed its looks over the years. Originally it was one story, later the wrought-iron railing was added, and the landscaping has changed through the years.

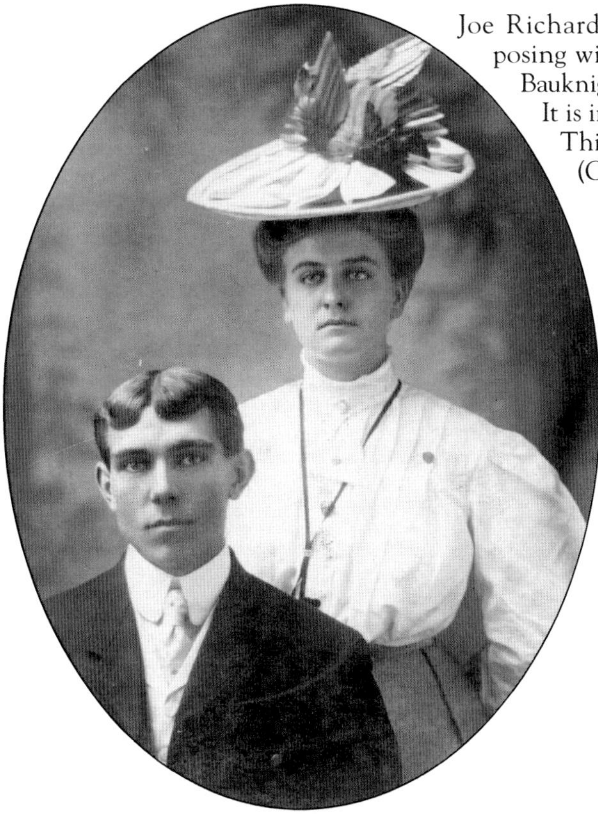

Joe Richards, cousin to Madison Bauknight, is posing with his wife. These are relatives of the Bauknights who lived near Farming Creek Road. It is interesting to see the fashions of the day. This was probably around the early 1900s. (Courtesy of Ann Cameron.)

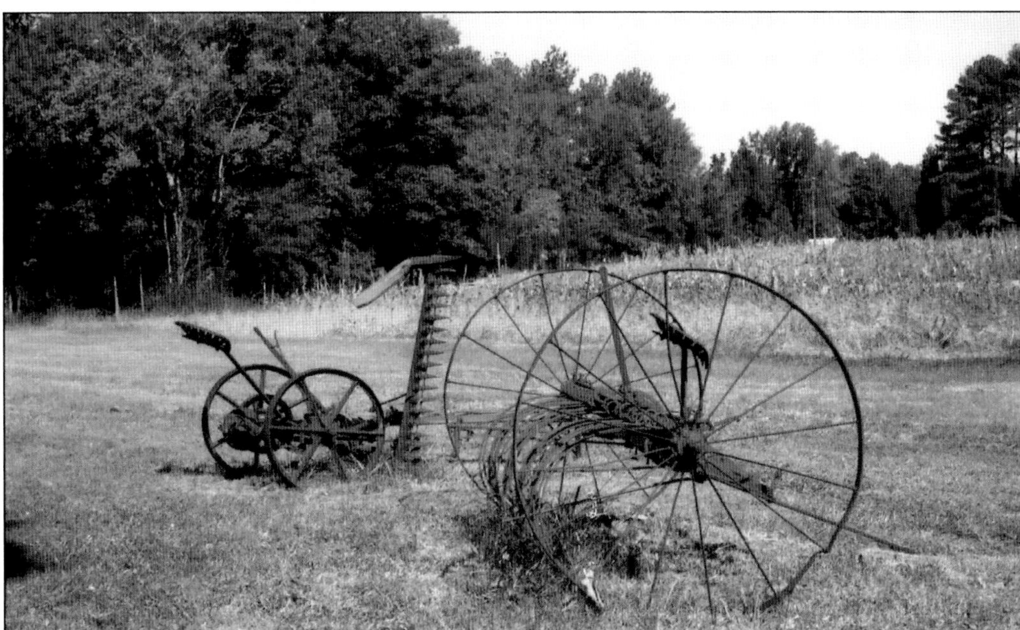

The antique hay rake and hay mower shown here originally were horse drawn. (Courtesy of Quentin Meetze.)

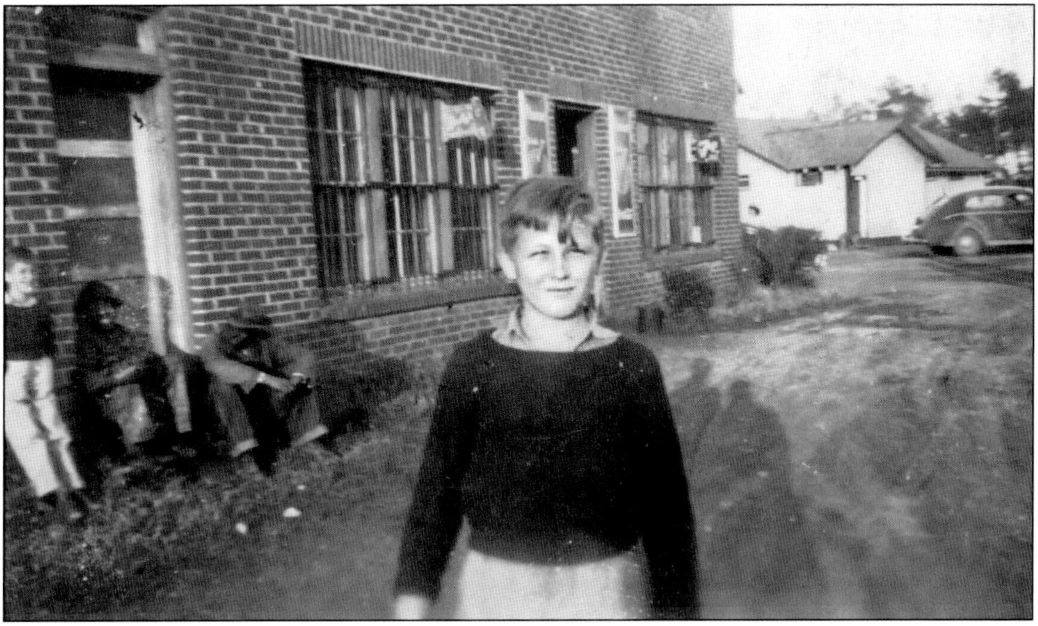

Larry Bailey is standing in front of the Sebe Metts's garage. The back of the building was where Sebe worked on cars, and in front, he had a store and sold snacks like soft drinks, crackers, and Moon Pies. Larry and his sister Lucy loved to follow their father to his sawmill. They were gone so much their mother called them "Go Went and Gone." (Courtesy of Lucy Lindler.)

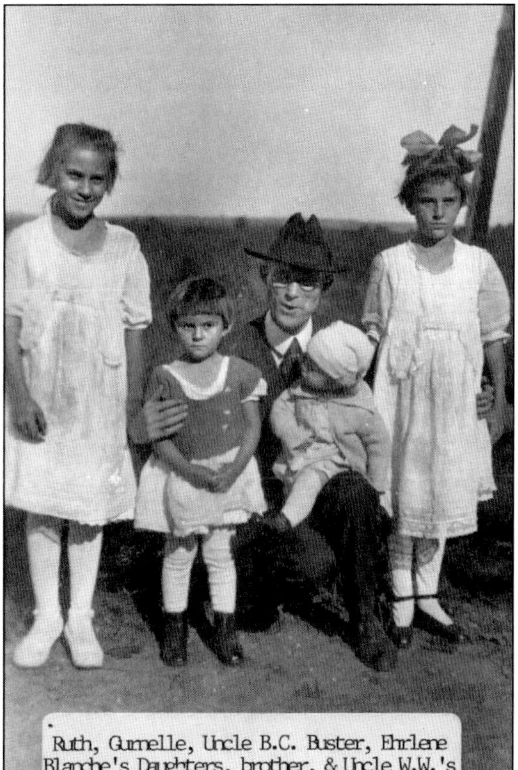

Here, from left to right, Ruth Sheely, Gurnelle Sheely, and Ehrlene Sheely are with their uncle Ben Amick and cousin Buster Amick. It was always a treat when their uncle Ben visited, as he worked for the Claxton Fruitcake Company (before it was called Claxton) and he always brought samples. All the family would get together when he came to visit. (Courtesy of Kay Shealy.)

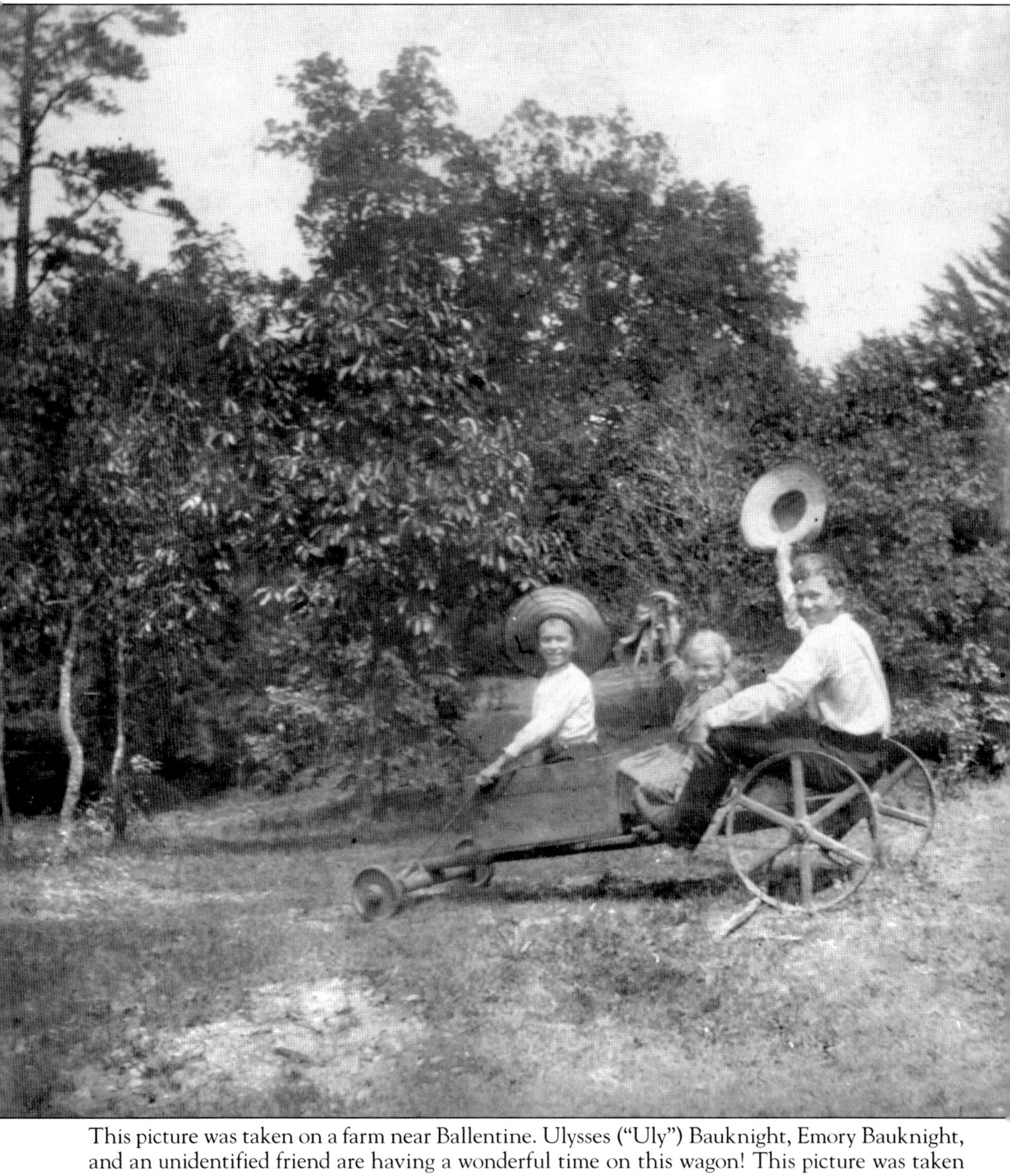

This picture was taken on a farm near Ballentine. Ulysses ("Uly") Bauknight, Emory Bauknight, and an unidentified friend are having a wonderful time on this wagon! This picture was taken in the early 1900s and is a great action shot. Many of the photographs of that time seem to be posed. (Courtesy of Ann Cameron.)

Ollie Mae Arnold Quick is with her little dog in front of her house. In the photograph, the right side of the porch appears to be enclosed. That is a room that had a separate entrance and was called a parson's porch. The room was originally built for the traveling preacher because, years ago, ministers served several congregations and had to travel, so he would stay with parishioners. There was a separate entrance so he could come and go without disturbing the family. (Courtesy of Ann Cameron.)

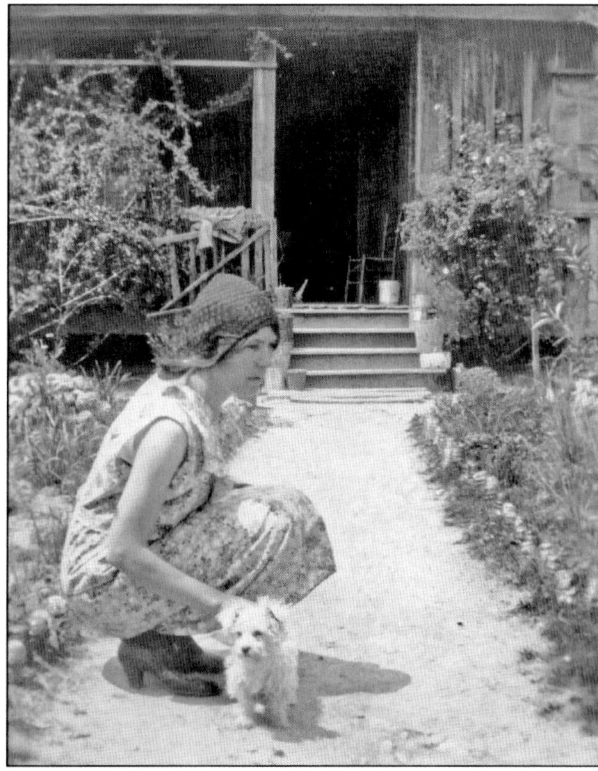

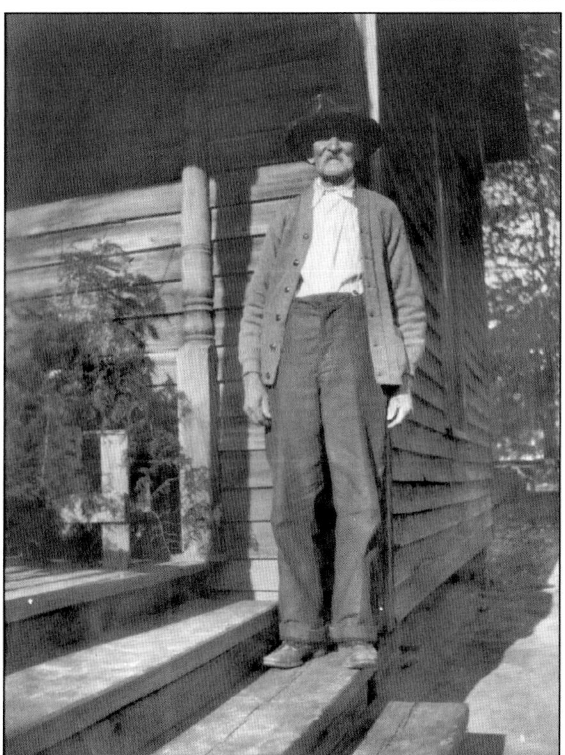

Drayton Ballentine is shown standing in front of the Ballentine house in the early 1920s before the house was remodeled in 1927. He was the father of Eusebius, Lonnie, Willie, Minnie (Haltiwanger), Sallie (Sease), Lila (Palatty, James), and Corrie (Frick). Drayton married Elvira Koon Ballentine, the widow of his brother John and had two stepchildren, Walter and Mary Alice. His brother was killed in the Civil War in 1862. Drayton also served in the Civil War, enlisting when he was only 16.

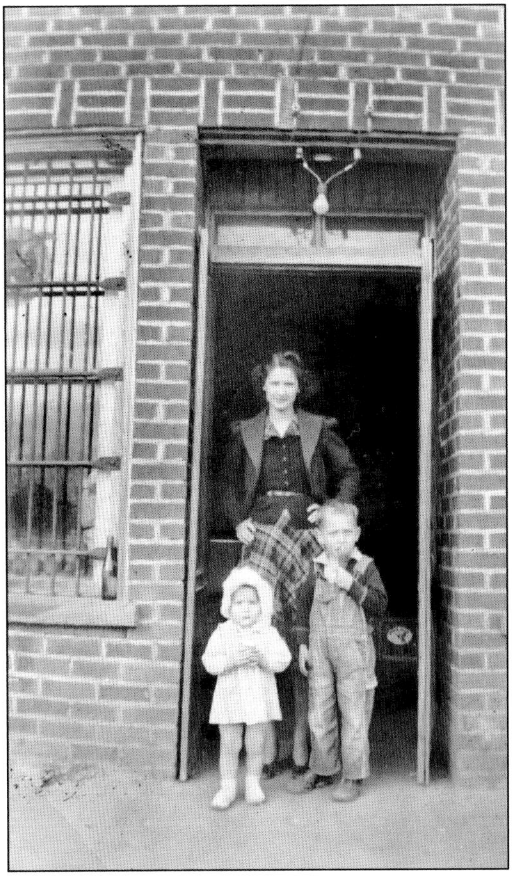

Bonnie Stevenson, Marilyn Shealy, and William Sheely are standing in front of the E. A. Ballentine general store in the late 1930s. Notice the light fixture above the door, the old soda bottle sitting on the ledge of the window, and the clothing. The store was built in 1929 and remodeled in 1938.

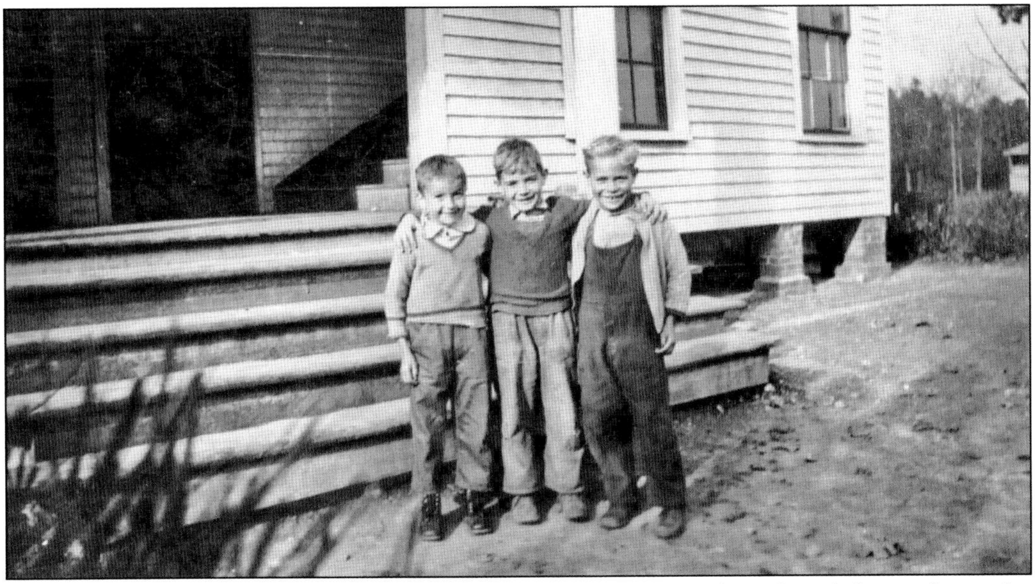

Good friends Bo Koogler, Fred Lindler, and Miller Yenny are standing, from left to right, at the side the Piedmont School. They were in the fourth or fifth grade, and it was the mid-1930s. This was around the time Babe Ruth announced his retirement. (Courtesy of Lucy Lindler.)

Frank Bouknight is shown wearing his Clemson College uniform. He attended Clemson in the 1930s. Clemson Agricultural College was established in 1889 after Thomas Clemson left most of his estate to establish a college that would teach scientific agriculture and mechanical arts to the young people of South Carolina. In 1893, Clemson College was formally opened with an enrollment of 446. From the beginning, the college was an all-male military school and remained that way until 1955, when the change was made to "civilian status" and Clemson became a coed institution. In 1964, Clemson was renamed Clemson University. More than a century later, the university is so much more than the founder could have imagined or hoped. The university not only provides an educational opportunity for the people of the state, as Clemson dreamed, but also throughout the world.

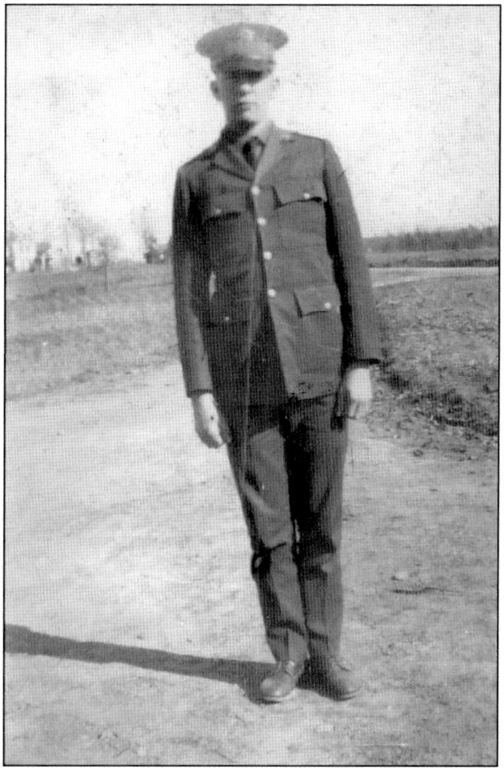

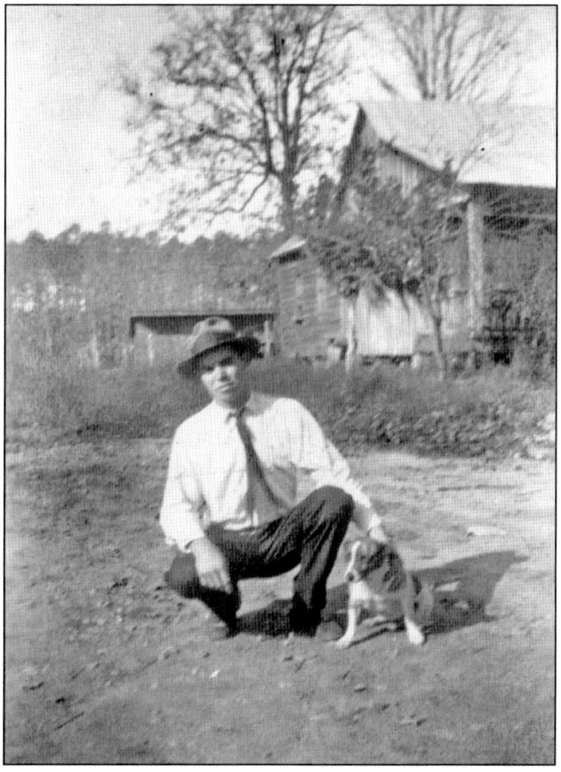

This photograph was taken around 1935; Homer Quick is in front of Ollie and Will Quick's home on Farming Creek Road. (Courtesy of Ann Cameron.)

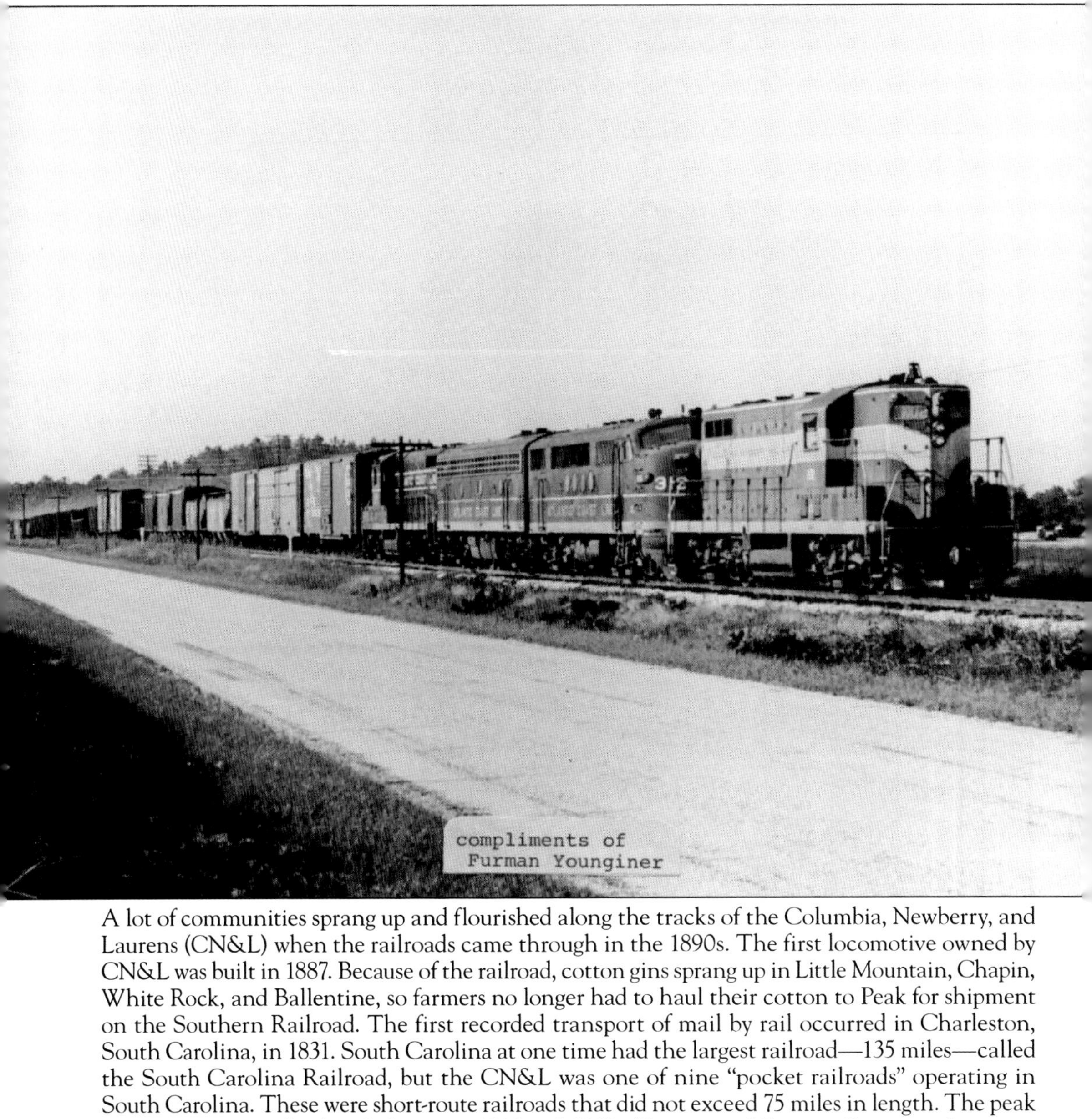

A lot of communities sprang up and flourished along the tracks of the Columbia, Newberry, and Laurens (CN&L) when the railroads came through in the 1890s. The first locomotive owned by CN&L was built in 1887. Because of the railroad, cotton gins sprang up in Little Mountain, Chapin, White Rock, and Ballentine, so farmers no longer had to haul their cotton to Peak for shipment on the Southern Railroad. The first recorded transport of mail by rail occurred in Charleston, South Carolina, in 1831. South Carolina at one time had the largest railroad—135 miles—called the South Carolina Railroad, but the CN&L was one of nine "pocket railroads" operating in South Carolina. These were short-route railroads that did not exceed 75 miles in length. The peak passenger era was the decade between 1910 and 1920. (Courtesy of Furman Younginer.)

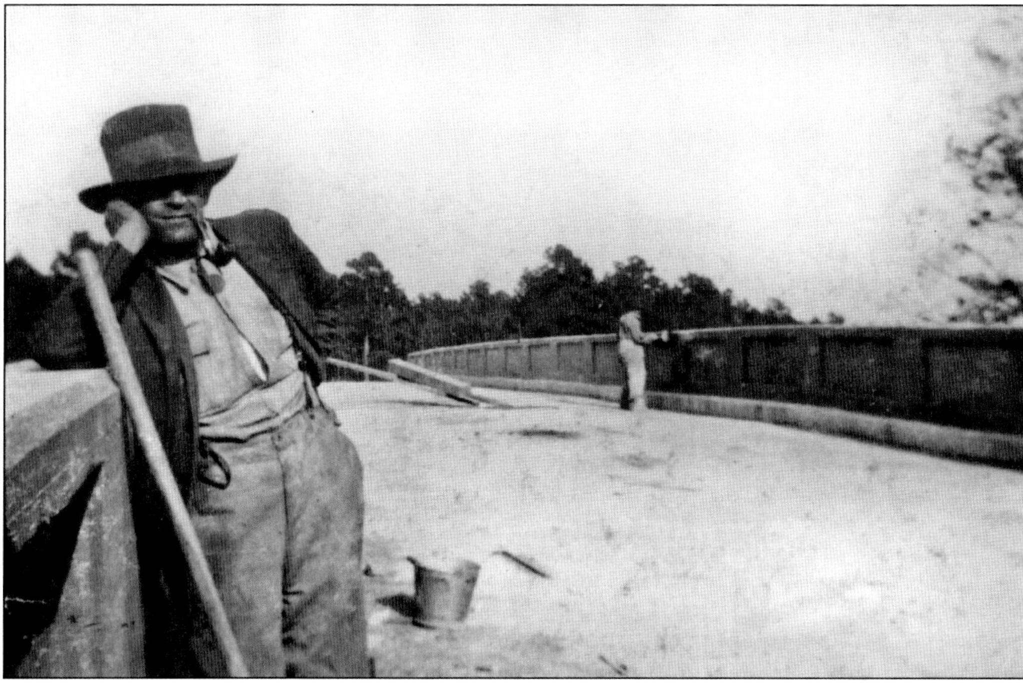

"The Captain," as John Green Hiller was known, is shown here standing on the first bridge in Ballentine with his walking stick. He worked for the highway department, but it is not clear if he was working that day or visiting friends. (Courtesy of Jonnie Mae Sites.)

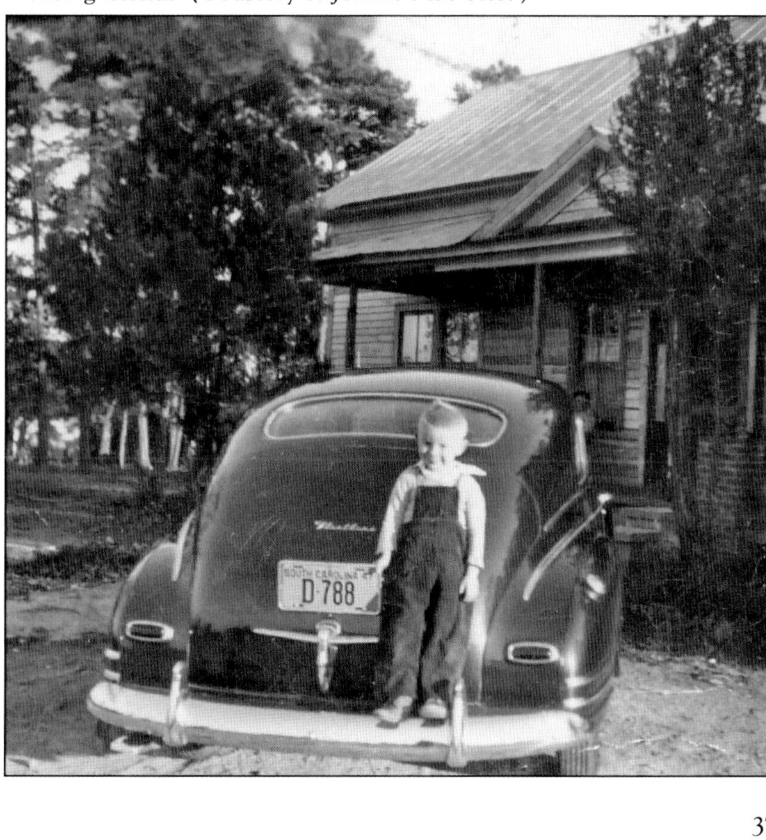

Dick Lowman is standing on the back of his family's car, and the building in the background is the original Ballentine School and his home. After the school closed, the Lowmans lived there for a period of time. There have been many stories of how old buildings such as schools, churches, and warehouses are being restored as homes because of the distinctiveness and quality of the structures. (Courtesy of Dick Lowman and Pat Derrick.)

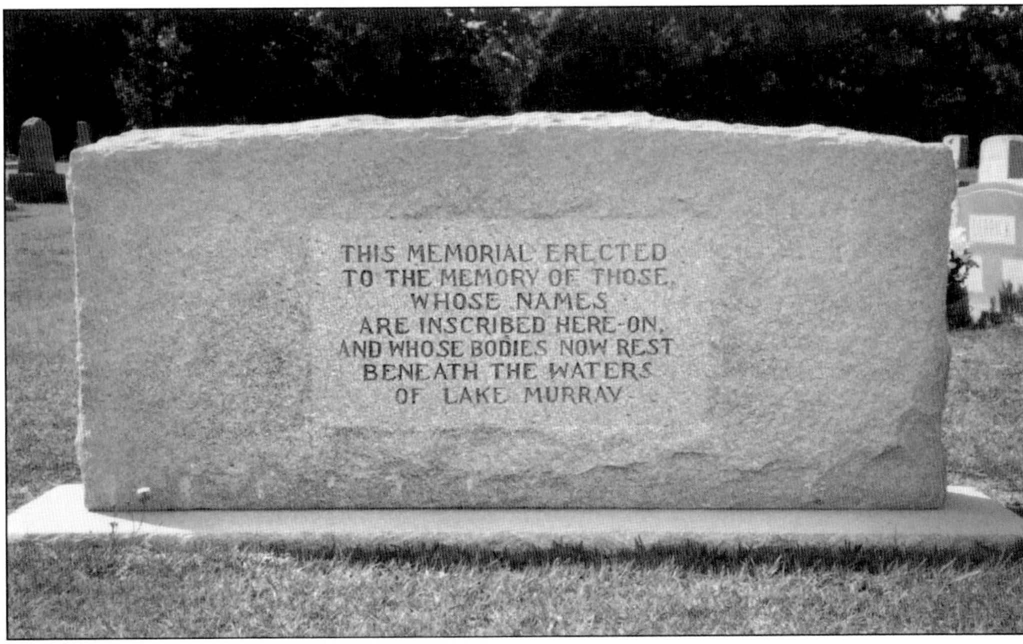

This memorial is located in the Bethel Lutheran Church Cemetery and was provided by the Lexington Water Power Company. It is dedicated to the 50-plus graves left under the waters of Lake Murray. The Bethel High Hill Church and cemetery had to be moved as a result of the development of the lake. It was necessary to work all night to dam up the water around the cemetery so the graves could be moved. The power company had agreed to move all the graves of those whose families wished it. (Courtesy of Jacob Dean.)

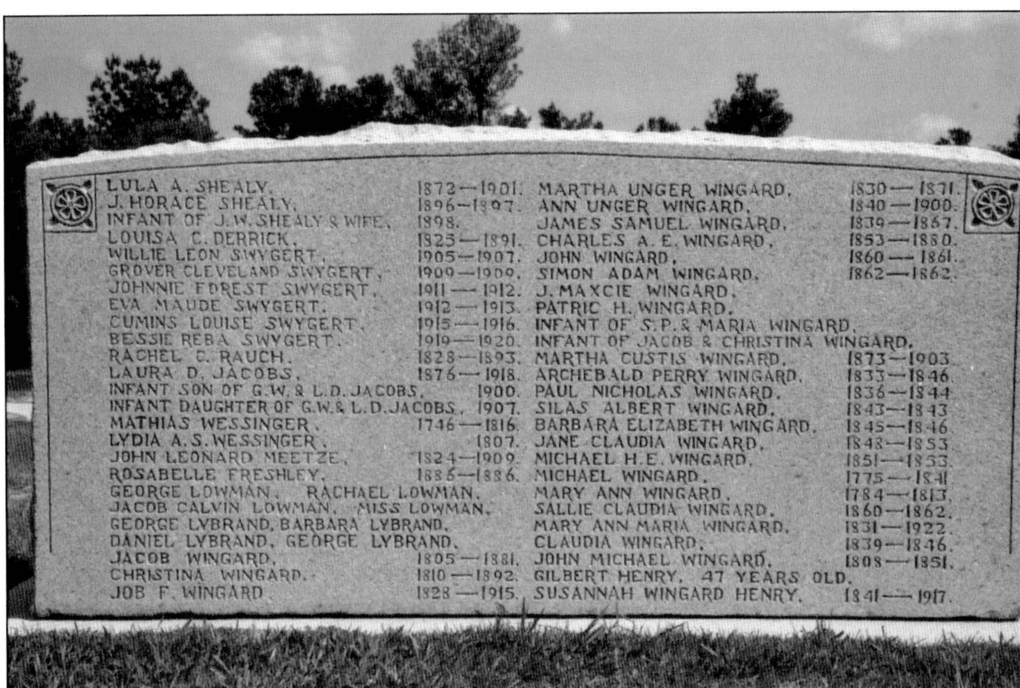

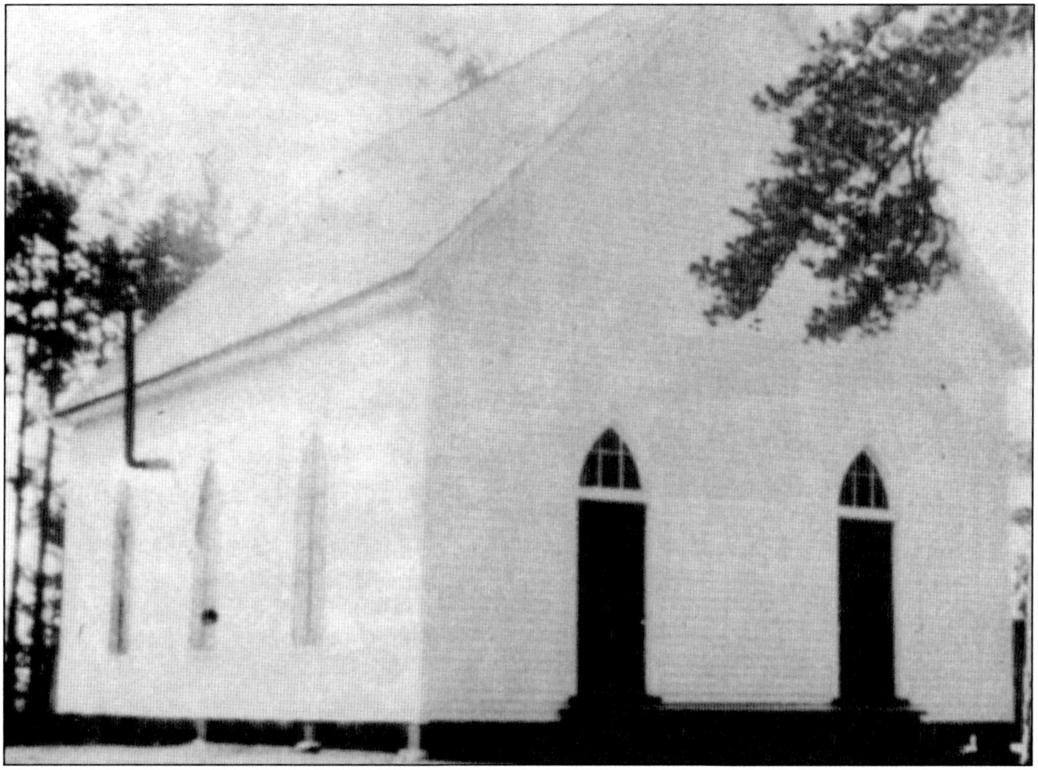

Salem Church was established in 1863. The first pastor was J. Claude Miller, and the first congregation numbered 56 people. The old white church was replaced by the brick building, and this has been recently remodeled. (Courtesy of Barbara Thomas and Dutch Fork Methodist Church.)

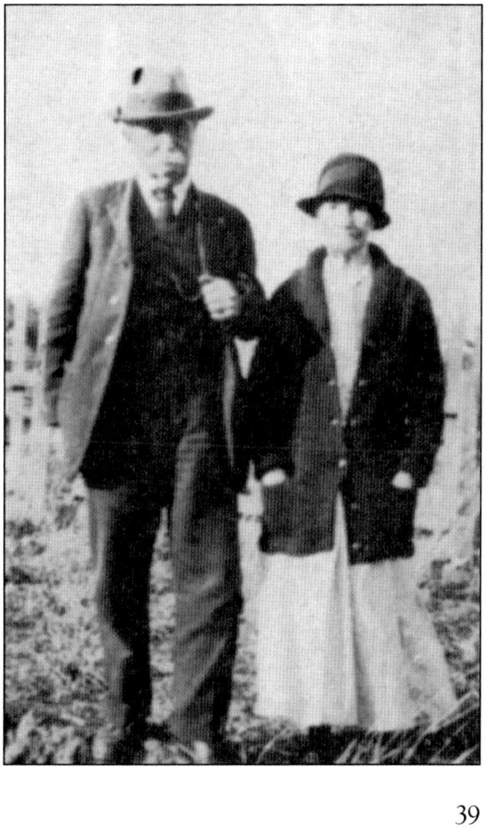

Quentin Meetze's grandparents, John Fletcher (October 10, 1856–October 19, 1941) and Emma Isabel Riddle Meetze (February 26, 1861–September 21, 1959), were a typical couple of the area. She was a housewife, he was a farmer, and they had nine children. The first three children—Jacob Matthew, Sara Eugene, and Lee Augustus—were born in an old log cabin, and the other children—Joseph Eusbuis ("Seab"), Eva Belle, John ("Johnnie") Wilbur, Oscar Riddle, Mary Ann, and Vern Smith—were born in what is now called the old homestead. The original spelling of the last name was Metz, but it was later changed to Meetze. (Courtesy of Quentin Meetze and Barbara Thomas.)

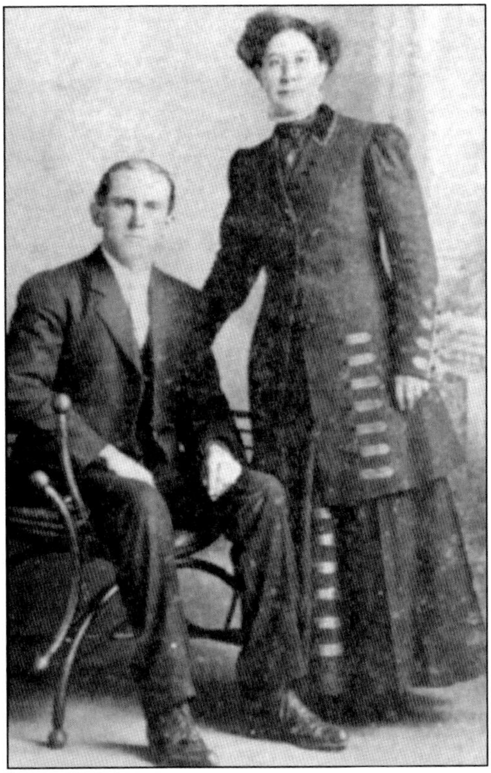

Gus and Lola Haltiwanger Bickley, parents of Harper Bickley, are buried at Salem Methodist Church. Harper Bickley was a local resident and farmer, who passed away several years ago. The Ballentine Elementary School now sits on a parcel of the Bickley property. (Courtesy of Barbara Thomas.)

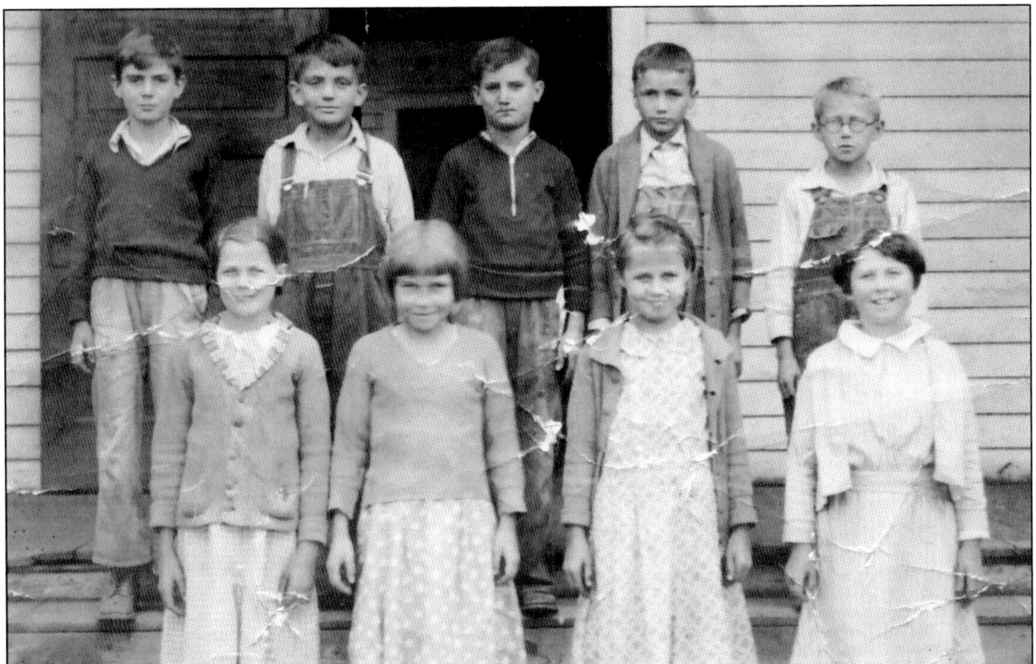

This is a group of children in front of the Piedmont School in the 1930s. Several have been identified: Fred Lindler, Keith Ballentine, Jimmy Lee, and Ruby Daily. (Courtesy of Lucy Lindler.)

S. Wyman Boozer, owner of Wyman Boozer Realty, was a major developer of the St. Andrews area. He had the foresight to buy and develop land in Lexington and Richland Counties for a shopping center (Boozer Shopping Center), rural properties, and Lake Murray tracts, including Ballentine Estates. Ballentine Estates was originally farmland owned by Eusebius Ballentine.

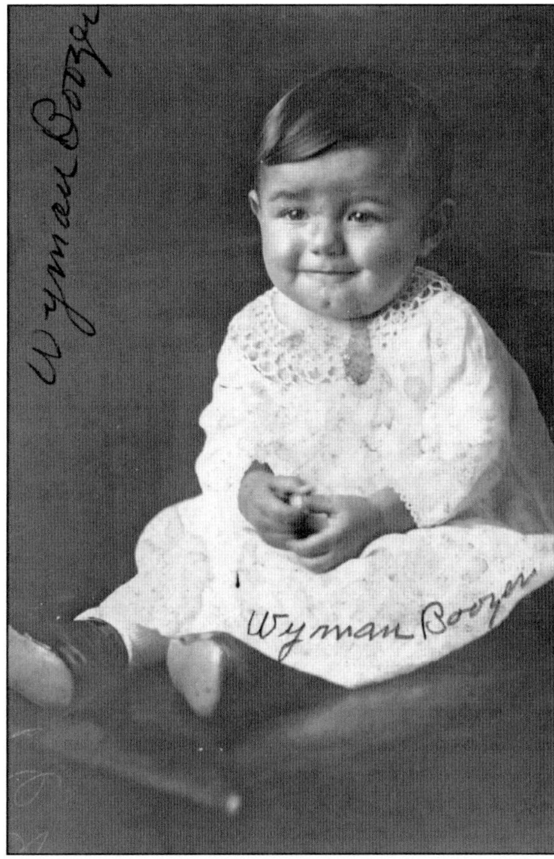

This Allis Chalmers tractor, originally built in 1948, has been lovingly restored by Roswell and Richard Meetze. The building in the background is estimated to be around 175 years old and was used to store horse gear and buggies. (Courtesy of Quentin Meetze.)

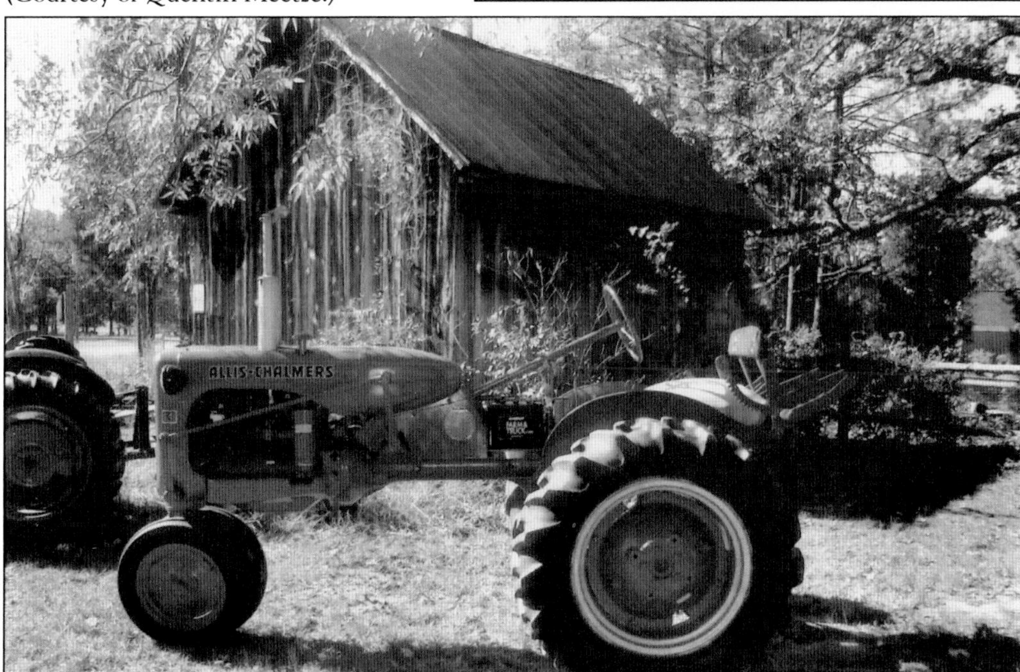

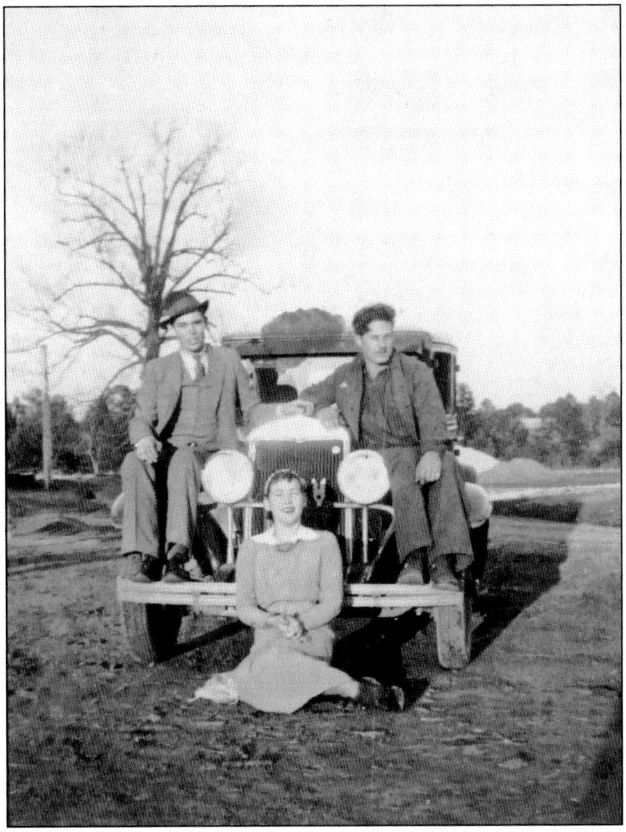

From left to right, Homer Quick, Jessie Lawhorn, and Joel Quick are shown posing in front of this early-model car. Not many candid pictures were made in the earlier years, but it seems nearly every family had a picture taken in front of a new car. It seemed to be the thing to do. (Courtesy of Ann Cameron.)

John Riddle and his family lived in this house for many years before it was torn down. The house had stood empty for several years before the land was sold, a new road was cut where the house once stood, and new retail shops came to Ballentine. Note the unique posts holding the porch roof up. There were several homes in the area with that type of design. (Courtesy of John Riddle.)

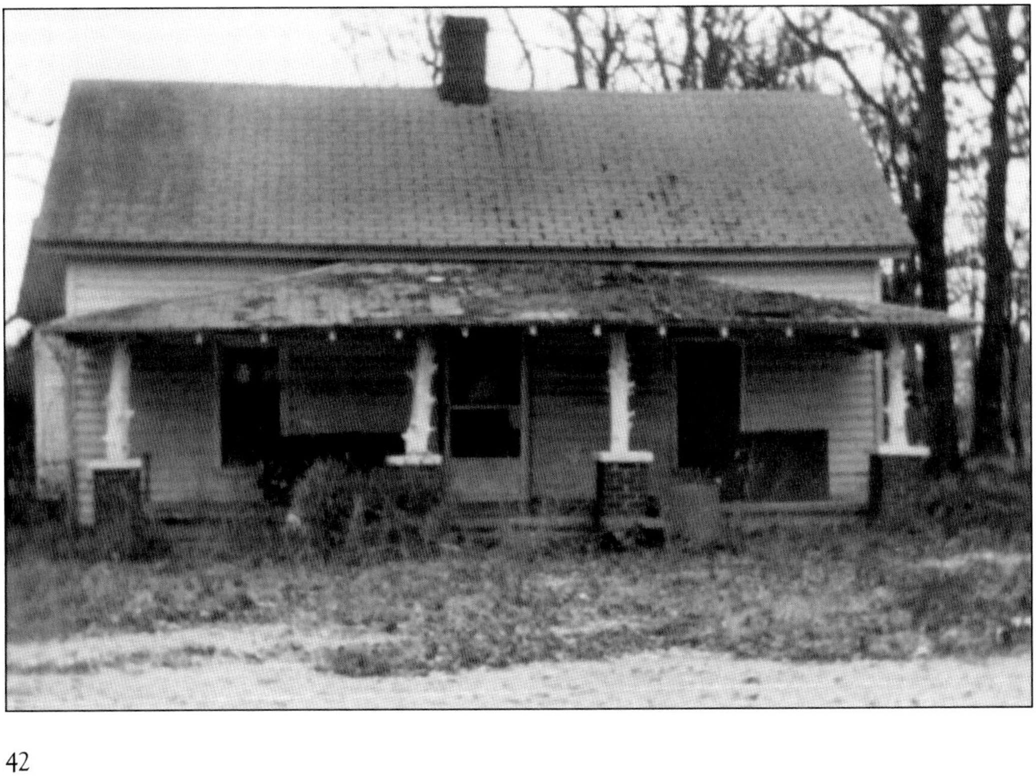

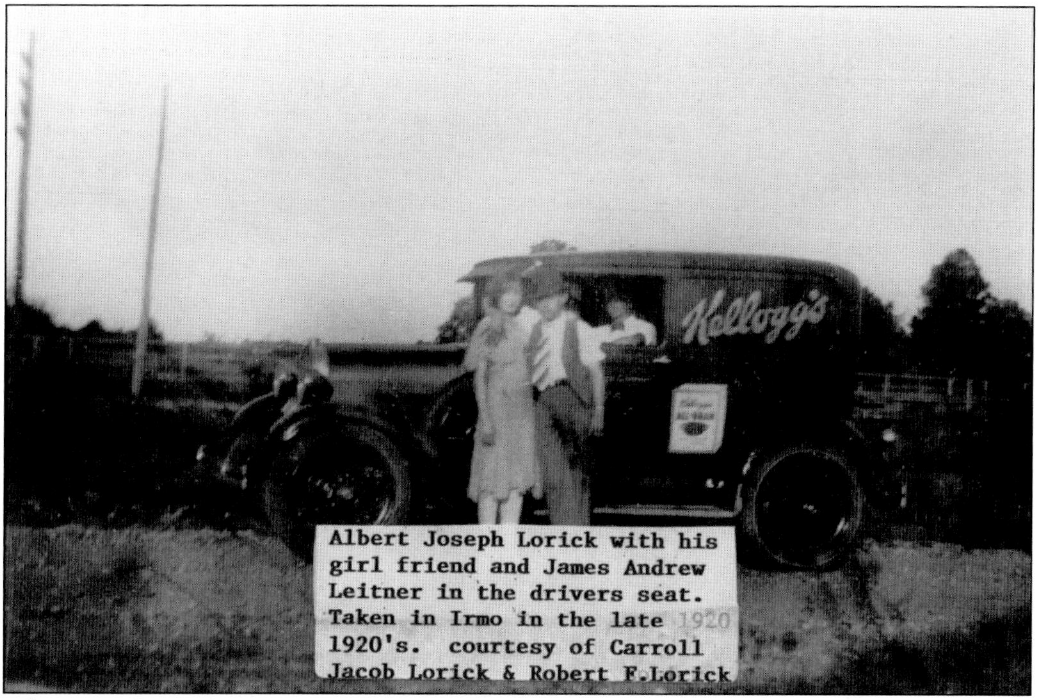

Albert Joseph Lorick, James Andrew Leitner, and Albert's girlfriend pose with the Kellogg's truck in Irmo, South Carolina. The Kellogg's Battle Creek Toasted Corn Flake Cereal was the original name of the company. In 1922, the company was renamed Kellogg's. (Courtesy of Carol Jacob Lorick and Robert F. Lorick.)

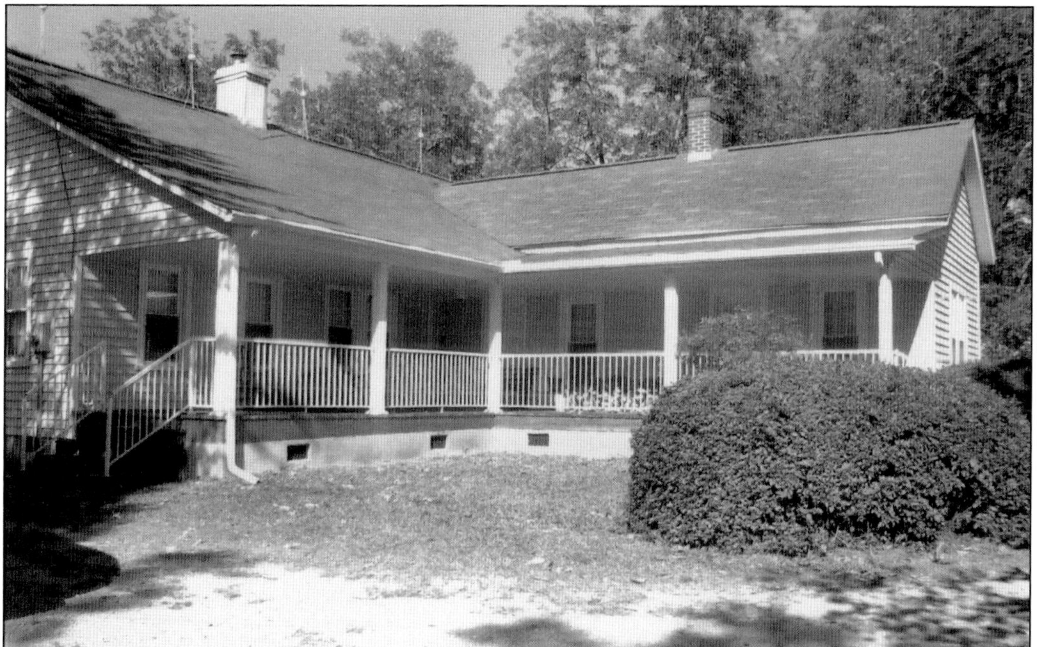

This is the Meetze family house as it appears today. It has been remodeled, and a new wing was added years ago. (Courtesy of Quentin Meetze)

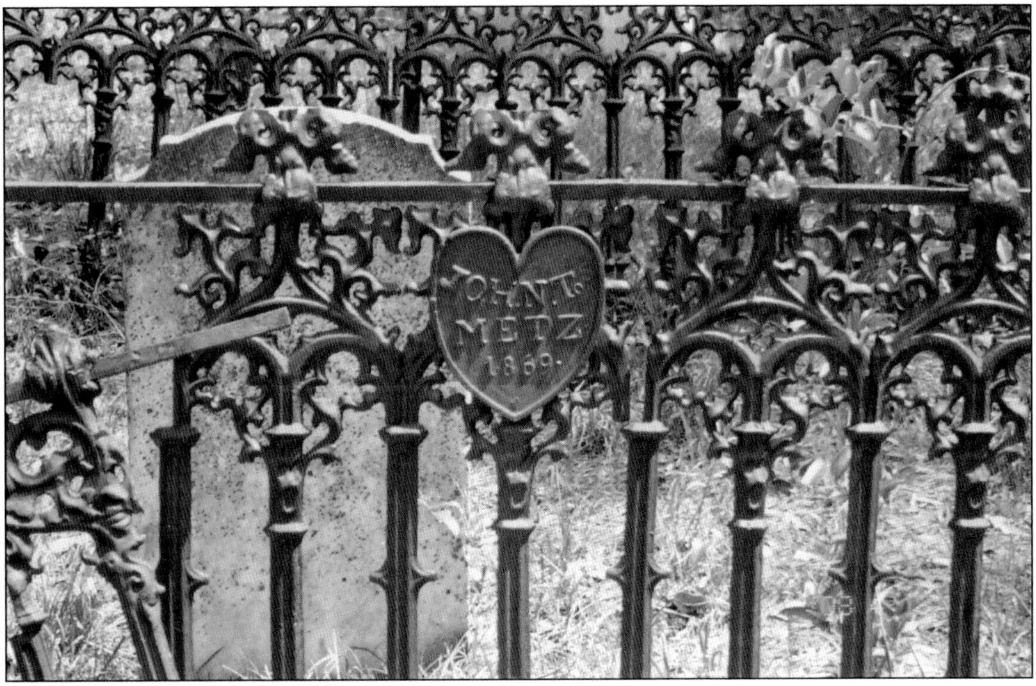

This is the John T. Metz family cemetery. The iron gate and fence were made in 1869 in Charleston, South Carolina. According to residents, the Metz family once had a large farm in the area. The land had been acquired by a land grant. (Courtesy of Ann Cameron.)

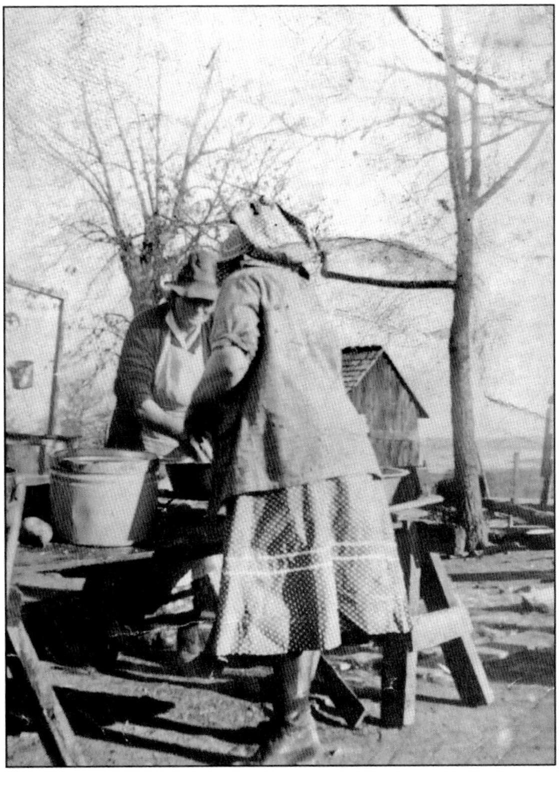

Lena Bailey and Mary Riddle are outside getting ready for butchering. Years ago, neighbors and families would get together for butchering. It was a social and practical event. A pig born in the spring was ready for slaughter in early winter, eliminating the necessity for carrying any livestock other than breeding stock over the winter. Compared to other animals, hogs were efficient in converting grain to meat for butchering. The weather had to be cold enough, and this usually occurred in the late fall/early winter. (Courtesy of Lucy Lindler.)

The back of this photograph states, "Summer fun in creek near barn in Shady Grove area." It is not clear who the boys are—one of them may have been Ulysses ("Uly") Bauknight—but it is a wonderful photograph of days gone by. (Courtesy of Ann Cameron.)

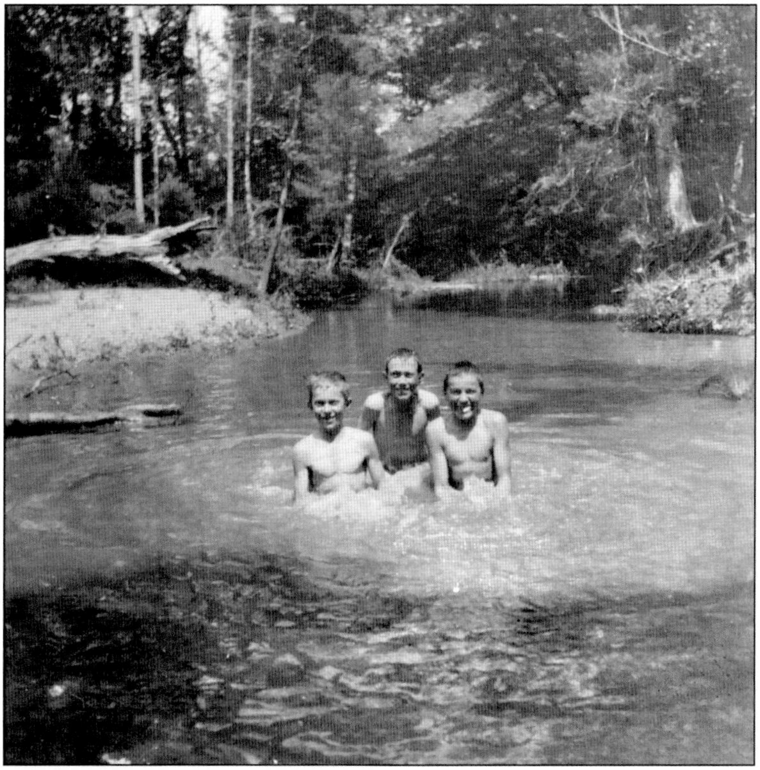

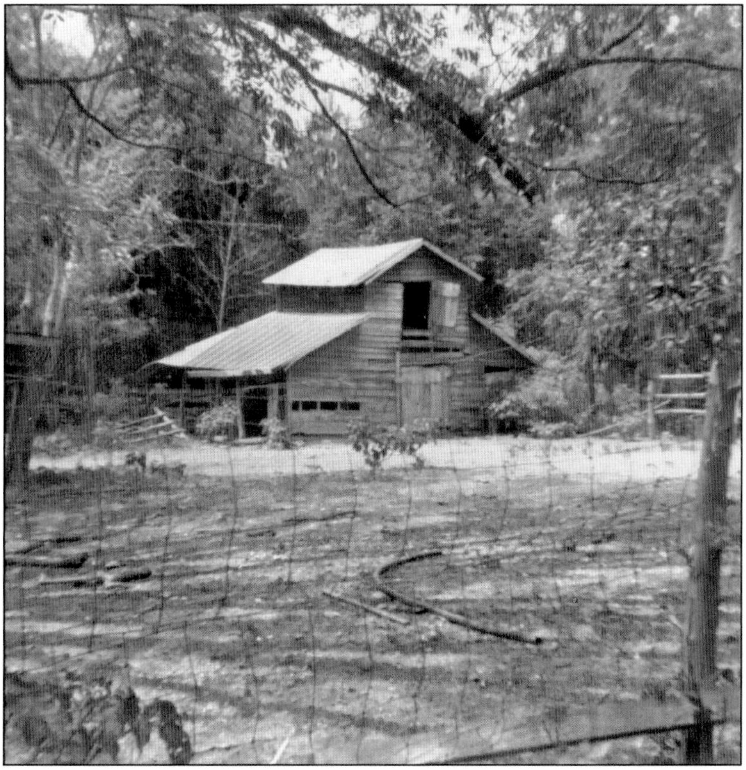

The George Milledge Lindler barn was probably built in the early 1900s. It is the standard style of the barns around the Dutch Fork area. There are still several barns around the area that are almost identical to this barn. (Courtesy of Lucy Lindler.)

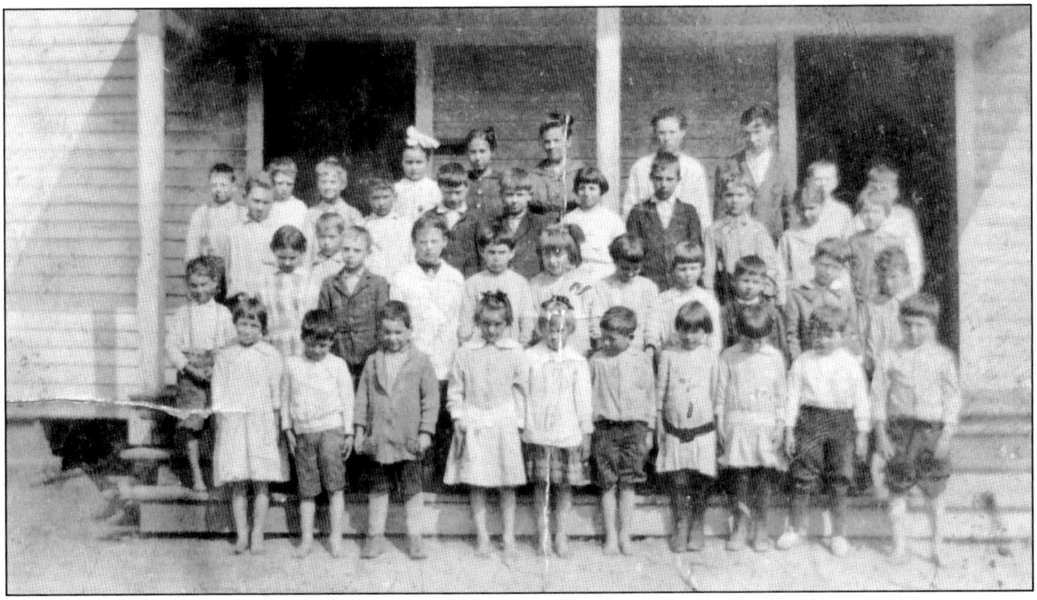

According to several of the original residents, this is the Piedmont School. It was located near the fork of Highways 76 and 176, where the district office now sits. The school consolidated with Ballentine, and grades one through four went to Piedmont and five through seven went to Ballentine. The classrooms were located on the first floor, and an auditorium was upstairs. A Ford Model A school bus transported children to the schools. (Courtesy of Lucy Lindler.)

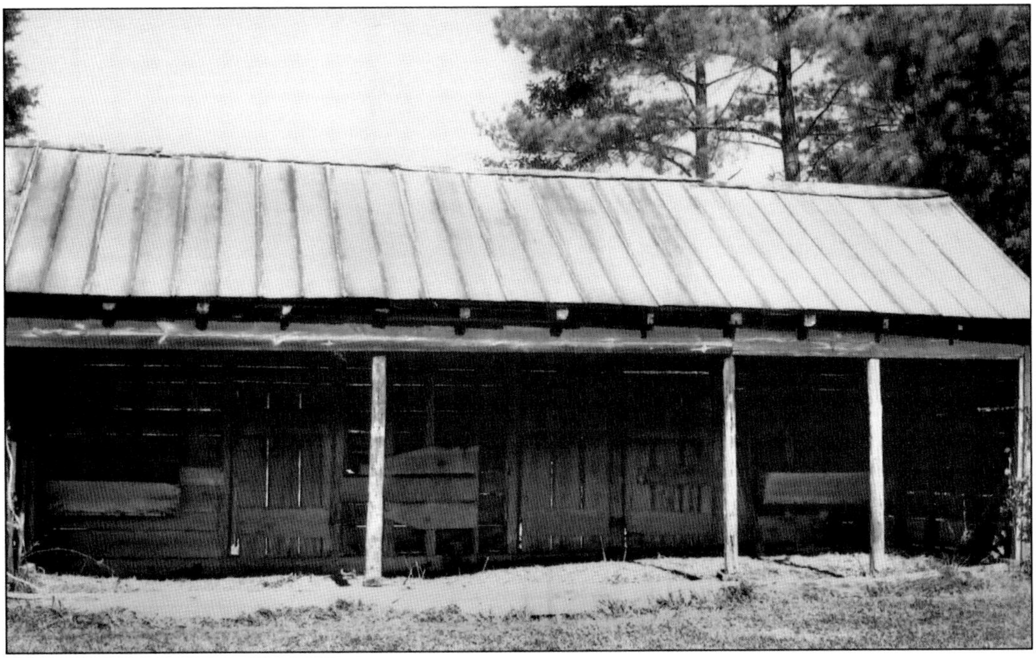

This is one of the original buildings on the Meetze property. This was what they called the horse and mule station. There are many historical buildings on their property, and most are estimated to be more than 150 years. This farming family had their own blacksmith shop; shoe shop; "tater house," which stored canned goods and vegetables; and a syrup pit, where they cooked the juice from the sugar cane to make syrup. (Courtesy of Quentin Meetze.)

Two

FOXHUNTING

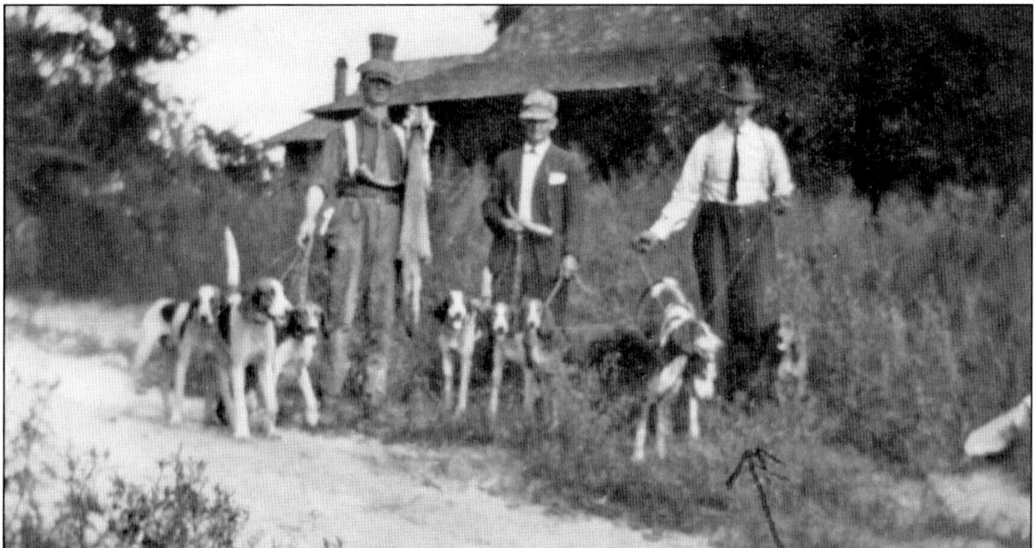

From left to right, Claude Lowman, John Dreher, and Sebe Ballentine are posing with their hunting dogs. Claude Lowman, holding the fox, is apparently the winner of this hunt. There are now over 173 member hunts (including both registered and recognized) in the United States, 18 of them in North and South Carolina. Sebe and probably Claude and John were members of the South Carolina Fox Hunters Association. There are two types of foxes found hereabouts, the red fox and the gray. According to Sebe, the gray fox was a wary creature whose main defense was to outfox the dogs pursuing him by running through yards, hiding out among the cattle, or running on pavement, hopefully causing the dogs to lose the trail. On the other hand, the red fox, lacking the inborn cunning of the gray fox, used his tremendous speed to save him.

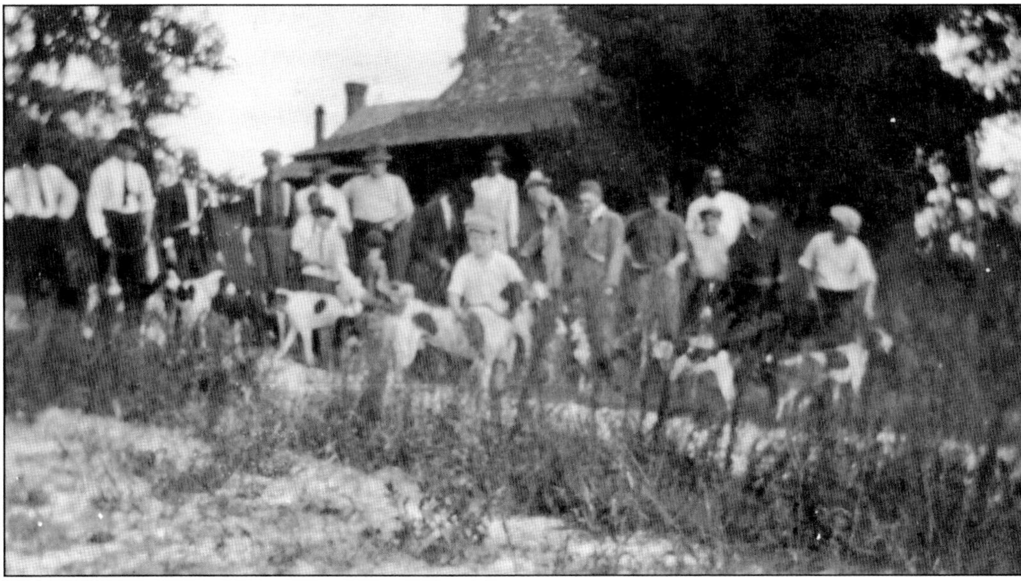

A group of fox hunters are shown with their hounds. Usually they would get together and eat breakfast before the hunt began. It is unclear if this picture was taken before or after the hunt, but from the dogs' reaction, it looks like it is before the hunt. They look eager to begin.

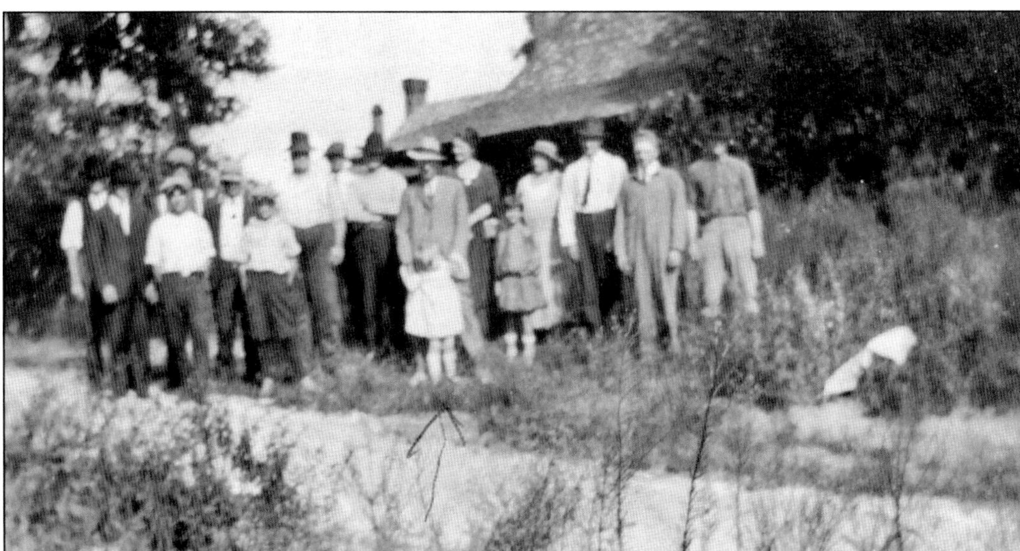

This is one of the foxhunts in the early 1920s in Ballentine. Not all of the people were identified. The small child was Julia Barnette, behind her was her father, and the tall lady behind him was her mother. They were good friends from Columbia. The other child was Bonnie Stevenson, and the lady behind her was her mother, "Mama Jennie." Next to her are, from left to right, Sebe Ballentine, Bill Swygert, and John Dreher.

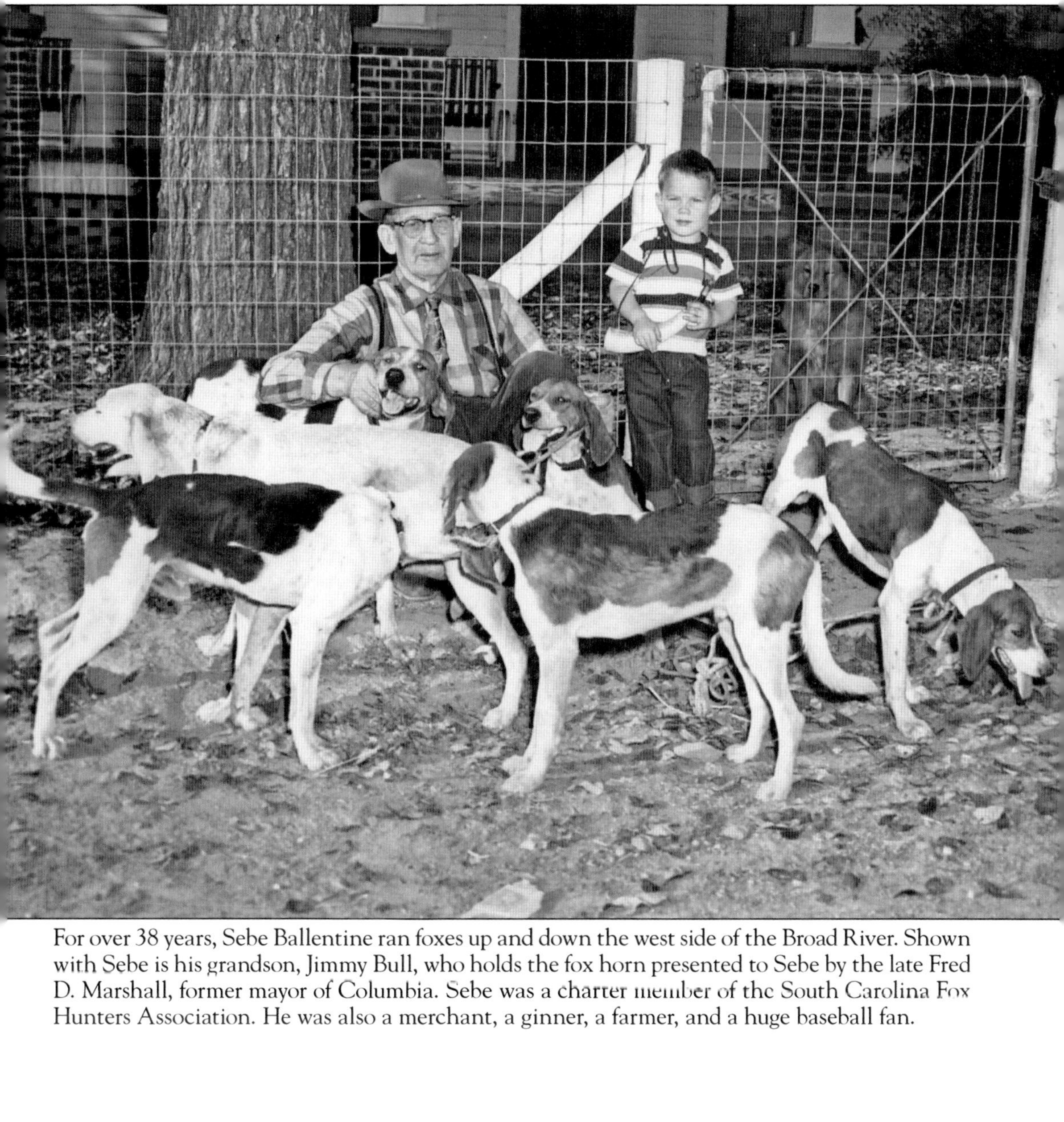

For over 38 years, Sebe Ballentine ran foxes up and down the west side of the Broad River. Shown with Sebe is his grandson, Jimmy Bull, who holds the fox horn presented to Sebe by the late Fred D. Marshall, former mayor of Columbia. Sebe was a charter member of the South Carolina Fox Hunters Association. He was also a merchant, a ginner, a farmer, and a huge baseball fan.

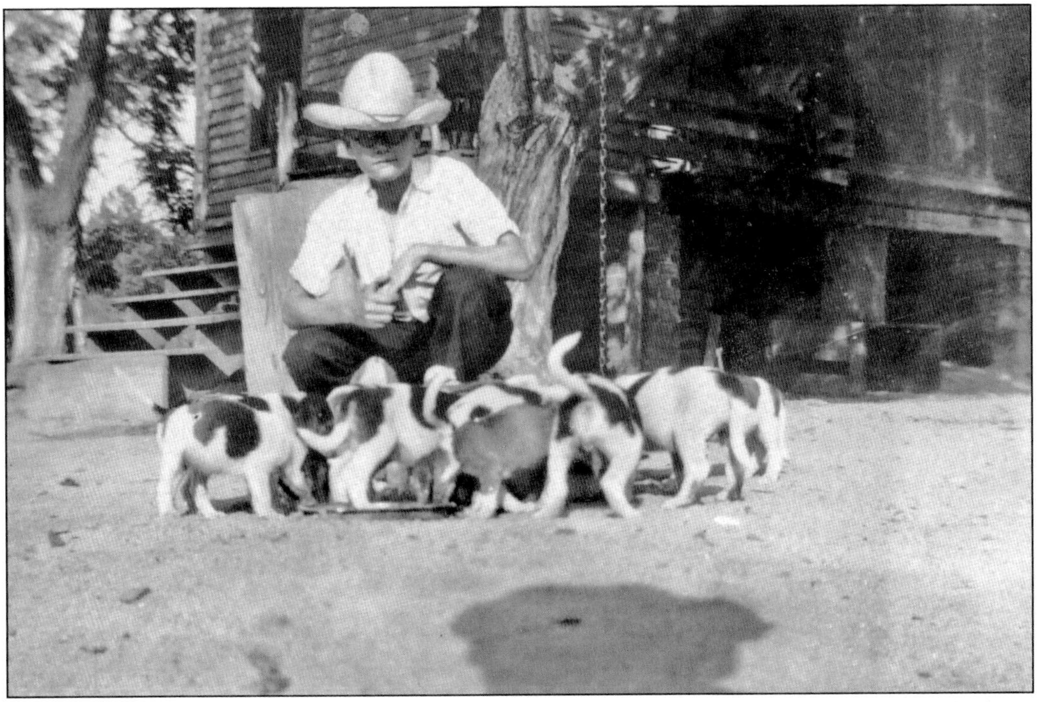

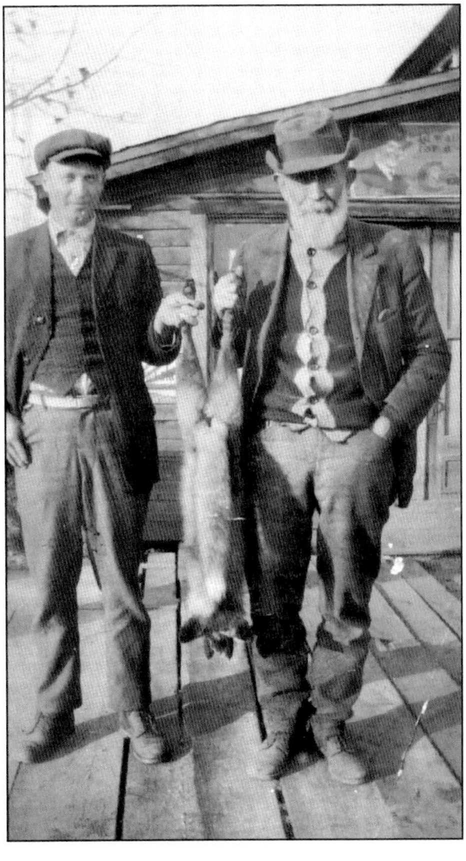

Max Ballentine's nephew "Baby" Kohn is feeding the young litter of hound puppies. The American foxhound is descended from the English, Irish, and French foxhounds and is the oldest sporting dog in America. They are black, white, and tan in either a tricolor or bicolor pattern.

Two unidentified gentlemen are posing with the fox caught during one of the many foxhunts around Ballentine in the late 1920s. Some older residents believe this picture was taken in front of the old two-story building that was located near High Noon where the Bull Oil tanks were.

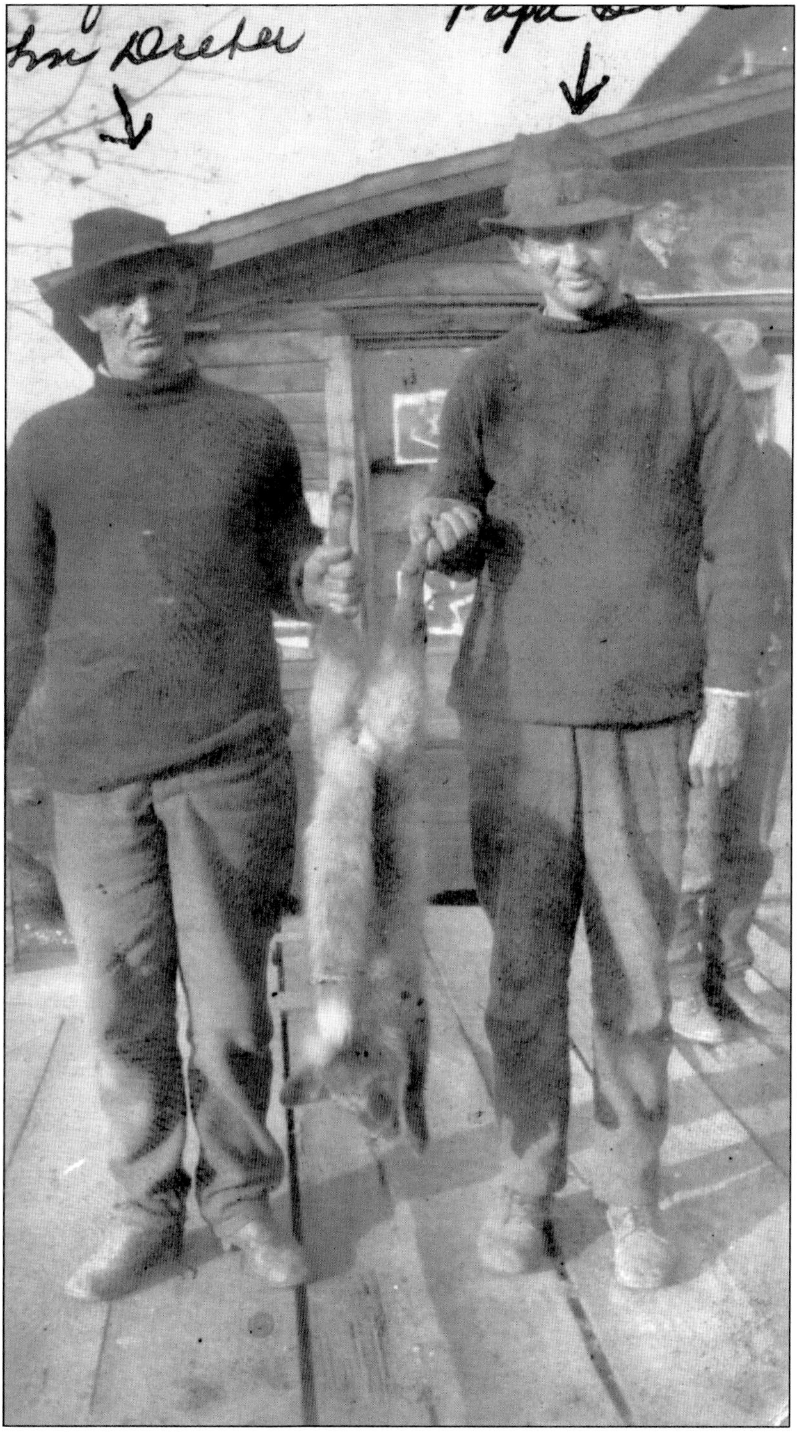

John Dreher and Sebe Ballentine were avid fox hunters. According to family members, they went foxhunting whenever the opportunity arose. They would sometimes go down to other parts of the state, especially the lower part, for hunts, and fox hunters from other areas would come to Ballentine.

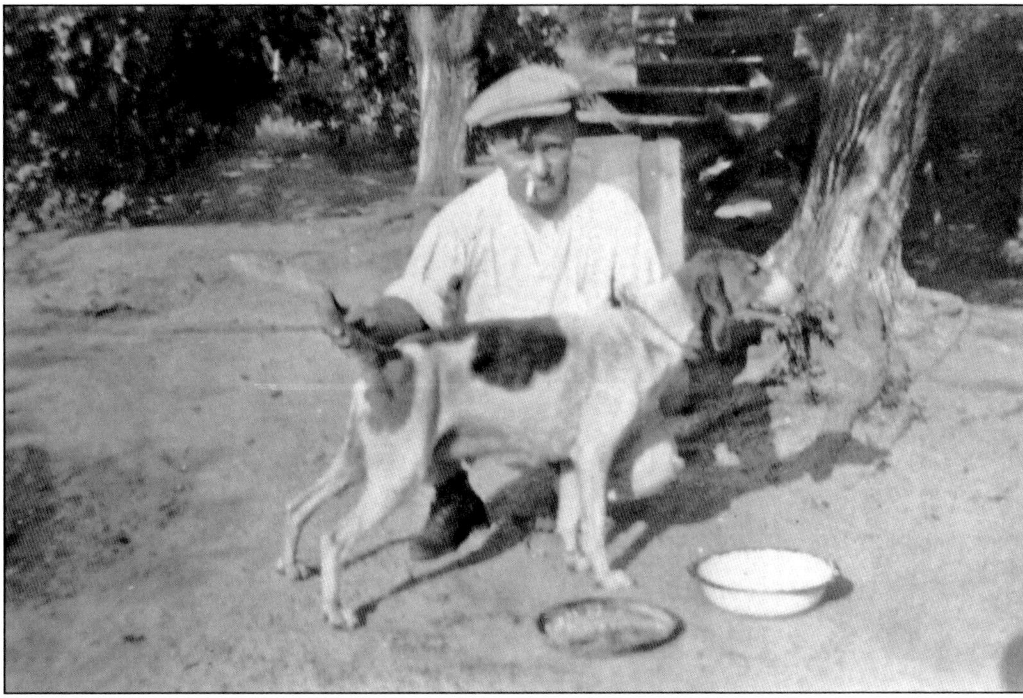

Max Ballentine is shown with one of his prize hunting dogs. Max was one of the regular fox hunters and loved it as much as Papa Sebe. According to some older residents, it was not the actual catching of the fox but the chase that was so much fun.

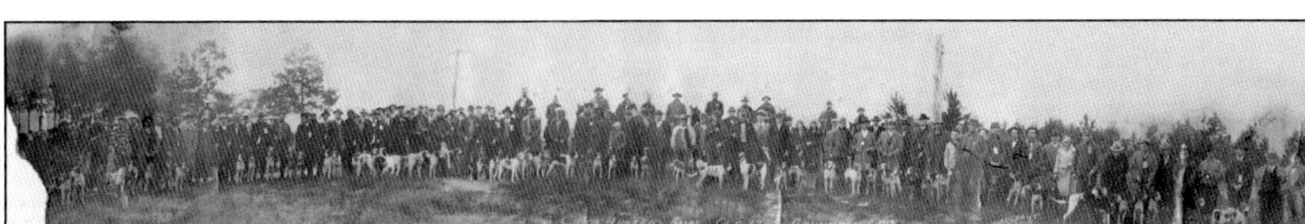

Members of the South Carolina Fox Hunters Association of 1928 are shown posing with their dogs. Several women and young boys were members of the association.

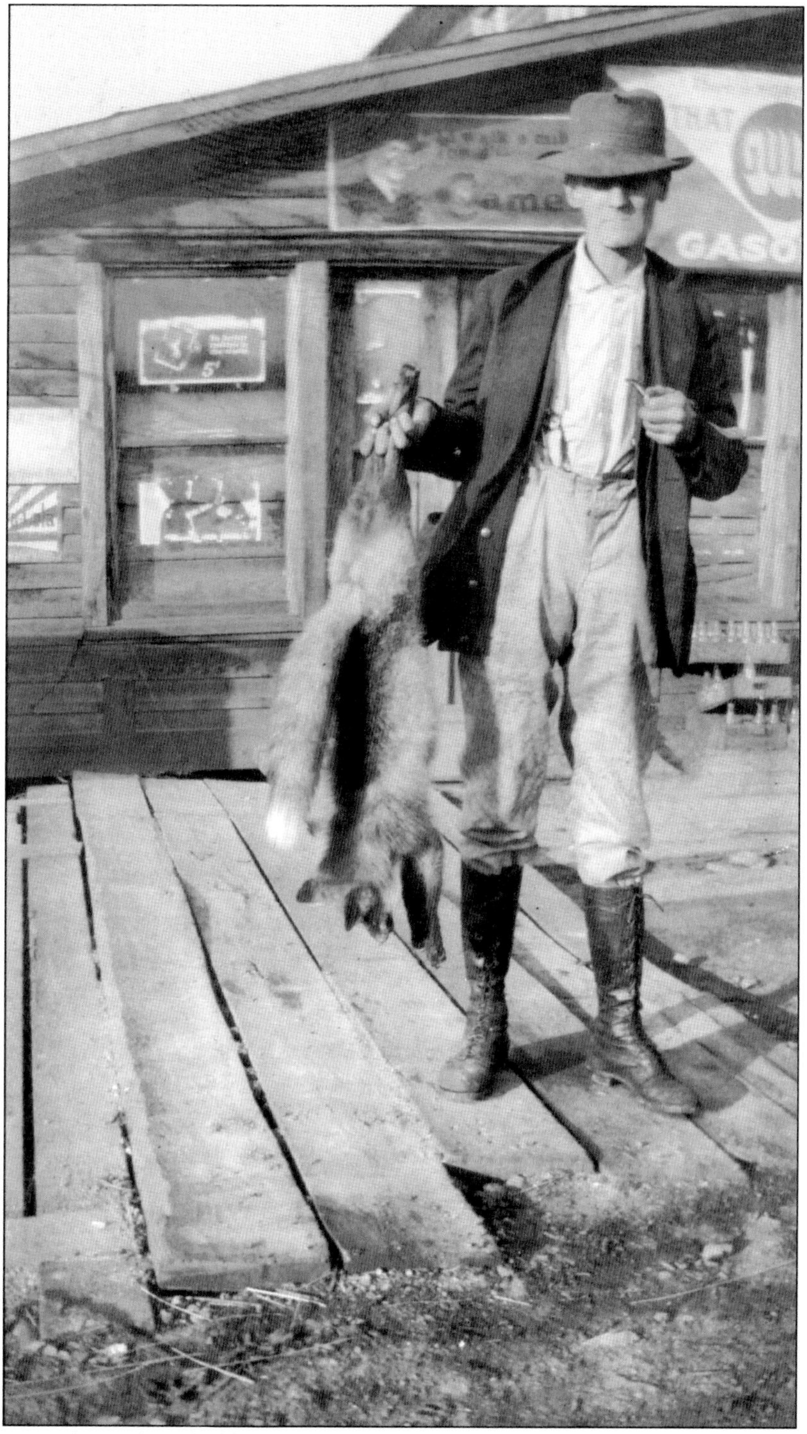

Sam Lowman is shown here holding a fox caught during one of the many foxhunts in Ballentine. It is believed he is standing in front of the shed that was attached to the two-story general store (behind where High Noon now sits). Later the Woodmen of the World would hold meetings in the upper story, and the Keith family lived in the lower story.

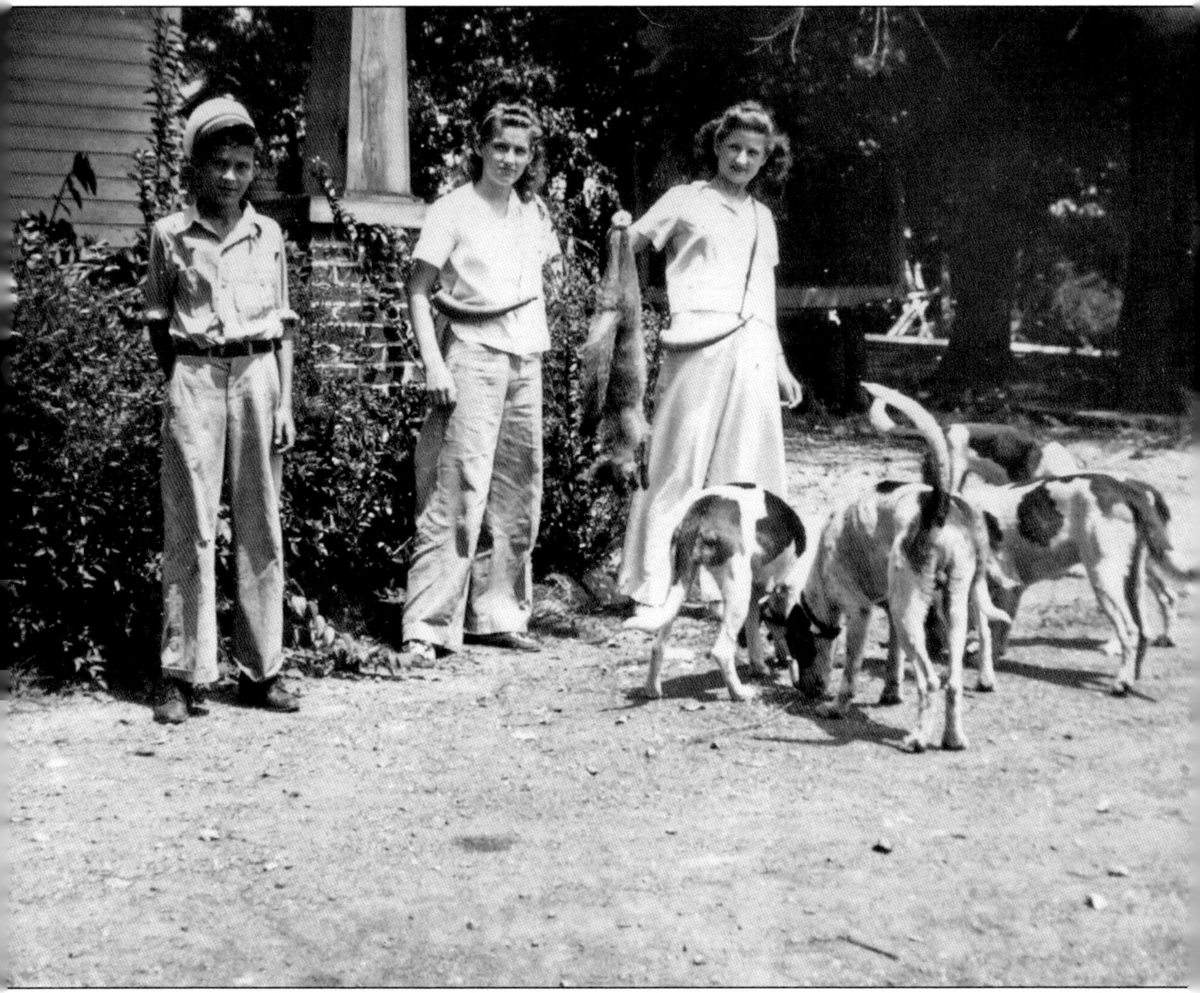

From left to right, John B. Lowman Jr., Myrtle Ballentine Bull, and Marie Still Buist are standing outside of Myrtle's house with her daddy's hounds. Marie loved to go foxhunting with Papa Sebe and went whenever she could. Marie was originally from Blackville but spent a lot of time in Ballentine with her sister Martha and her brother-in-law Rudolph. This picture was taken in the mid- to late 1930s.

Three

Going to Town

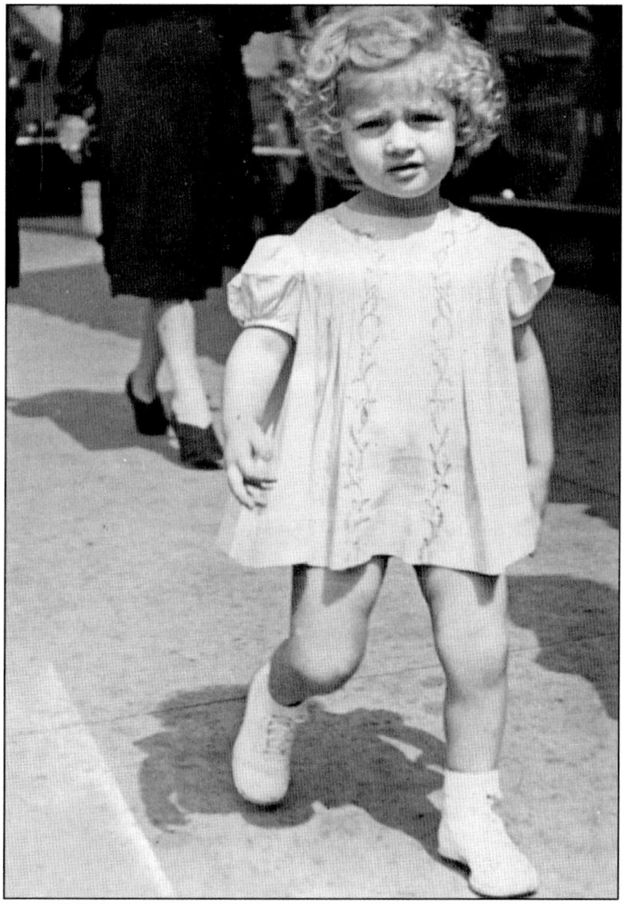

Carol Black is walking down Main Street of Columbia in 1940. She was an adorable two-year-old, and her mother, Miriam, wrote that Carol insisted on sending this photograph to her aunt, Myrtle Ballentine Bull.

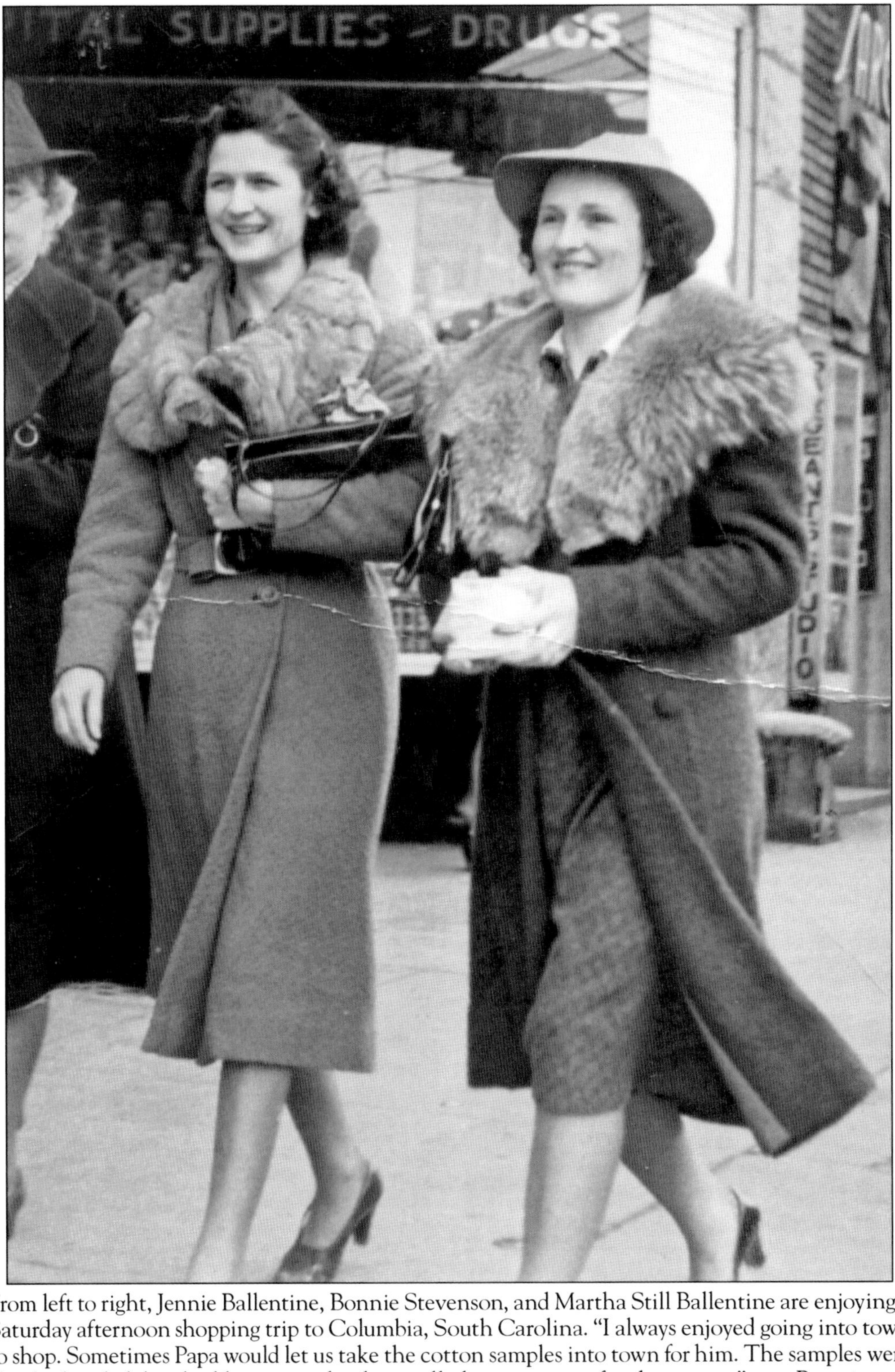

From left to right, Jennie Ballentine, Bonnie Stevenson, and Martha Still Ballentine are enjoying a Saturday afternoon shopping trip to Columbia, South Carolina. "I always enjoyed going into town to shop. Sometimes Papa would let us take the cotton samples into town for him. The samples were checked and if they had long strands when pulled we got more for the cotton," says Bonnie.

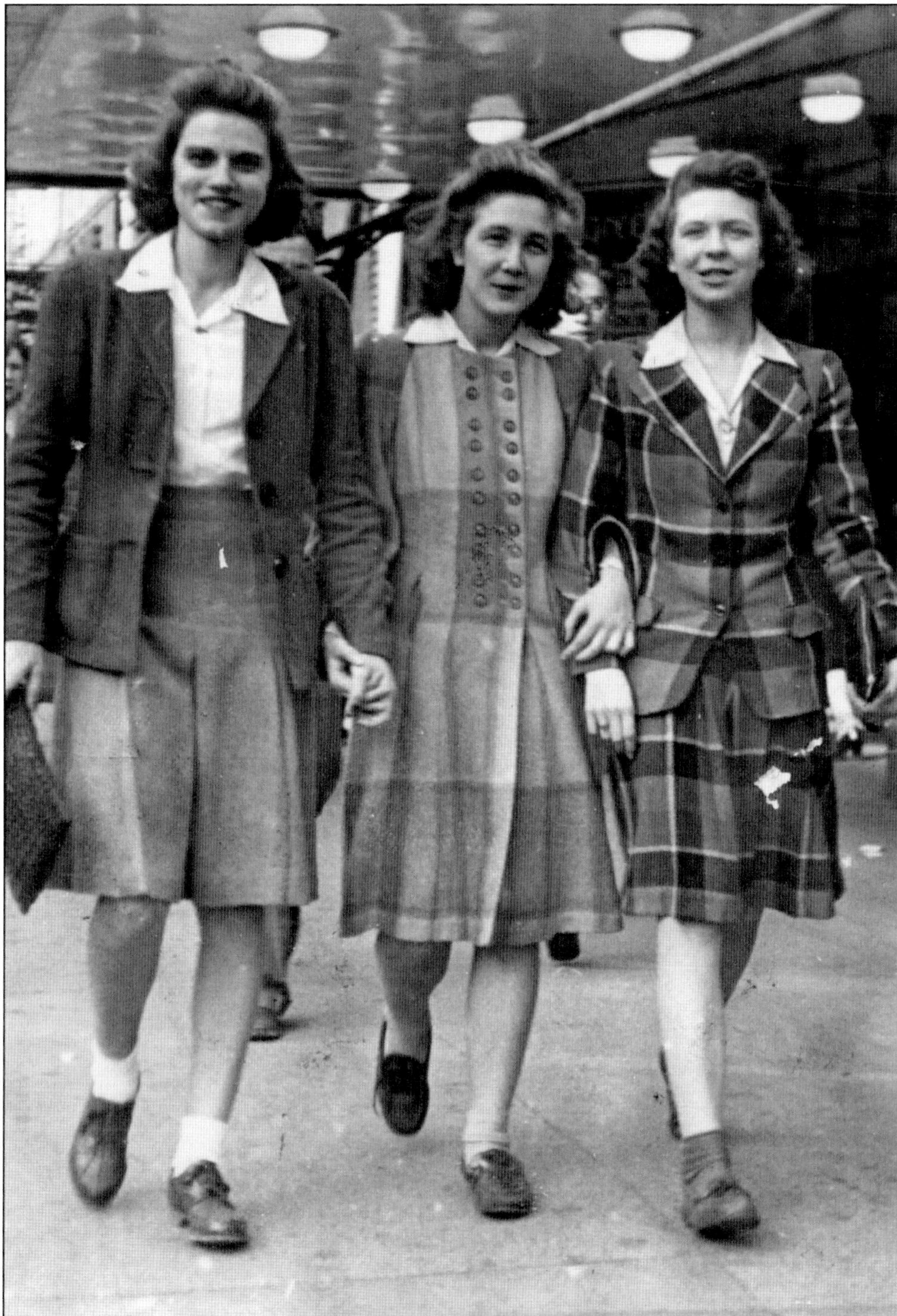

From left to right, Marjie Troutman, Lucy Lindler, and Catherine Koon are happily strolling down Main Street in Columbia. The year was 1945, and apparently they had a lot to be happy about. It was the year World War II ended, and friends and family members would be returning home. (Courtesy of Lucy Lindler.)

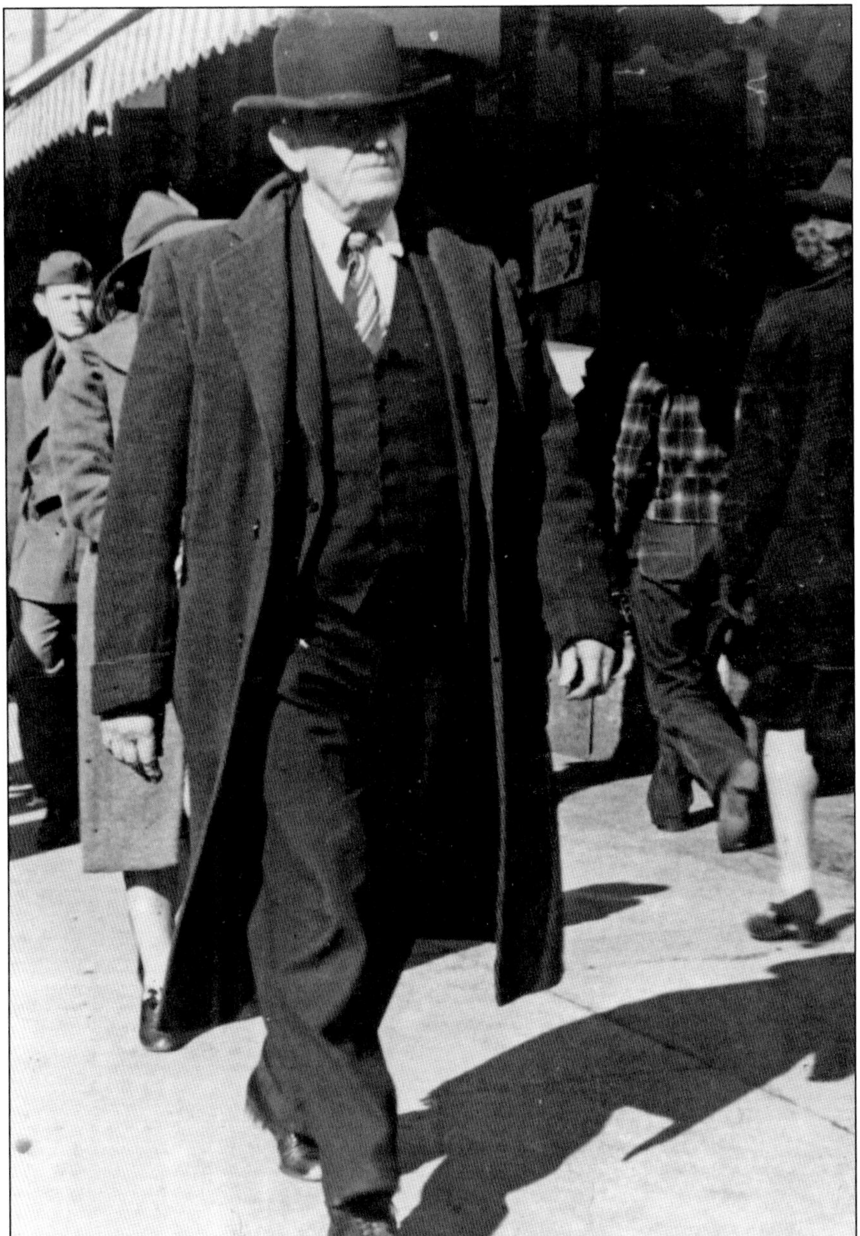

John Green Hiller is walking down Main Street in Columbia in the 1940s. Some people called this "candid camera." A photographer would go up and down Main Street taking various pictures of people passing by. The subjects would buy the picture, and he would mail the pictures to them. The back of the photograph was like a postcard with a place for the postage and could be sent through the mail. When it was cold, John Hiller always wore his black J. B. Stetson hat and long overcoat. Hiller was known as "the Captain," and he got the name from a black man name Fred "Crusty" Richardson, who worked for him at the highway department. Sometimes Hiller would tease Crusty and say he was going to tell his wife, Rugie, on him if he did not behave. Crusty would say, "Oh Captain, don't do that." (Courtesy of Jonnie Mae Sites.)

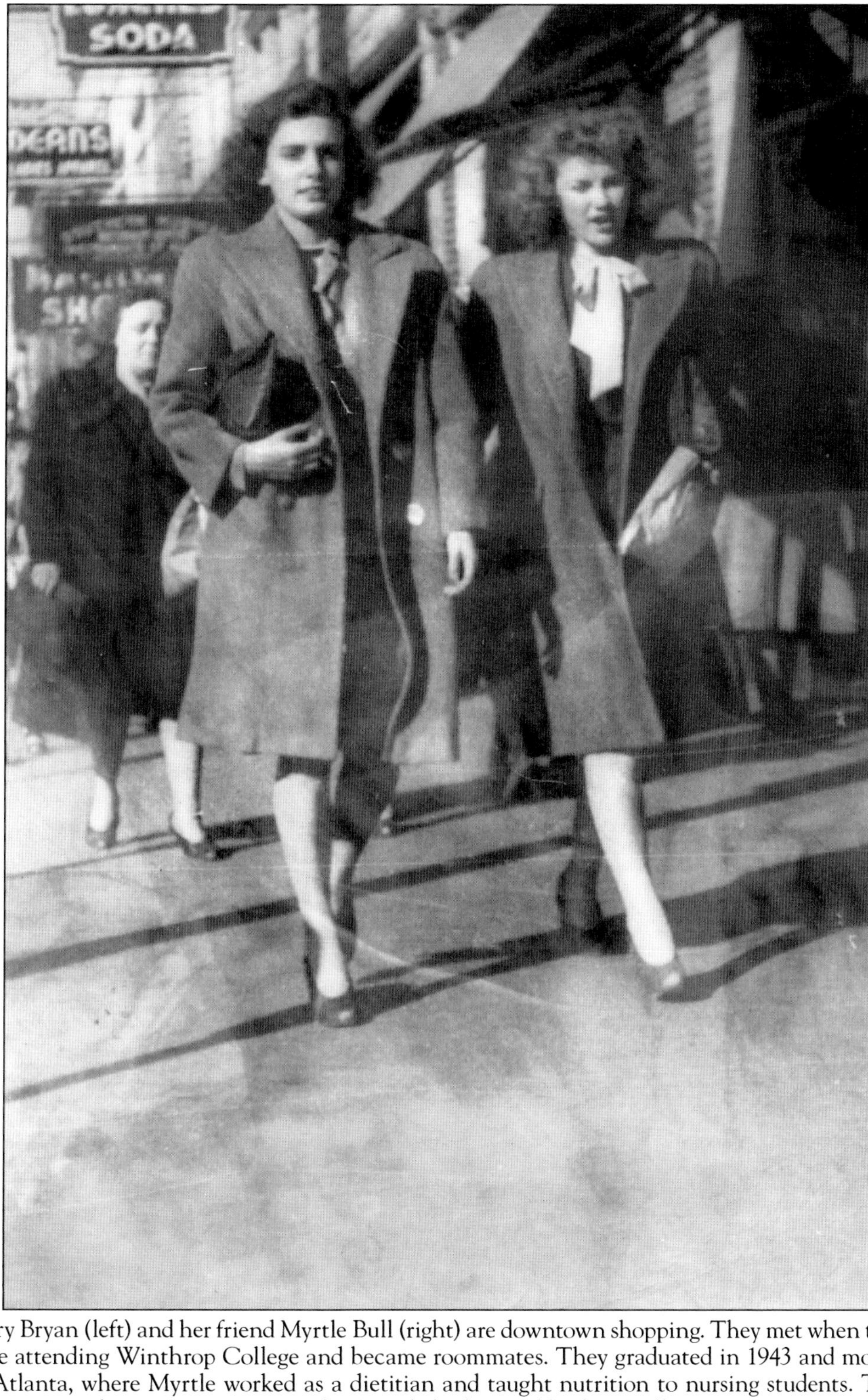

Mary Bryan (left) and her friend Myrtle Bull (right) are downtown shopping. They met when they were attending Winthrop College and became roommates. They graduated in 1943 and moved to Atlanta, where Myrtle worked as a dietitian and taught nutrition to nursing students. This picture was taken in January 1946 after Myrtle had moved back to Ballentine.

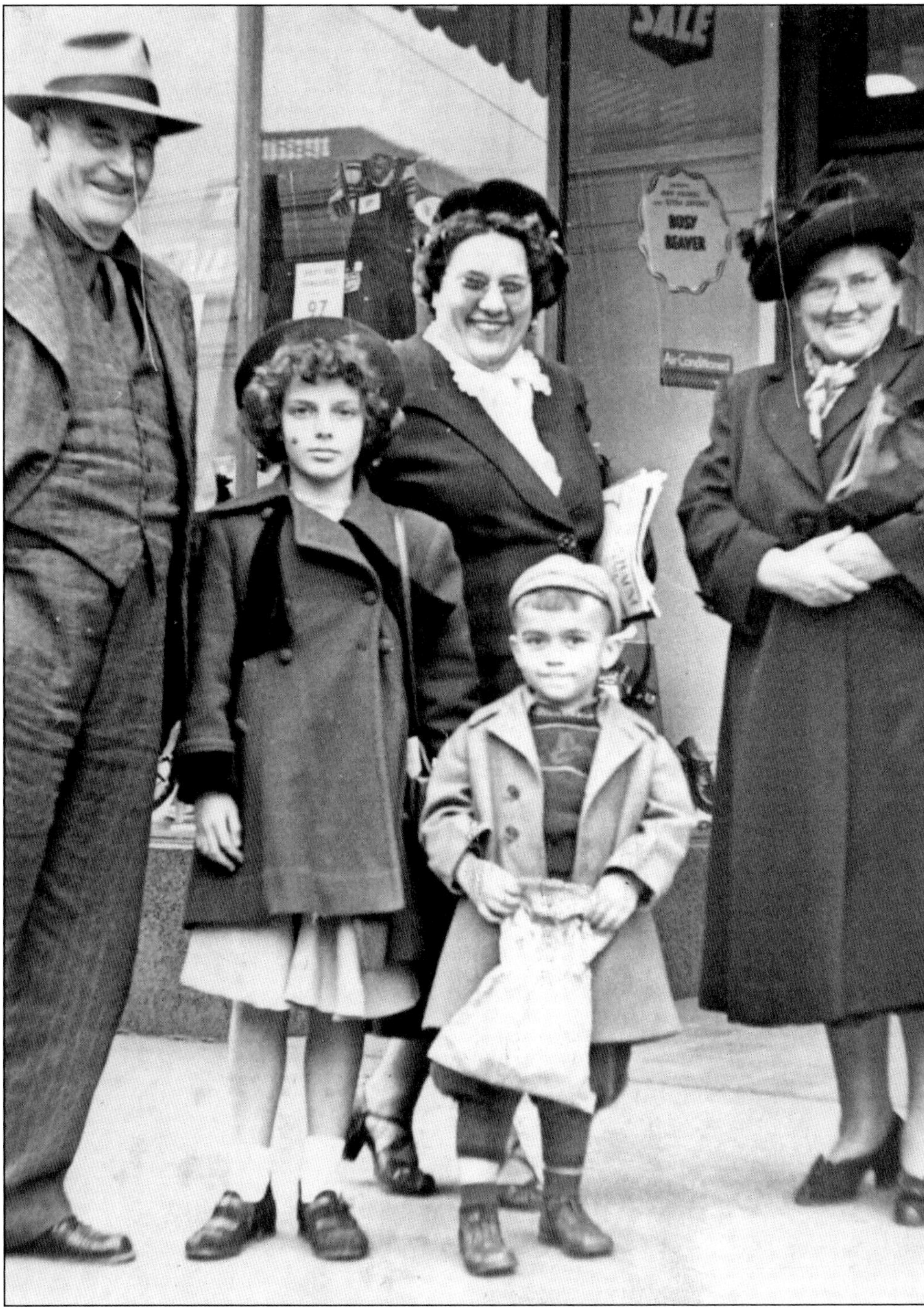

Kay Barr and her family are shopping downtown. The year was 1951. From left to right are Kay's grandfather G. J. Sheely, Kay, Kay's mother Ruth, a cousin Terry Coker, and Kay's grandmother Blanche. Kay said it was always a big deal when they went to town and people always dressed up. Her grandmother always stressed the importance of looking your best when you went to town. The photographer on Main Street was always out taking pictures, and this tradition carried on into the 1960s; it had apparently started in the 1930s. (Courtesy of Kay Shealy.)

Four

1920s to Present

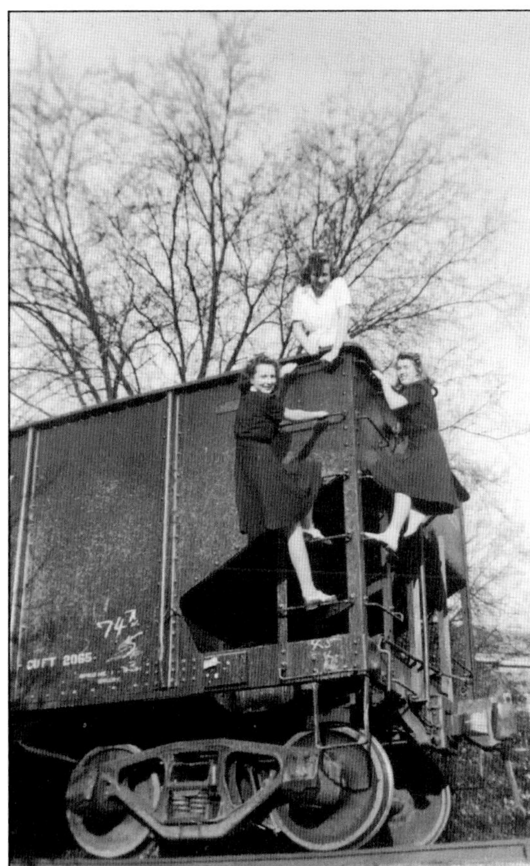

These three unidentified girls are having a great time posing on the train. The train was stopped in Ballentine, and the girls apparently could not resist climbing aboard. Trains have always held a fascination for many. The stamp date on the back of the photograph is April 1941, just a few months before the United States would be attacked at Pearl Harbor.

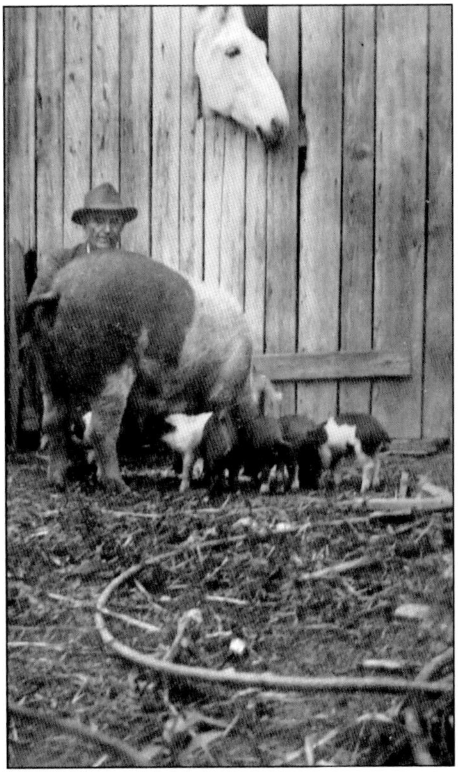

George Johnston Sheely is petting the mother sow and her piglets while "Old Gray" looks on. Old Gray is the horse with his head sticking out of the stall. Johnston loved his animals and took good care of them. His life was farming. Even on his deathbed, he was still concerned about them. Sheely was also hardly ever seen without his pipe. (Courtesy of Kay Shealy.)

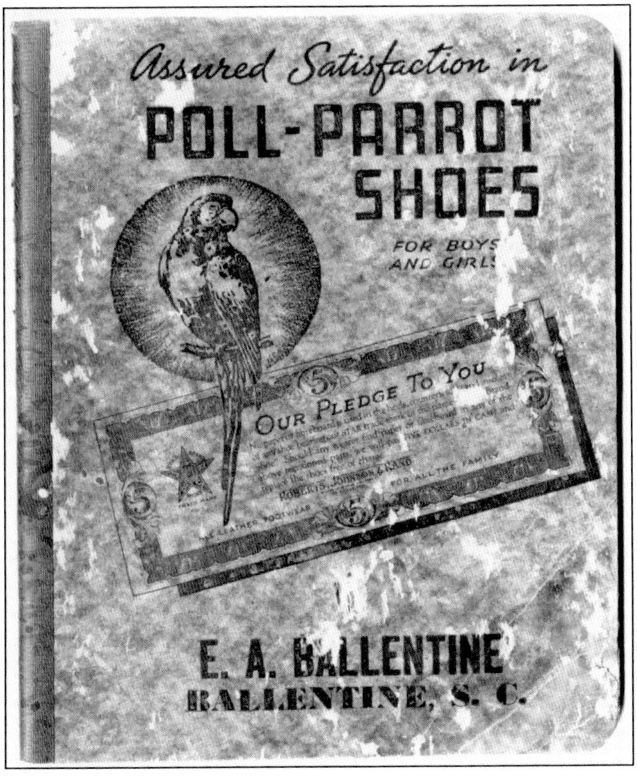

Sebe Ballentine sold Poll-Parrot shoes in his store in the 1940s and apparently this was some type of advertising for the shoes. This Poll-Parrot notebook also had Sebe Ballentine's store name on the front. On the back of the notebook was useful information such as the tables of multiplication, table of time measure, table of dry measure, table of paper measure, table of circular measure, table of roy weight, and several other measurements.

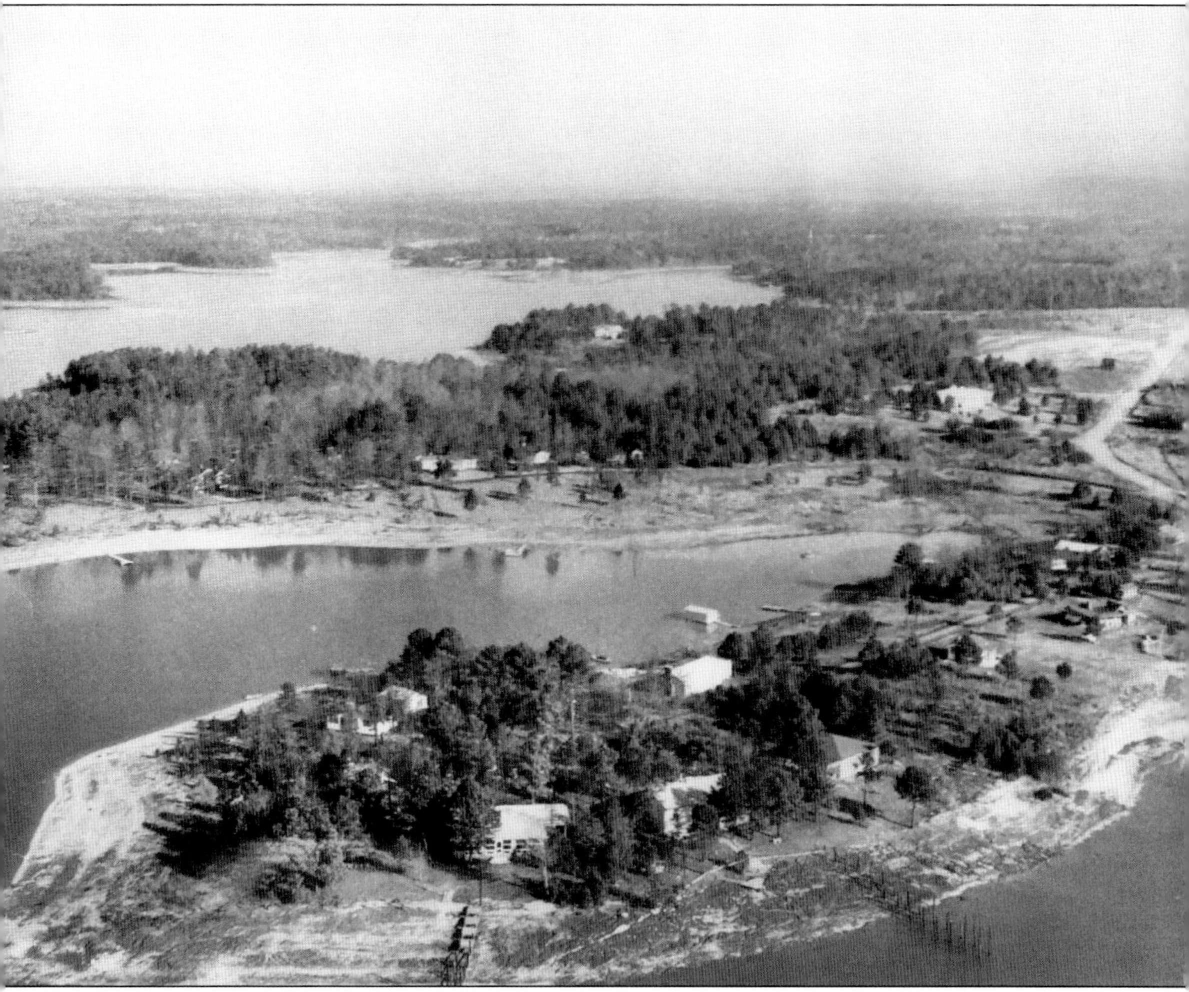

This aerial view of what is now called Marina Road was taken in the late 1930s or early 1940s. This photograph was found in Dr. Dotterer's house after he moved out. The whole Pebble Shore Road section was once known as Doctor's Point because all of the houses and lake cabins belonged to doctors. This land had previously been part of the Noah Shealy farm. Before the lake was formed, Marina Road continued on and connected with Bush River Road near High Hill Church. (Courtesy of Tom Rhodes.)

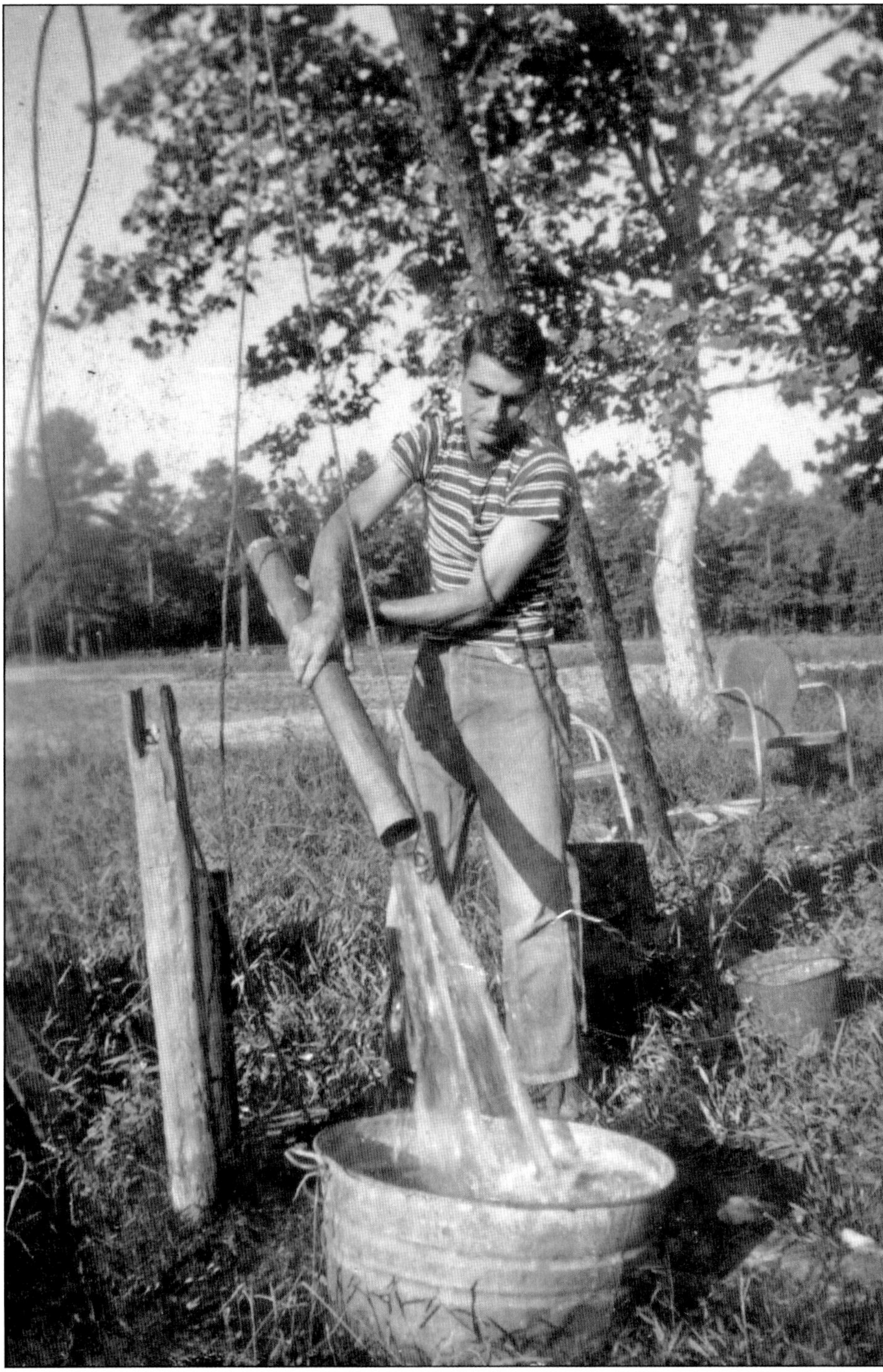

Fred Lindler is shown getting water from a punch well. A punch well was approximately 6 inches in diameter, with a hole punched into the ground instead of being hand dug or drilled. This picture was taken in the late 1940s, probably a year or so after Fred and Lucy were married. (Courtesy of Lucy Lindler.)

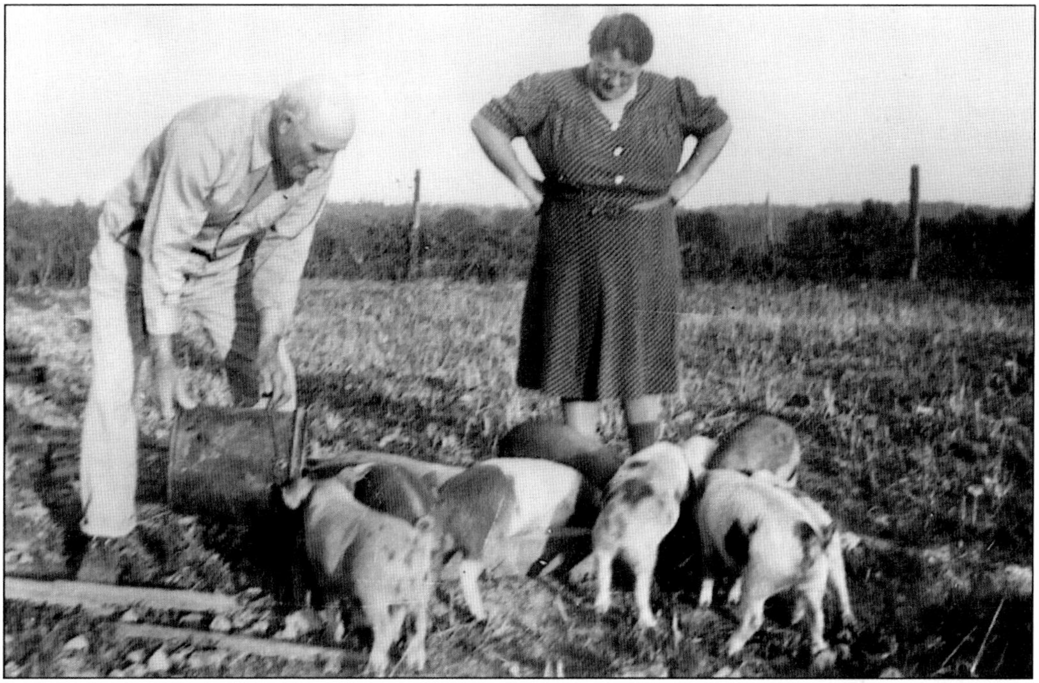

George Johnson Sheely and his wife, Blanche Sheely, are feeding their newest litter of pigs, or what some people call "slopping the pigs." Blanche was a homemaker who enjoyed growing flowers and was a very talented seamstress. She made many of her family's clothes and made a lot of the costumes for her granddaughters' plays. (Courtesy of Kay Sheely.)

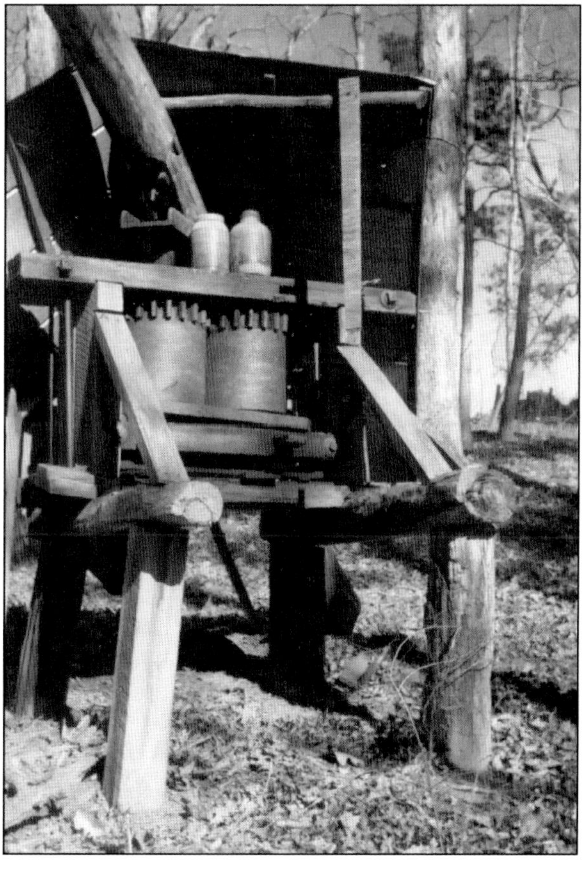

This is a cane press, used to press the juice out of the cane to make syrup. The cane was put in the cane mill and two mules would walk around the (animal-powered) press, causing the juice to be extracted. This press belonged to Owen Lowman. (Courtesy of John Bouknight.)

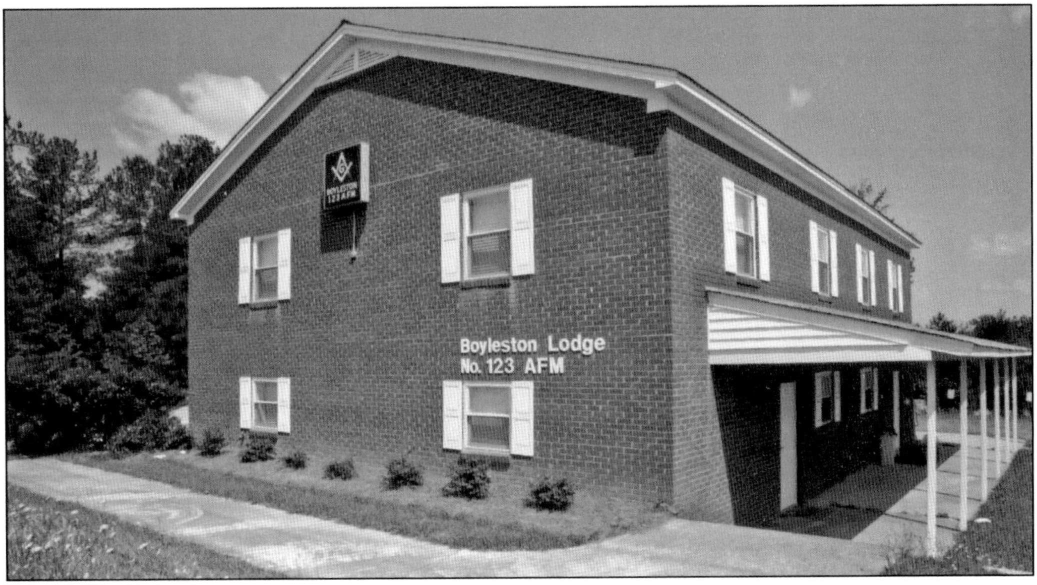

Boyleston's Lodge 123 was originally chartered on November 17, 1867, at Rocky Well in Lexington District, near what is now St. John's Lutheran Church on Highway 378. The meetings were held on the Saturday night preceding each full moon, as it was easier to travel at night under the full moon. The lodge was moved to Ballentine, and a new Masonic Lodge was built around 1920. On September 11, 1954, a dedication of the present lodge was held. Approximately 450 people (including wives and family members) attended the dedication and picnic. (Courtesy of Boyleston Lodge 123.)

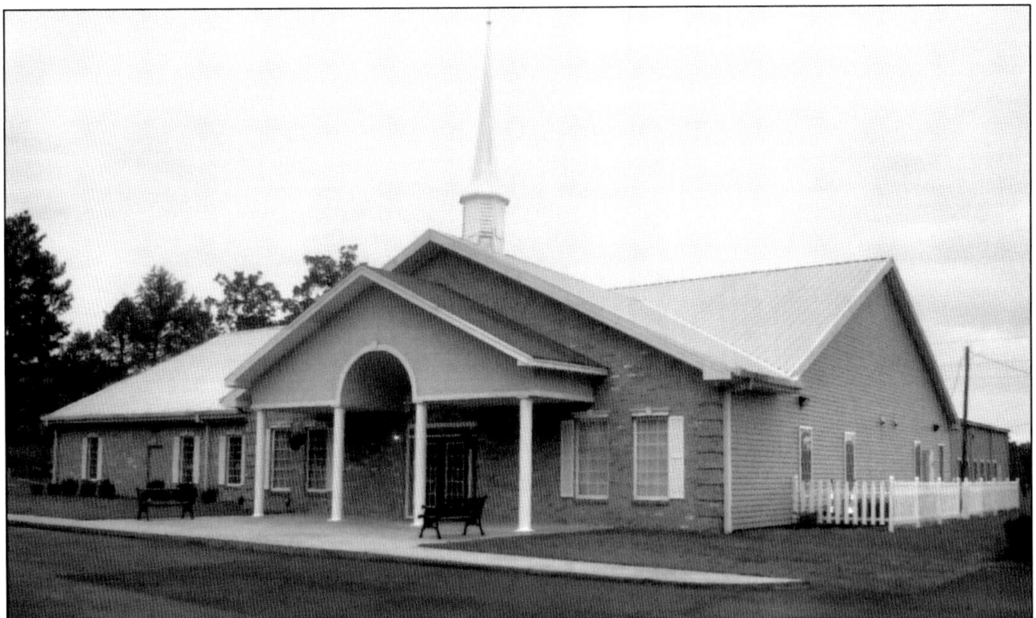

New Life Community Church started in 1990 in a storefront building and moved to its present location, 10809 Broad River Road, Irmo, in 1999. The mission statement of the church is "Loving God and Building People," and the church is affiliated with the Assemblies of God. (Courtesy of Marilyn Bull.)

This little black-and-brown terrier-mix dog seems to be a natural at driving the toy car, which was from the 1920s. According to Myrtle Bull, who was only three or four years old when this photograph was taken, he liked to be pushed and he would steer the car.

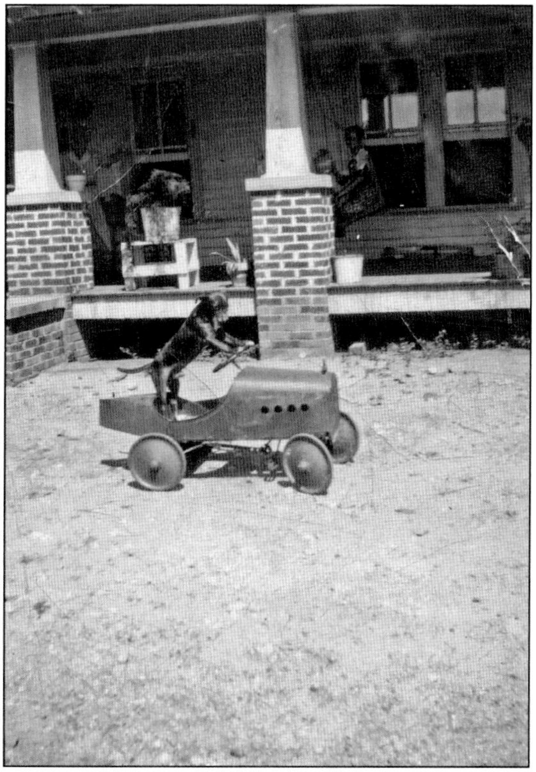

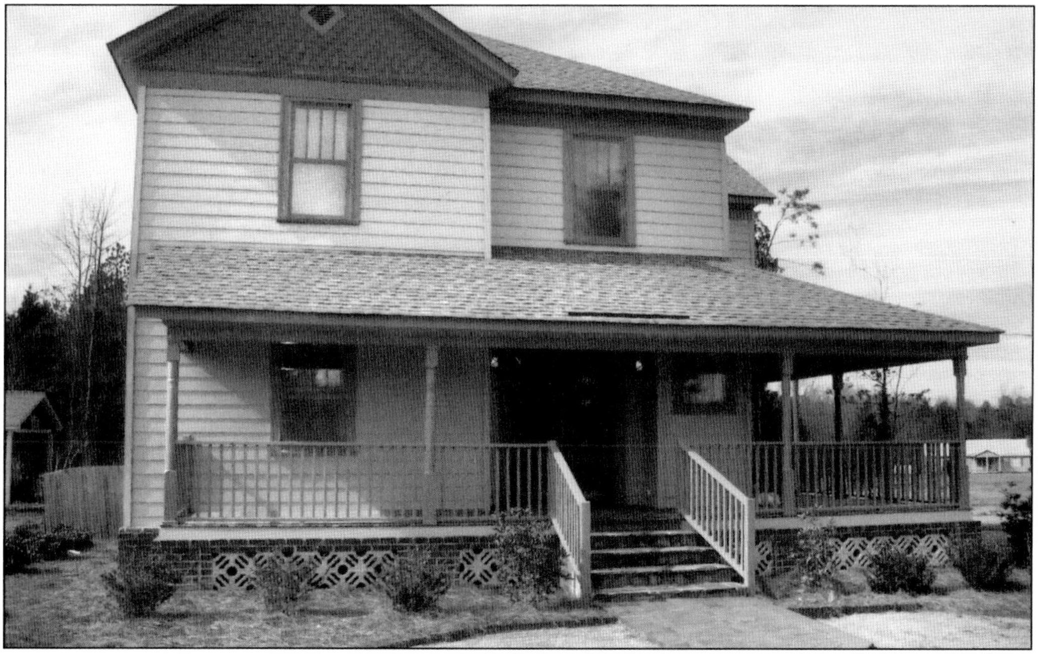

This is the Bickley home after it was restored by Jolene and Jimmy Smith. The home was originally located on the other side of Bickley Road where the new Ballentine Elementary School now stands. The Smiths moved the house to its present site, and Jolene Smith ran a decorating business from there. (Courtesy of Marilyn Bull.)

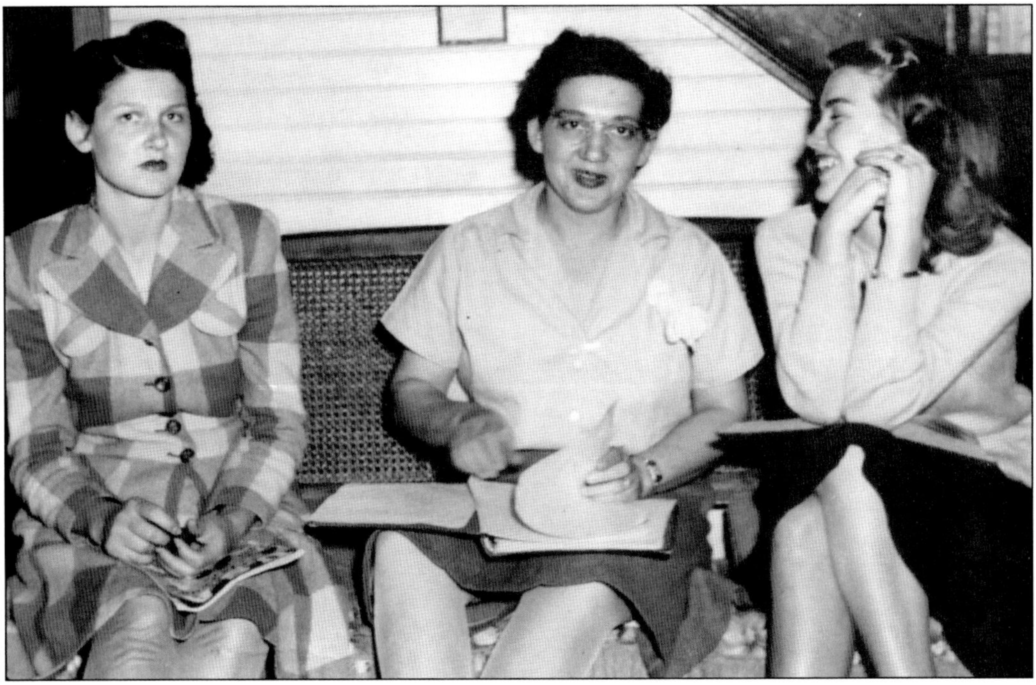

Verta Sheely is sitting between her two sisters Bonnie and Myrtle. Verta attended Summerland College and taught English at Newberry College and Chapin High School. She is helping her younger sister Myrtle with her homework.

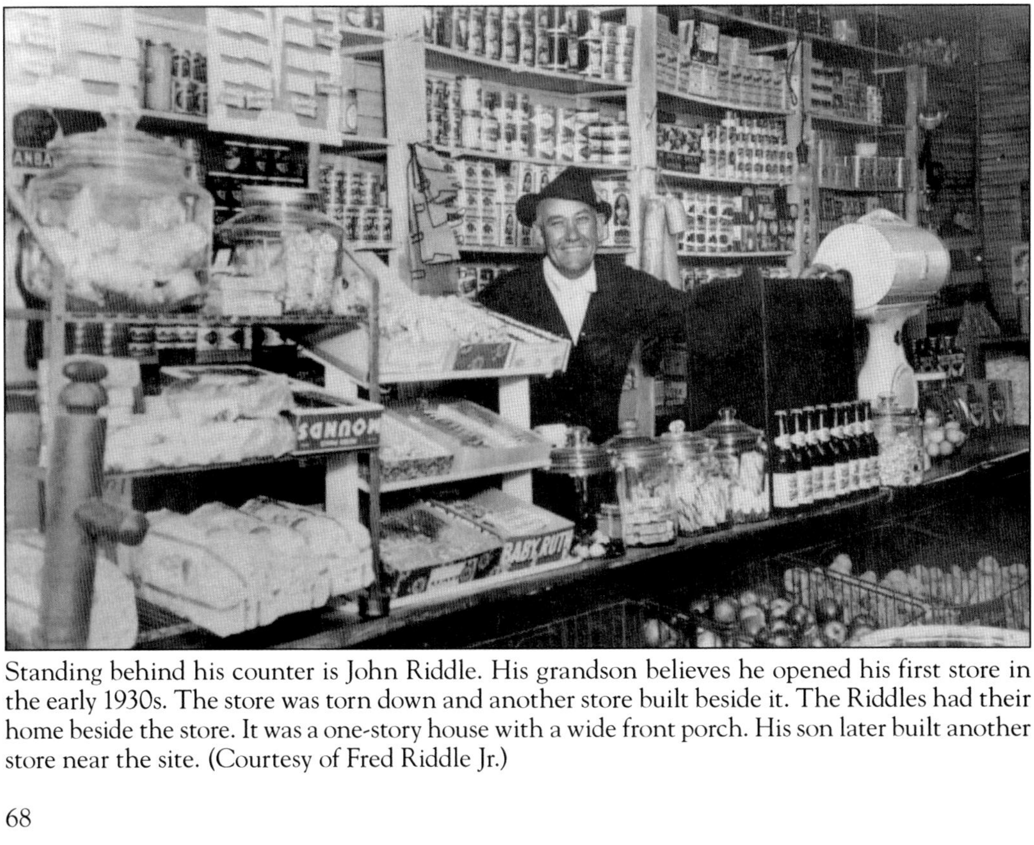

Standing behind his counter is John Riddle. His grandson believes he opened his first store in the early 1930s. The store was torn down and another store built beside it. The Riddles had their home beside the store. It was a one-story house with a wide front porch. His son later built another store near the site. (Courtesy of Fred Riddle Jr.)

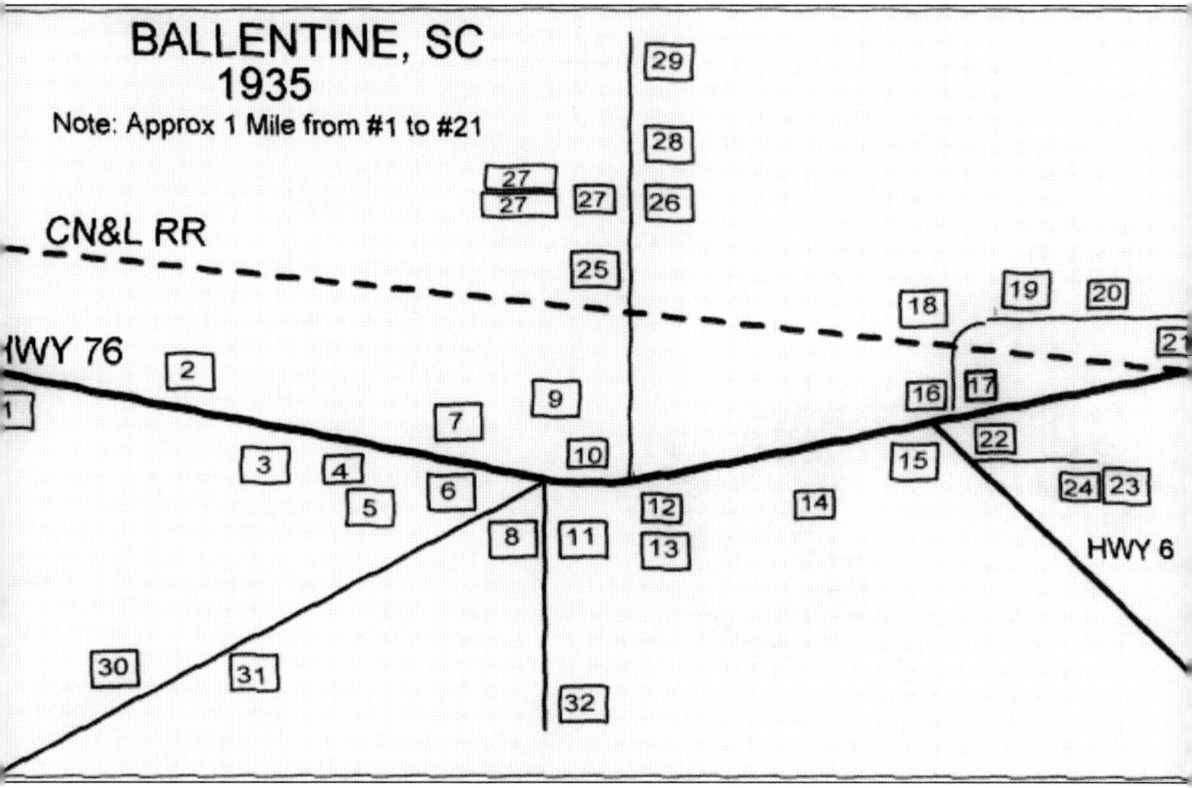

Bryson Lowman has re-created a hand-drawn map of Ballentine as he remembers it in 1935 and has listed all who lived there at that time: 1. Sallie Shealy; her son, Ellis ("Cy"); his wife, Catherine; their daughter Rebecca. 2. Rosabelle Wessinger; her sons James and Frank. 3. Anna Wessinger Lowman; her son, John Brooks; his wife, Dorothy; their two sons, Bryson and John Brooks. 4. L. (Lon) M. Ballentine Store. 5. L. M. and Bessie Keith Ballentine; sons Olin, J. D., and Keith; daughter Annie. 6. G. Johnson and Blanche Shealy; daughters Ruth and Gurnelle. 7. Dan and Maggie Stone. 8. Jim and Annie Swygert. 9. Andrew and Vivian Swygert; sons Donald and Johnny. 10. Andrew Swygert Garage. 11. Ballentine Elementary School. 12. John K. Riddle Store. 13. John and Eula Riddle; daughters Helen and Loraine. 14. Tenant house: Johnny Quattlebaum and mother. 15. Bob and Sallie Lowman; sons John and Jim; grandsons Grady and Ike. 16. E. A. Ballentine Store. 17. Two-story wood-frame house: old "Judge" Quattlebaum family. 18. Two-story building; upper story: Woodmen of the World; lower story: Frank Keith; his wife; son Von Ray Keith. 19. E. A. and Jennie Ballentine; sons Rudolph and Eugene, daughters Bonnie and Myrtle. (Note: Female teachers for the Ballentine School boarded here.) 20. Tenant house: Bill Smith family. 21. E. A. Ballentine cotton gin. 22. Masonic Hall. 23. John and Emogine Bouknight; daughter Vera. 24. Ballentine U.S. Post Office: Emogine Bouknight, postmistress. 25. Edgar Wise; his wife; son Eugene; daughters Katie and Margie. 26. Jim and Nora Wise; sons Frank Lee and Charlie. 27. Richland County Chain Gang Camp: Joe Lowman, captain. 28. Oscar Troutman; his wife; sons Thomas and Linel. 29. H. A. ("Gus") Bickley; his wife; sons Harper, Louie, and Archie; daughter Thelma. 30. R. Lester and Mary Derrick; son James; daughter Vernetta. 31. Bachman and Anna Derrick; son Weldon Derrick. 32. George Amick; his wife; son A. J. (Courtesy of Bryson Lowman.)

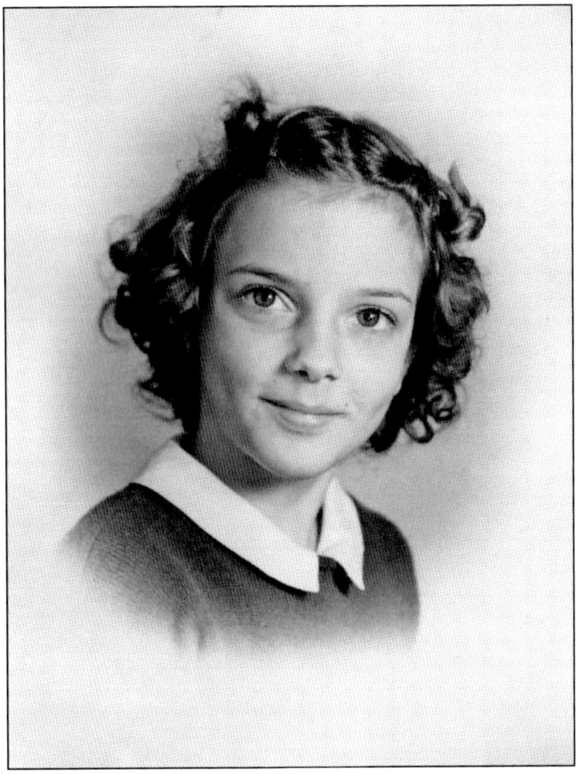

Kay Shealy said for this school picture she had rolled her hair in pin curls the night before. Her grandmother told her they would give her a comb before she had her picture taken and she could comb her hair out then. Unfortunately, according to Kay, she was not given a comb, so she had to have her picture taken without combing the curls out.

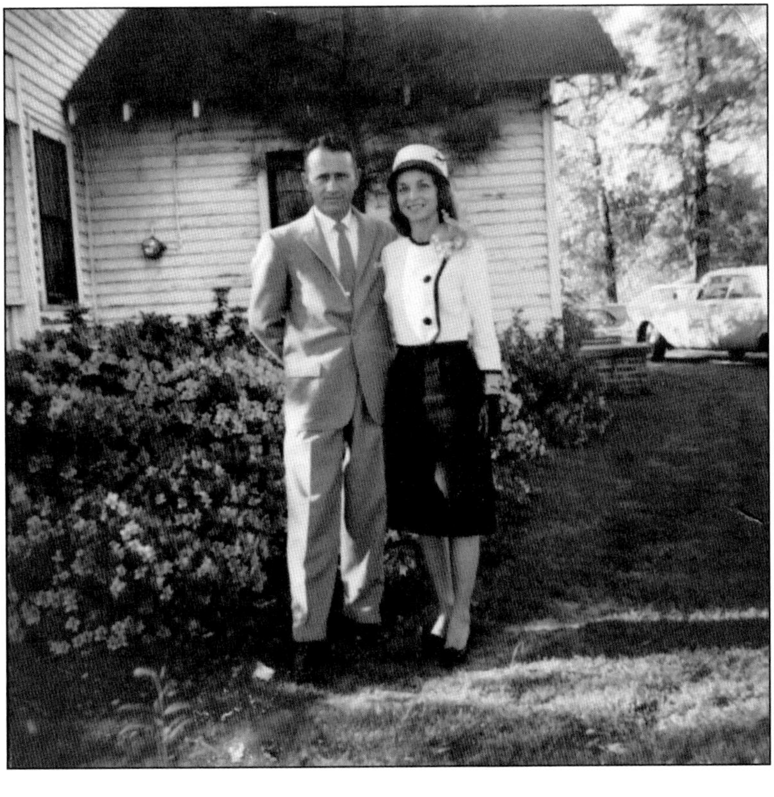

Alvin and Pat Derrick are standing at the side of the John and Blanche Derrick home. It was Easter Sunday, and the Derricks usually invited several friends over for breakfast. Previously, the house was home to Emogine Bouknight, the postmistress, and the section of the house shown was where the Ballentine Post Office was located. (Courtesy of Pat Derrick.)

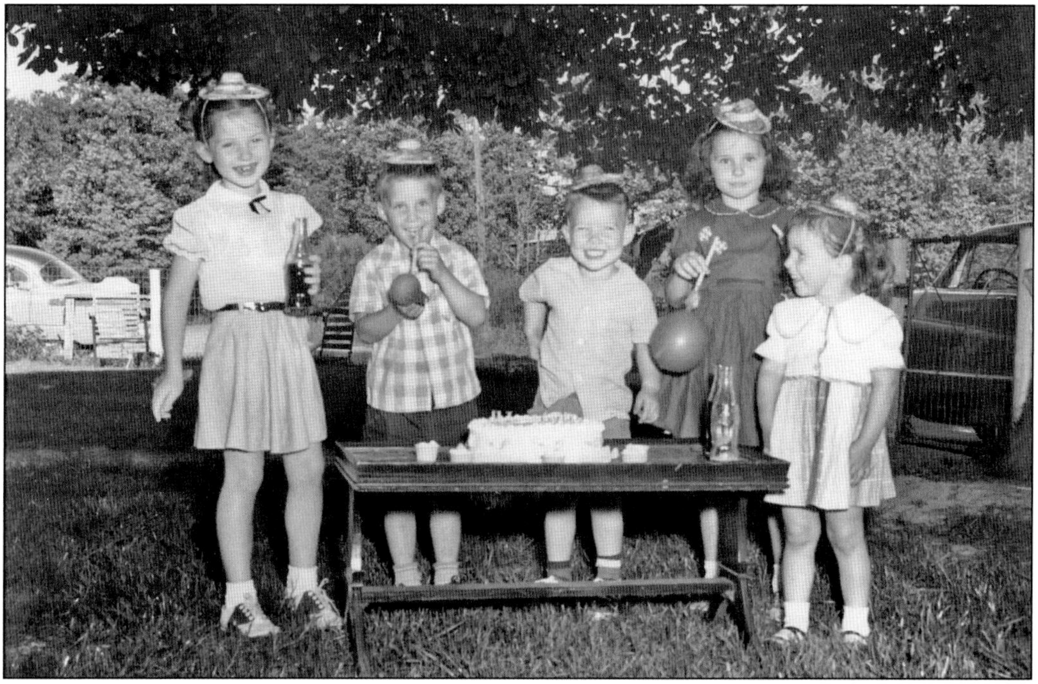

It was April 1954, and there was nothing better than celebrating a birthday with cake, Coca-Cola, balloons, and party hats. Helping Jimmy Bull celebrate are, from left to right, Genie Sosnowski, Koger Still, Jimmy Bull, Mary Margaret Still, and Patricia Still.

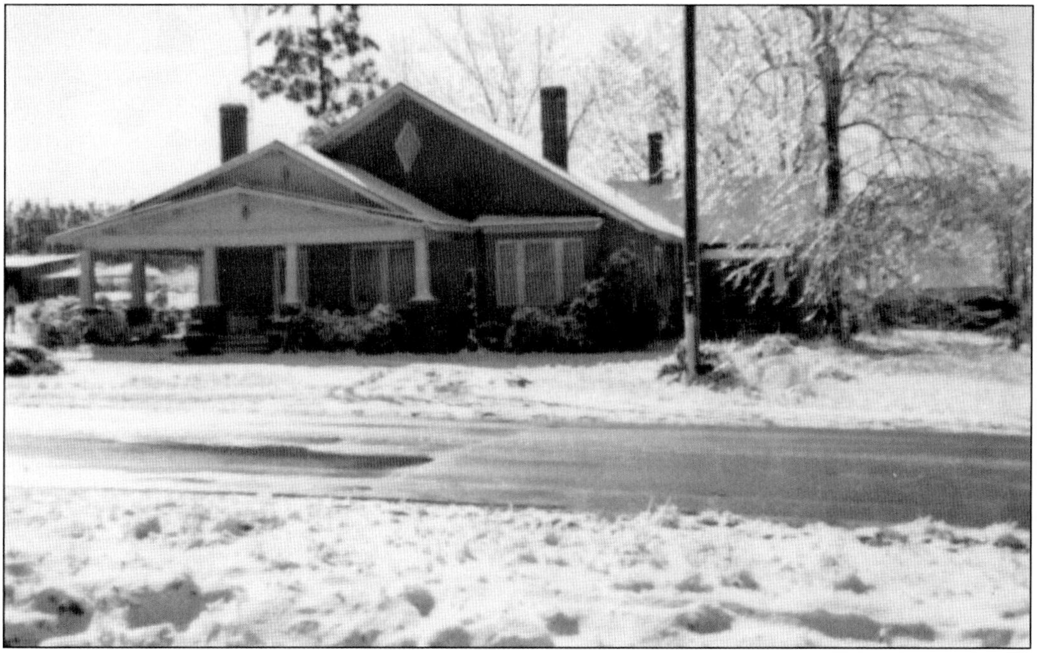

This craftsman-style house is the home of Barbara Porter. The home is believed to have been built in the late 1920s and was originally owned by the Lowmans. Barbara still remembers the first time she saw the house. She says she was not thrilled about living there, but after moving in and getting to know everyone, she fell in love with the area. (Courtesy of Barbara Porter.)

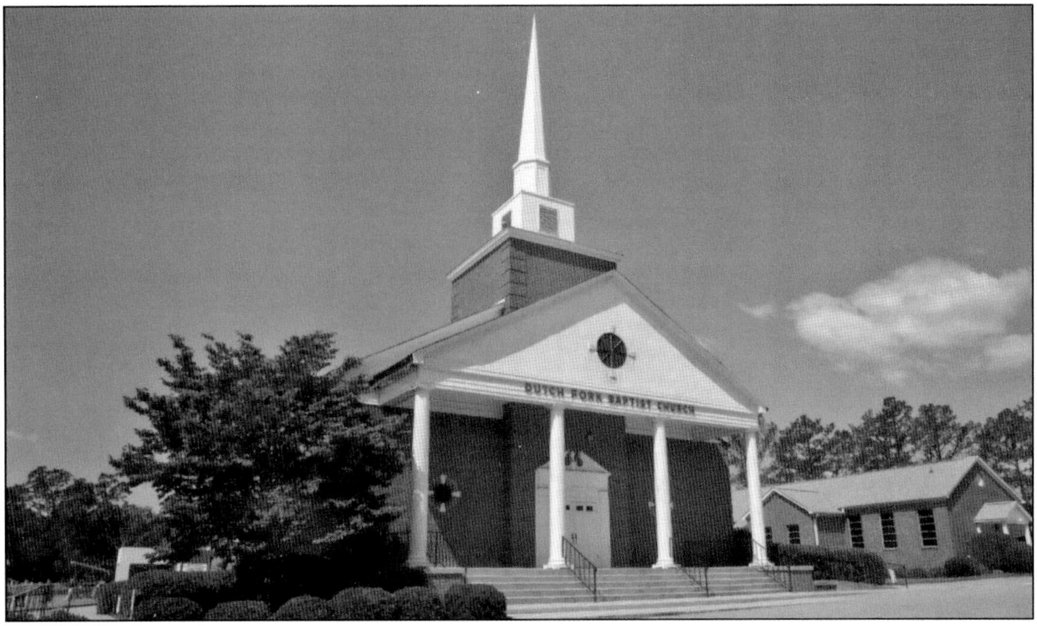

Dutch Fork Baptist Church's first building was dedicated April 20, 1958. Before the church was built, the congregation was known as the Dutch Fork Baptist Mission and had their first meeting on December 14, 1955, in the Old Dutch Fork School, where the school district offices are now located. The church grew rapidly, and in 1970, a mission committee was appointed to start a mission in the Chapin area. (Courtesy of Marilyn Bull.)

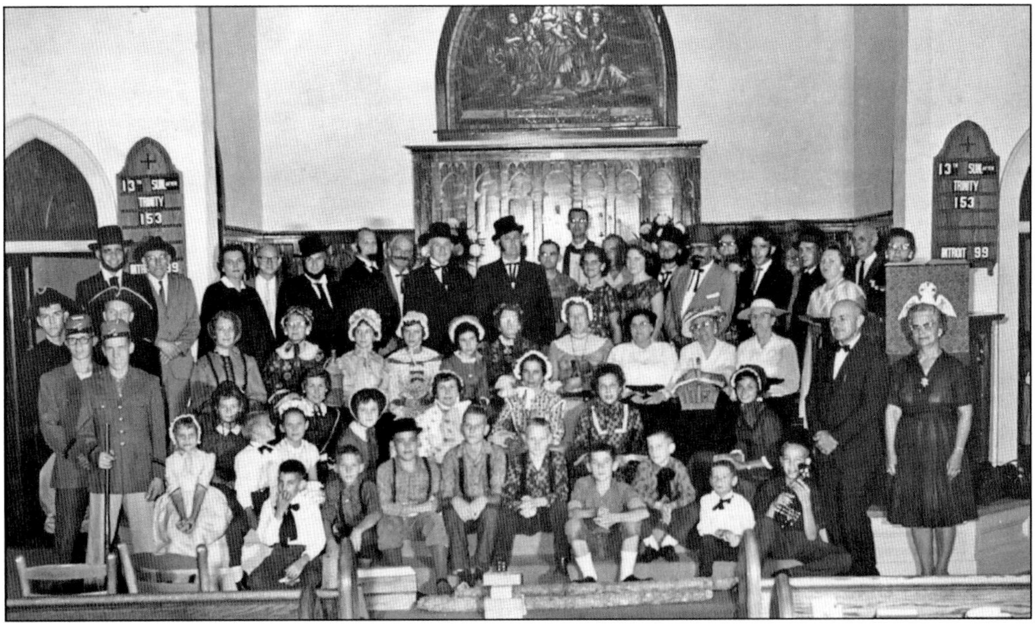

The Bethel Lutheran congregation celebrated the 200th anniversary of their church in 1962. Some members are shown here participating in the reenactment. Bethel Lutheran at High Hill was established in 1762. In 1928, Bethel merged with Mount Vernon. The new church was built in White Rock. Pastor Guy Cruse was the pastor of Bethel in 1959 and continued as pastor for over 30 years.

The Signets were a local band in the 1960s composed of Jim Bull (bass guitar), Wade Thompson (guitar), Ray Campbell (singer), Butch Trail (guitar), and Pat Simon (drums). They played locally, and one of their favorite groups was the Beatles—you can tell that from the hairstyles. (Courtesy of Jim Bull.)

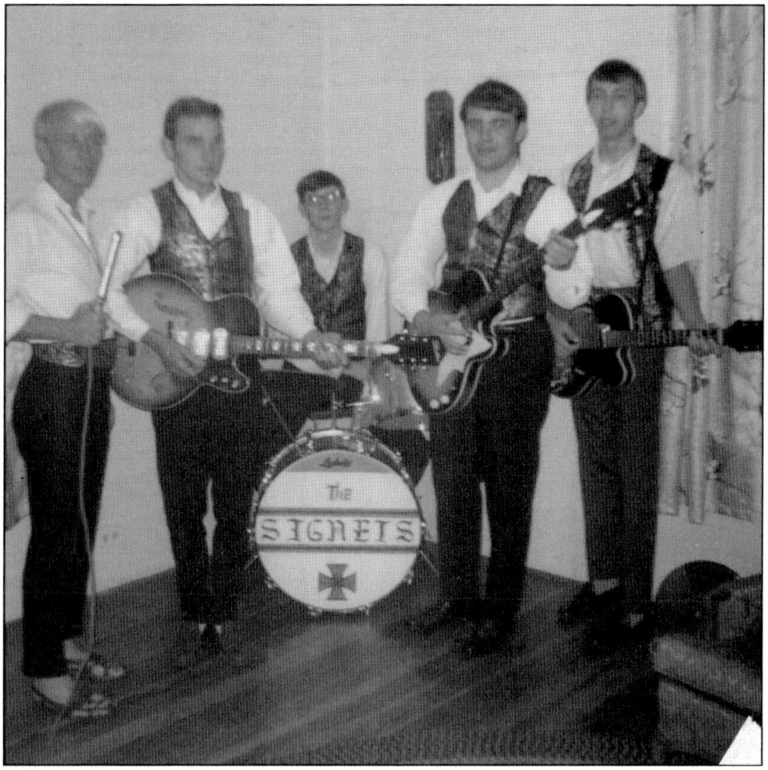

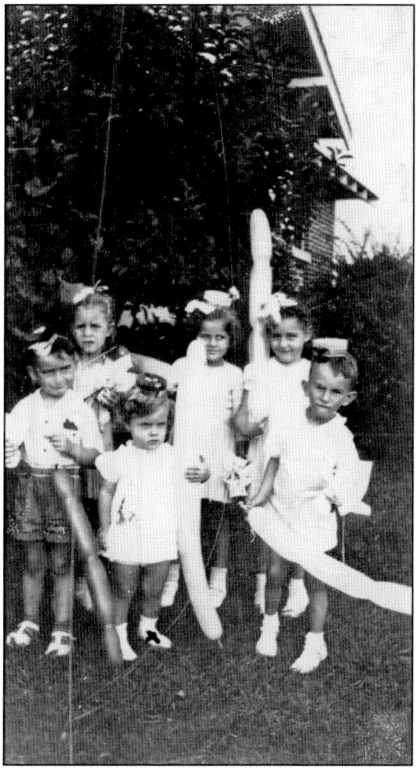

Jimmy Wessinger's birthday party in 1942 was attended by Marilyn Sheely (Shealy), Jane Cromer, Aldo Roy Stone, Donald Derrick, and Kay Barr (Shealy). Kay was almost two years old. (Courtesy of Kay Shealy.)

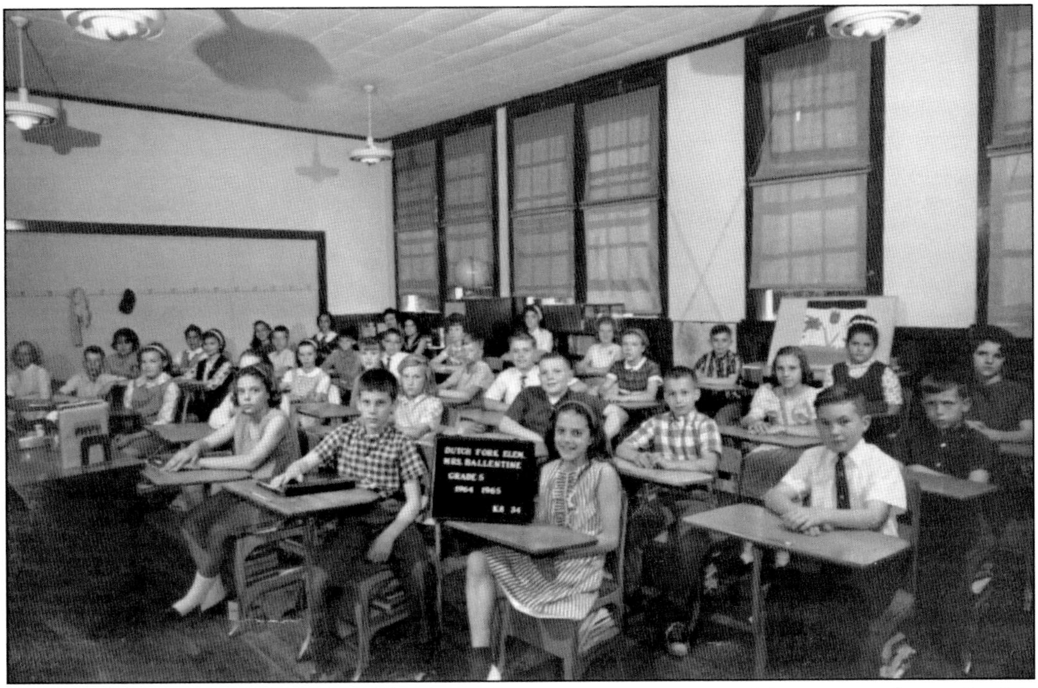

Precious Fulmer Mayer, who is seated next to the sign wearing a striped dress, seems happy in this 1964–1965 class photograph. The class was taught by Martha Ballentine, who recently celebrated her 97th birthday on January 26, 2009. (Courtesy of Mike Bull.)

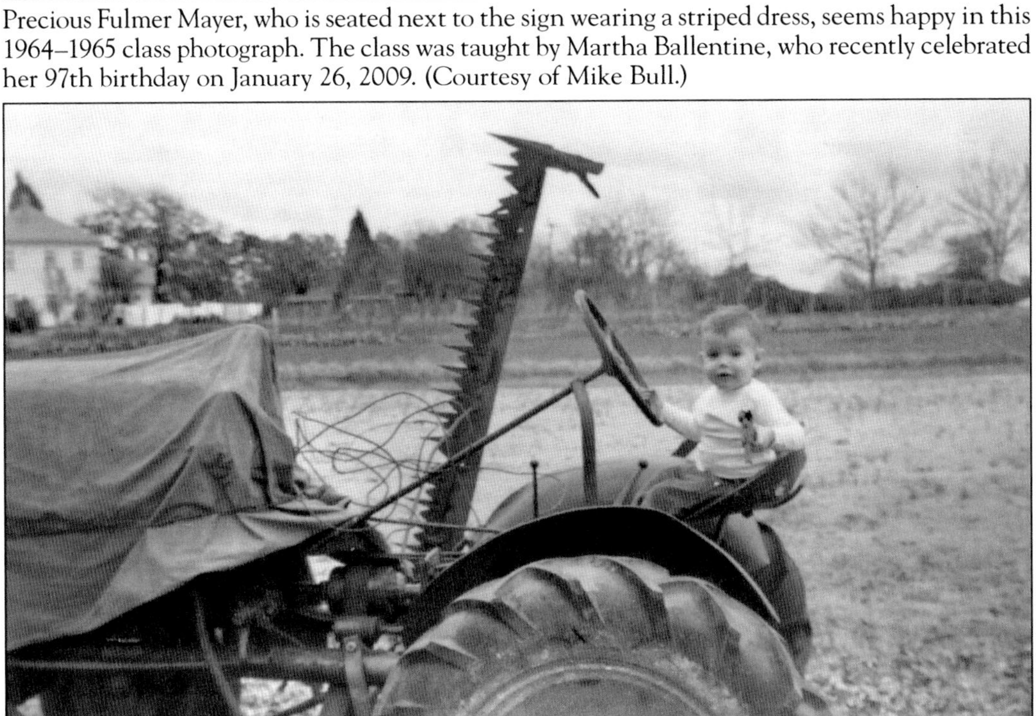

In the late 1960s, Van ("Mickey") Porter Jr. was just a toddler but he loved to ride on the tractor. His father, Van Porter, was an excellent photographer and was always taking pictures. In the background is the Shealy house, which was next to the Porters' house at the time this picture was taken. This is before the Marina Road entrance was changed. (Courtesy of Barbara Porter.)

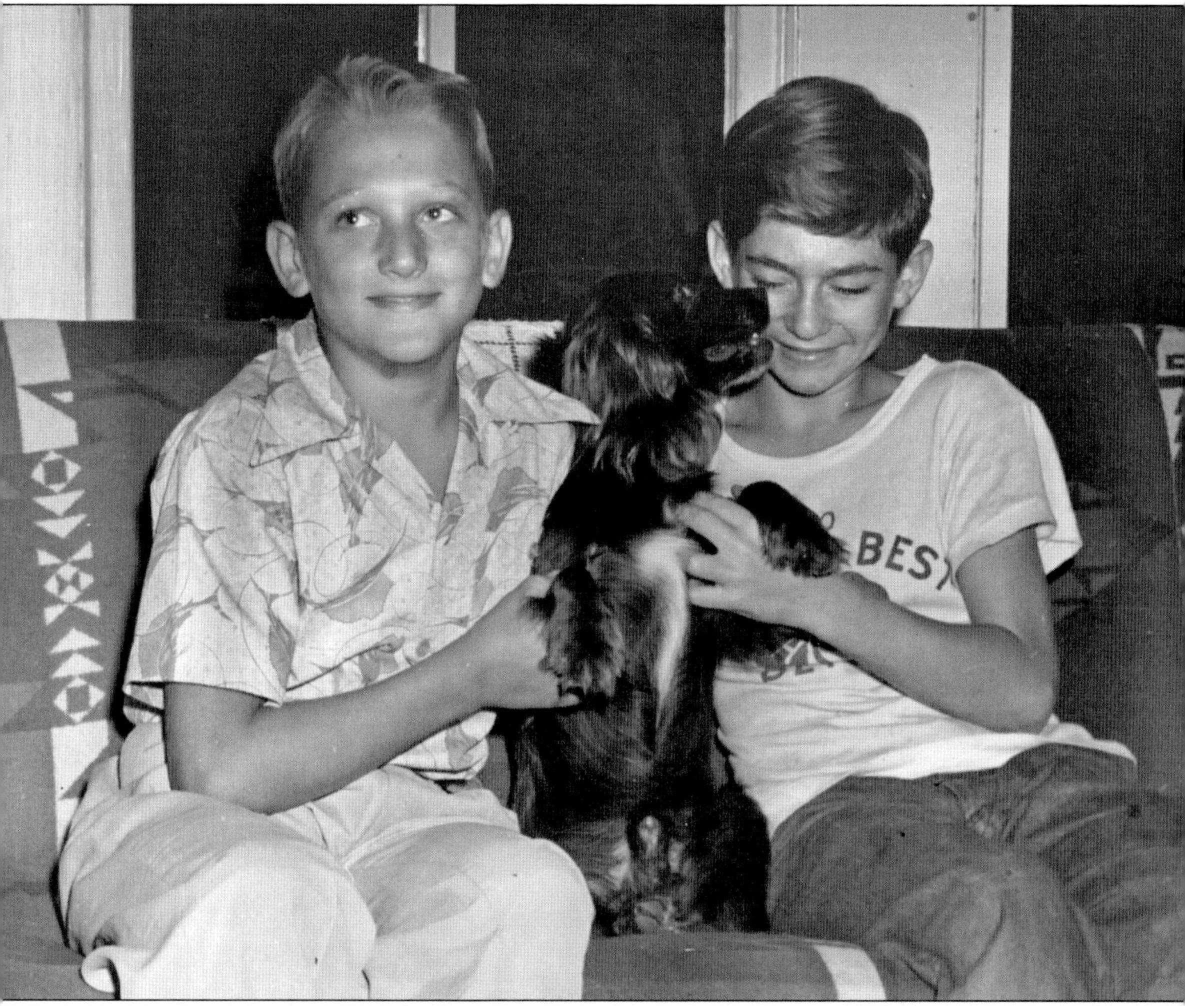

"Gus" was a popular, loyal, loving dog. He is giving Johnny Derrick a kiss while William Sheely helps hold Gus. Gus was a Boykin spaniel, sturdy, medium-sized, well-built dogs. The Boykin spaniel is designated as the official dog of South Carolina.

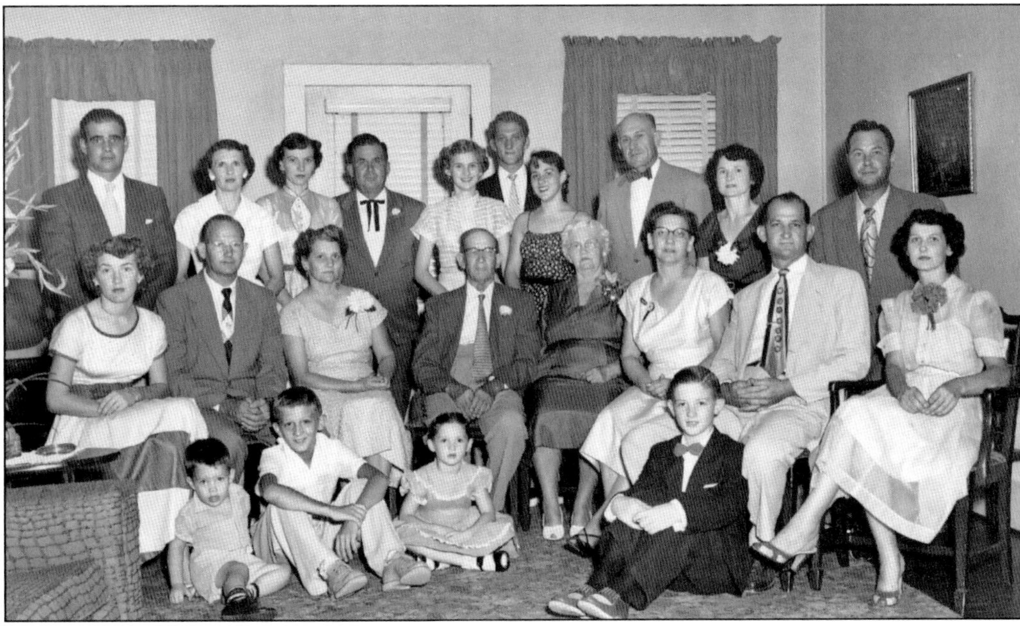

A special gathering was held on August 6, 1953, of the Ballentine family honoring the 50th wedding anniversary of Eusebius and Jennie Ballentine. They are surrounded by their children (sitting), children's spouses, and grandchildren. It was a dream of Sebe's for all of his children to go to college. All six did attend college, ranging from Newberry, Summerland, University of South Carolina, Winthrop, and Clemson.

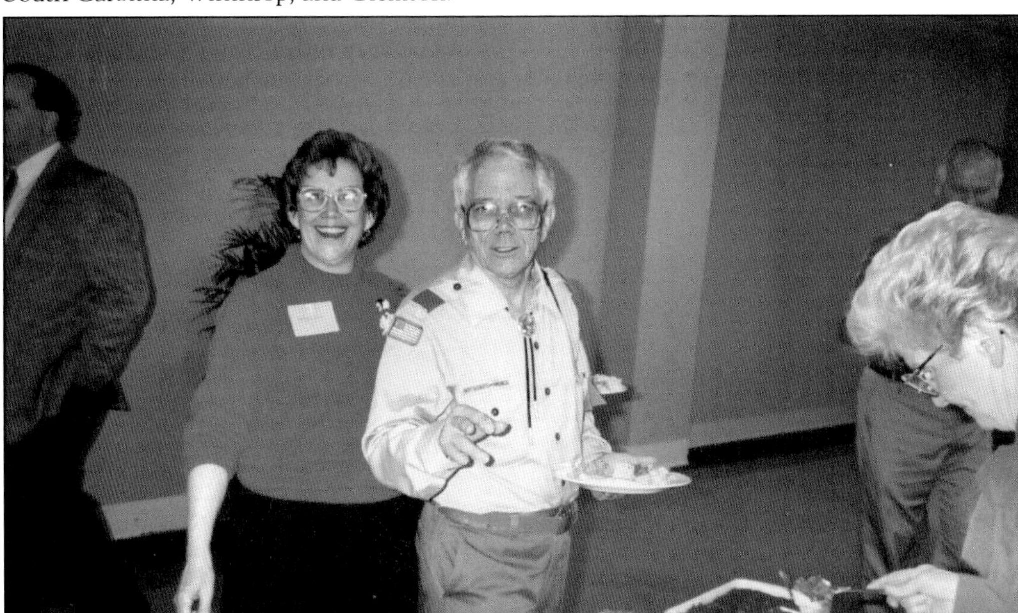

Barbara and Van Porter moved to the Ballentine area in 1960. Van worked for the school district as director of special services and before that worked at the state department. Barbara is a sign language interpreter and has had several positions. She worked for ETV for 20 years as the interpreter for the governor, taught sign language classes for USC and Midlands Tech, and is now the minister of special ministry for First Baptist Church. (Courtesy of Barbara Porter.)

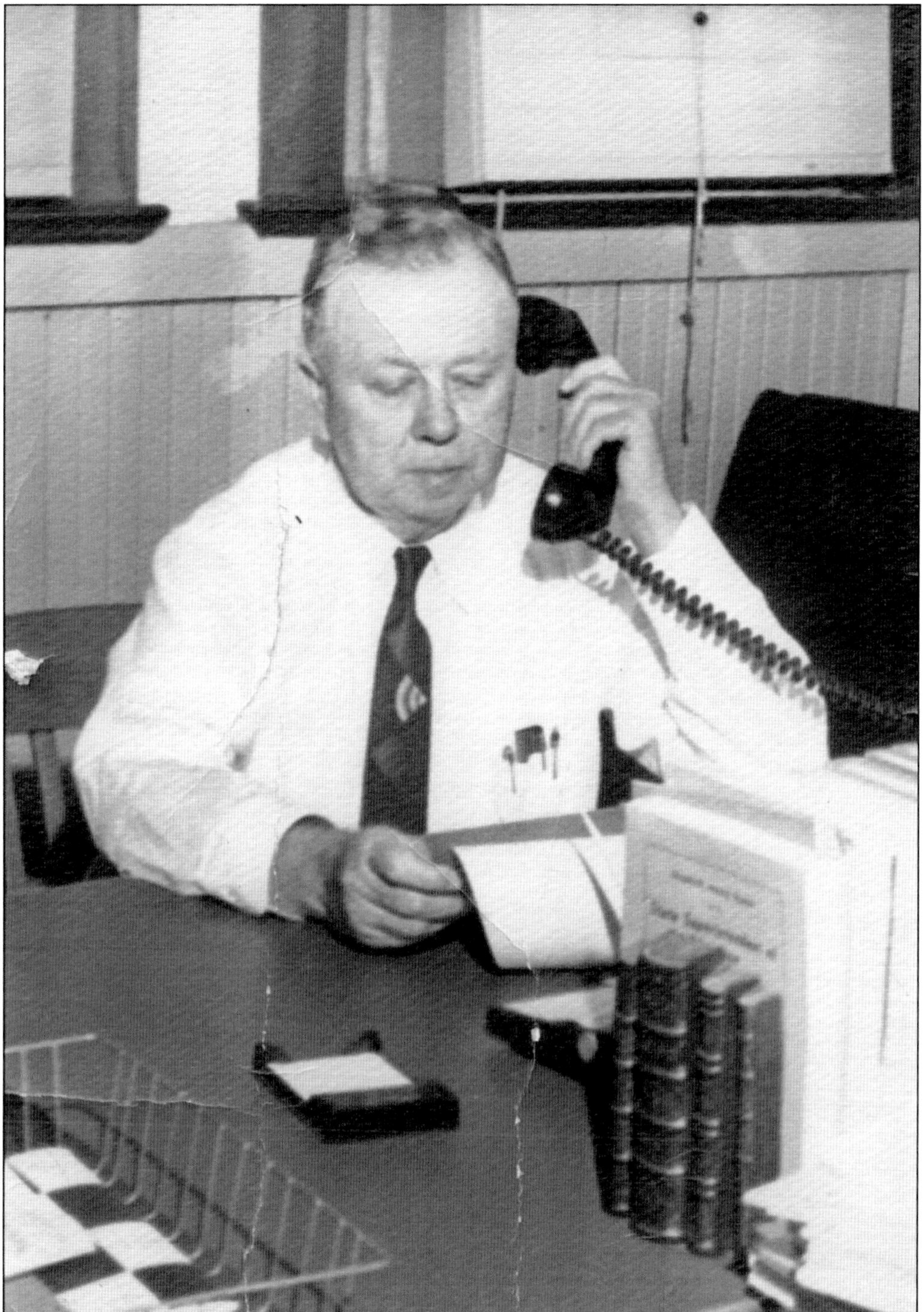

The first superintendent of Lexington-Richland School District 5 was Samuel Thomas Smith. He was followed by W. C. Hawkins, Dr. Hap Corley, Dr. Wendell Clamp, Dr. Dennis McMahon, and Dr. Scott Andersen. Currently the district superintendent is Dr. Herb Berg. (Courtesy of Lucy Lindler.)

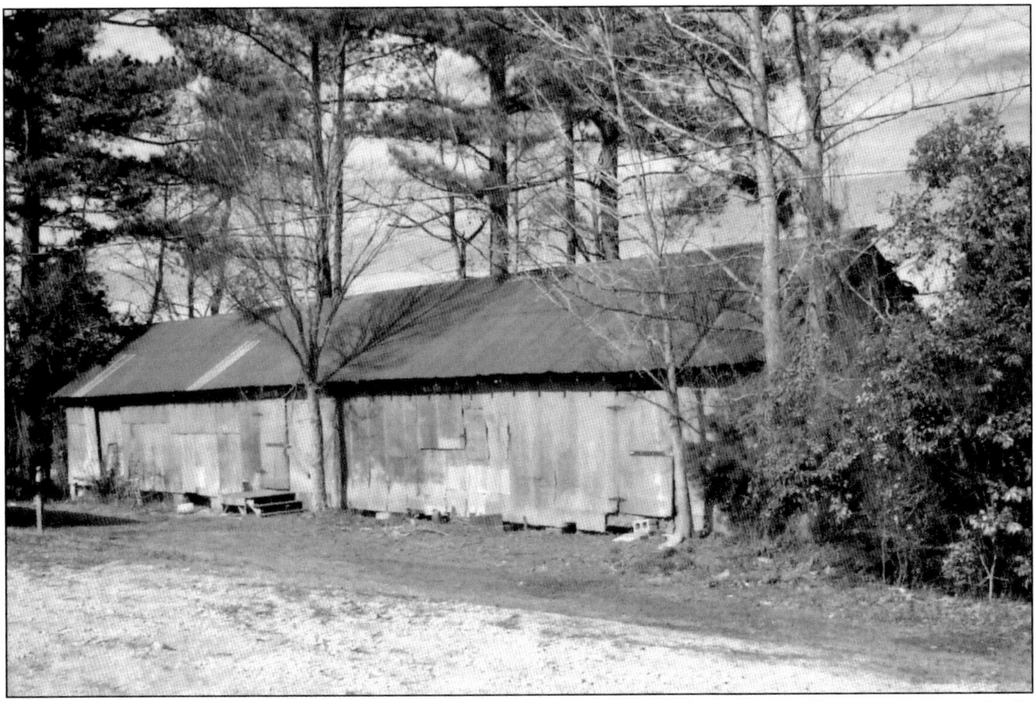

The old warehouse in Ballentine still stands today. It is behind the E. A. Ballentine Store, which now houses High Noon. It originally held cotton, then was used as general storage, and for a while was a woodworks business where old furniture was restored and new furniture was made.

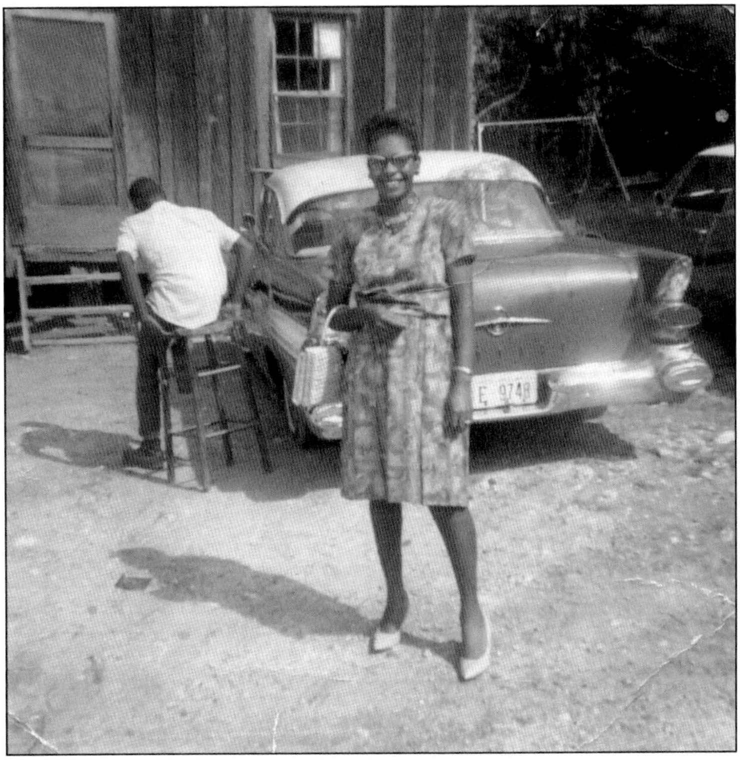

Marvie Quattlebaum is shown standing in front of her home. The home is still standing, but Marvie no longer lives there. This image was taken in the mid-1960s, and Marvie was raising her family and working several jobs, including with Myrtle and Jim Bull. She later worked for the post office. Looking back, Marvie says she does not know how she accomplished what she did and gives most of the credit to her faith in God and her church. She says faith is what carried her through the rough times. (Courtesy Marvie Quattlebaum.)

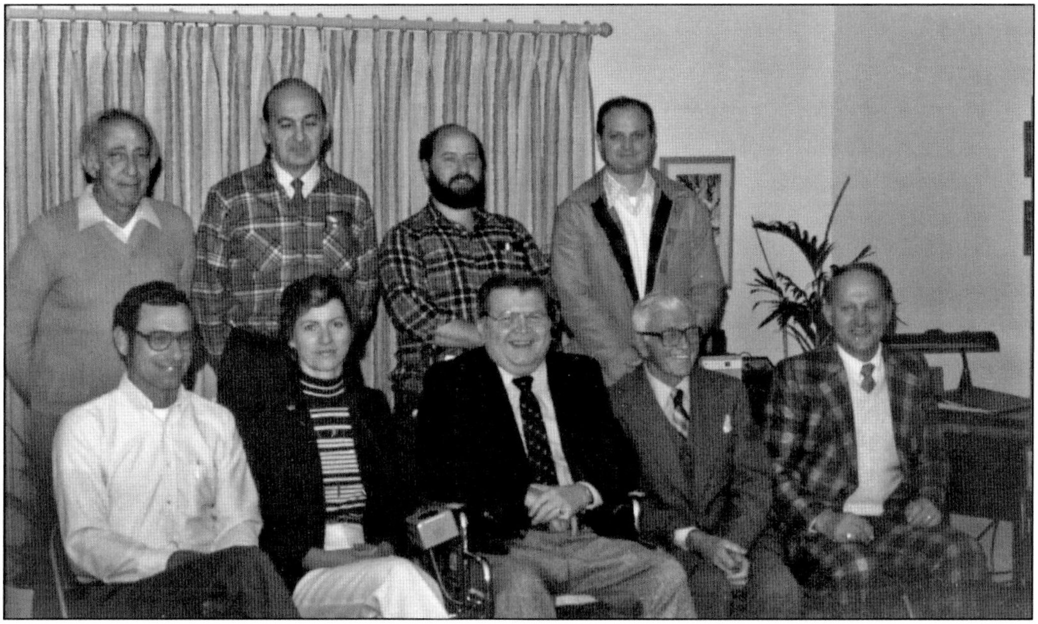

In the 1970s, the Ballentine Civic Association was formed and later became the Ballentine–Dutch Fork Civic Association. They had monthly meetings, and some said it was so the area could have more of a voice in the growth of the community. The civic association also sponsored several community events, such as the yearly Christmas party and spring and fall festivals. The officers for the year of 1983 were, from left to right, (first row) Larry Fulmer (treasurer), Shirley Fulmer (corresponding secretary), Claude Beckham (president), Lacy Gibbon (recording secretary), and William Sheely (vice president); (second row) Don Paul (past president), Robert Cook (director), J. A. Bouknight (director), and Bob Manley (director). (Courtesy of Ballentine–Dutch Fork Civic Association.)

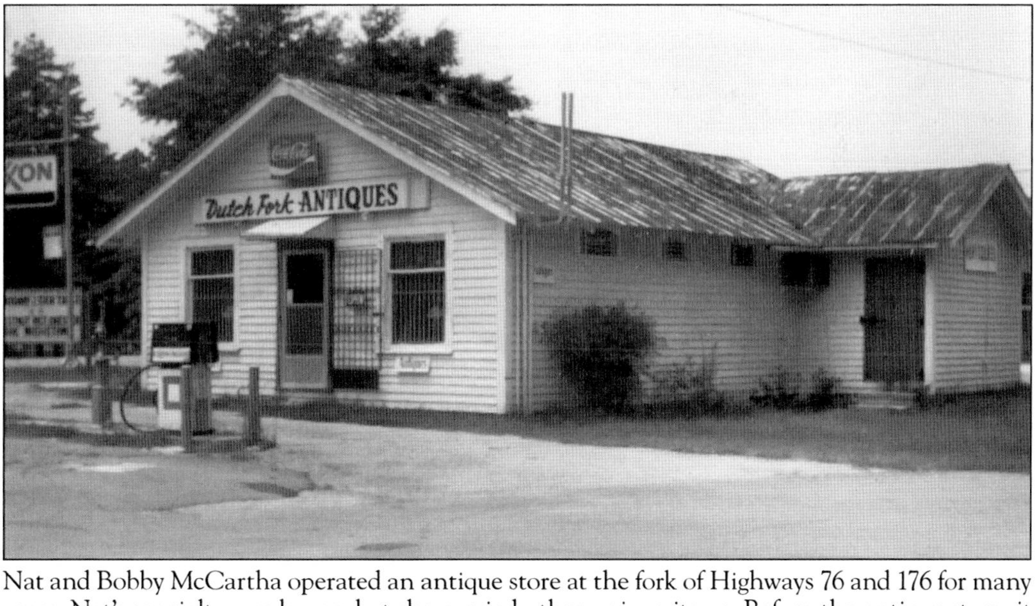

Nat and Bobby McCartha operated an antique store at the fork of Highways 76 and 176 for many years. Nat's specialty was lamps, but she carried other unique items. Before the antique store, it was a general store owned and operated by Milford Ballentine and his wife, Eula Mae. (Courtesy of John Bouknight.)

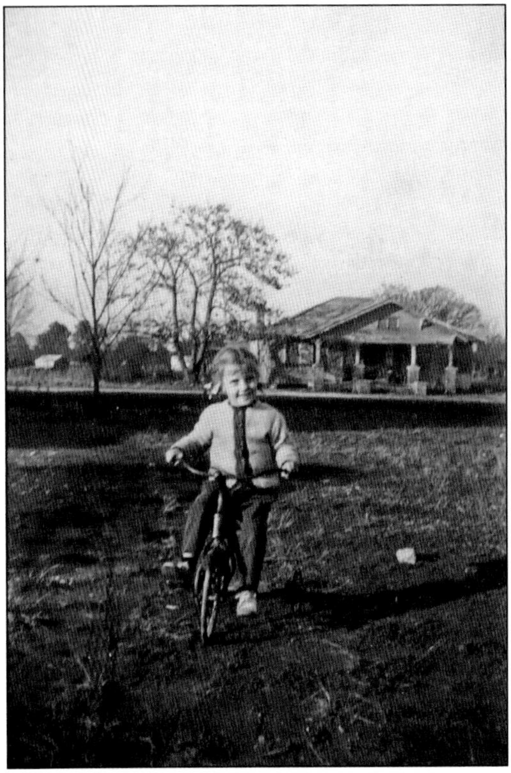

Riding her bike was a favorite pastime of Kay Shealy. In the background is the home of Maggie Stone, who made the best yeast rolls in the area. (Courtesy of Kay Shealy.)

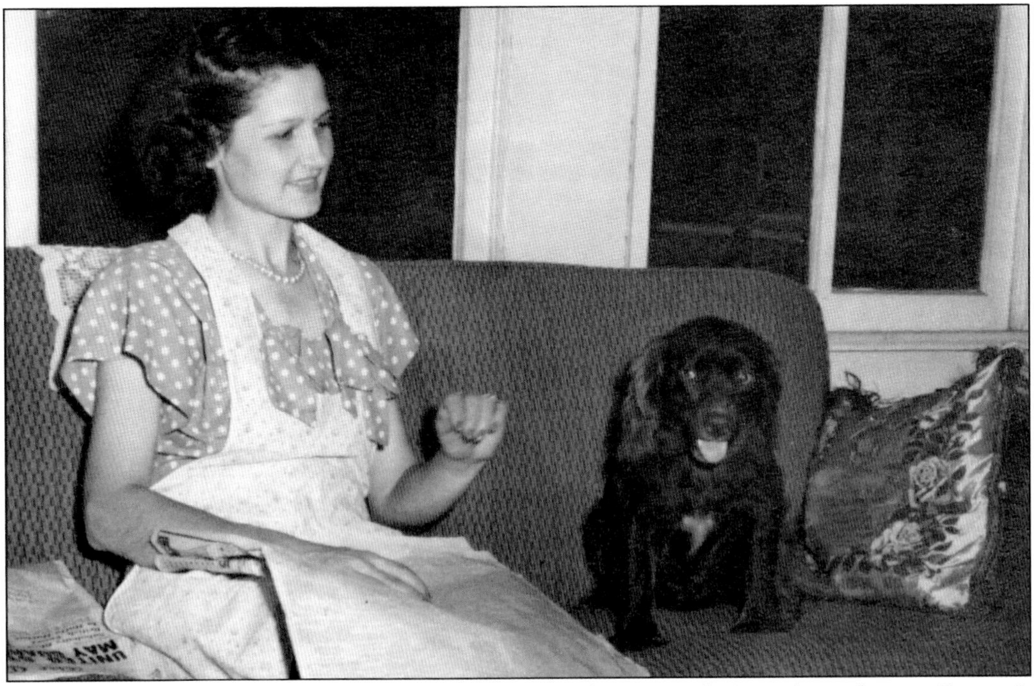

Bonnie Stevenson is sitting on the sofa with her Boykin spaniel, Gus. According to Bonnie's nephew Jim, Gus lived nearly 18 years. This photograph was taken in the early 1940s, so he had to be a very young dog when this was taken.

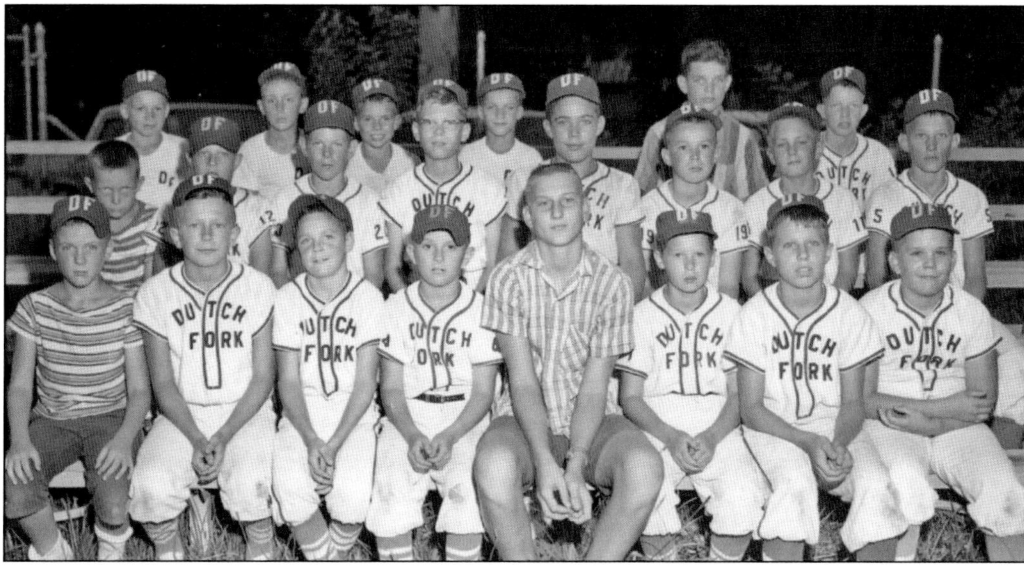

The Dutch Fork Dixie Youth baseball team was comprised of two teams—the regular and the peewees. These boys enjoyed playing on the Dutch Fork Dixie Youth and Pee Wee teams. They are, from left to right, (first row) Dick Watkins, Menal Bouknight, Jerry Meetz, Danny Roof, Larry Troutman (scorekeeper), Scotty Gable, Joe Desso, and Watson Sites; (second row) Leonard Bouknight, Harvey Amick, Hoyt Dailey, Eric Holmes, Jimmy Bull, Howard Coogler, David Matthews, and Bruce Troutman; (third row) Marshall Rowe, Cecil Rowe, Mike Bull, Dale Meetze, Roger Meetze, and Cliff Webb. (Courtesy of Jim Bull.)

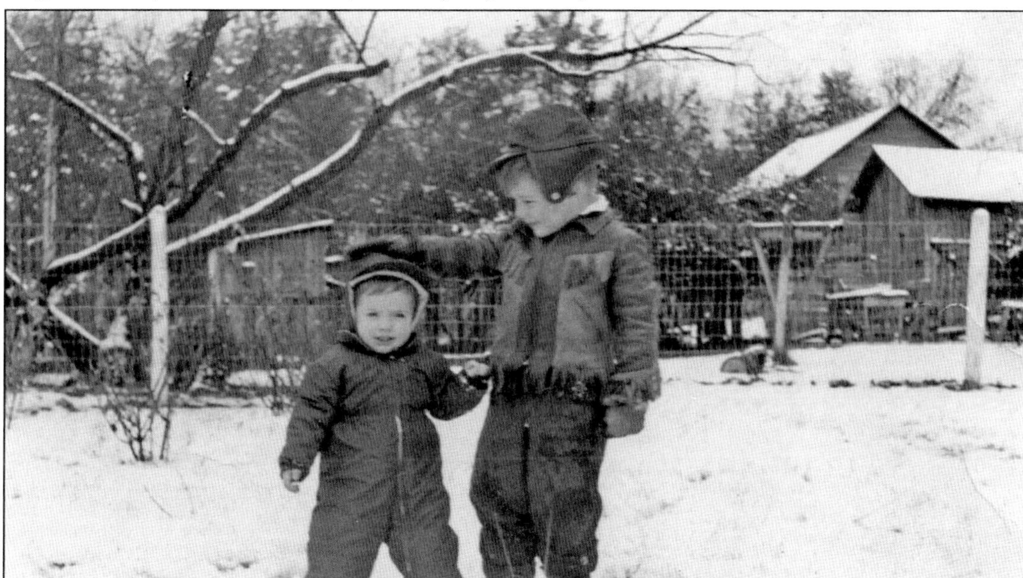

Occasionally, the Dutch Fork area does get some snow. In the mid-1950s, it got a very good covering. The contrast of the snow on the trees and barn with the dark wood underneath is so pretty, but these two little boys are just interested in playing in the snow. It looks like the older boy is taking care of the younger boy.

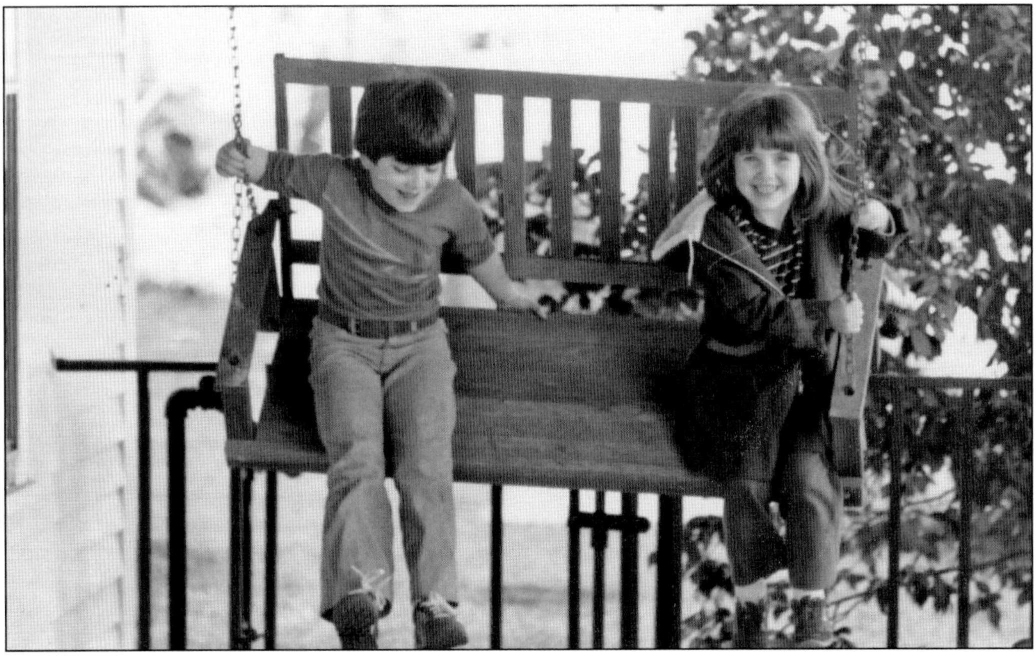

Jason Derrick and Jenny Bull are having a great time swinging on Mama Myrtle Bull's front porch. A lot of the older homes always had a swing on the front porch. The front porch was a gathering place, a place to get a cool breeze on a hot afternoon, or, for teenagers, a place for (spooning) dates.

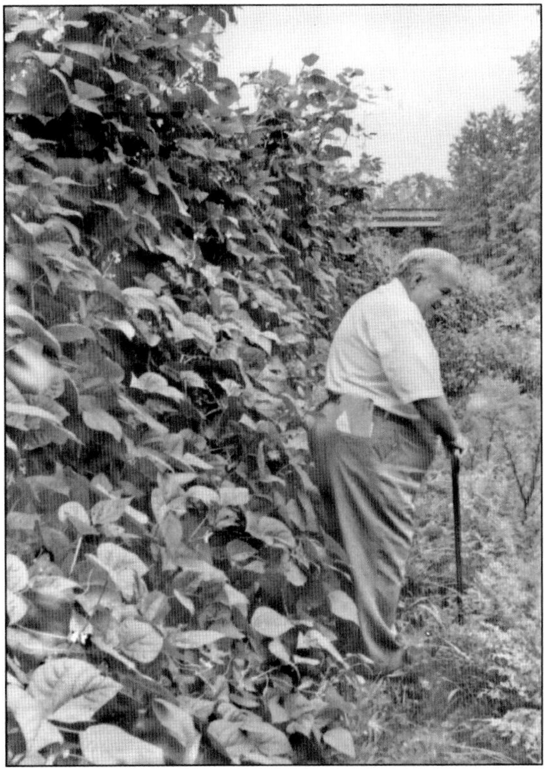

John Willie Derrick is walking around his garden. He and his wife, Blanche, always had a huge vegetable garden, where they grew corn, beans, tomatoes, and more. They also grew beautiful roses, which could be enjoyed by anyone traveling on Highway 6. They even had a few people stop and ask for cuttings of their roses. Their home was located at the intersection of Highways 6 and 76, where Walgreens now stands.

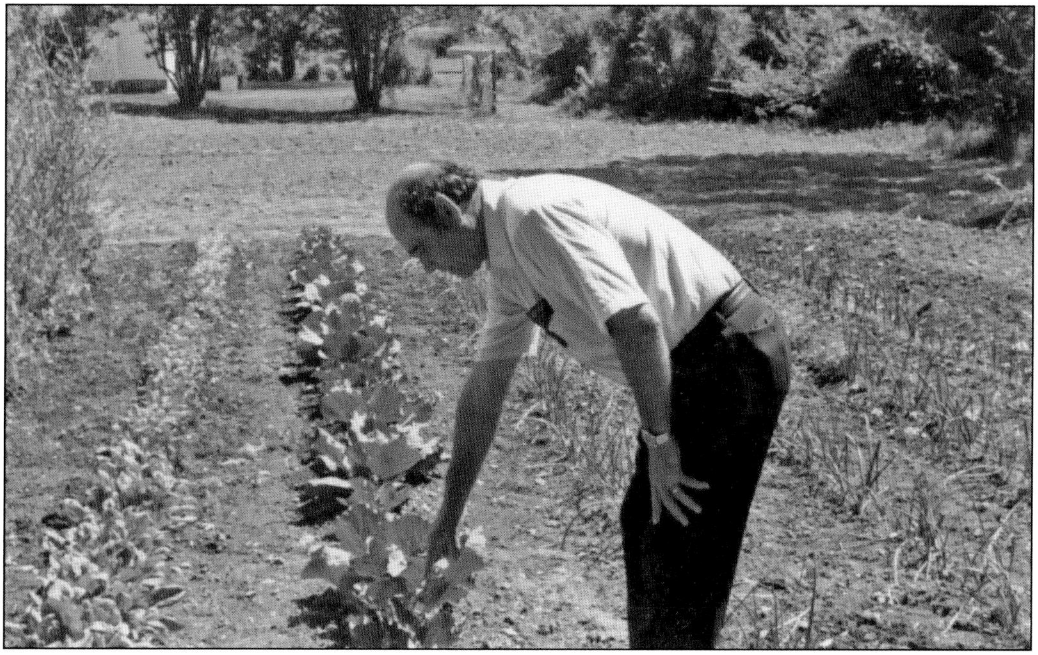

Shown checking his garden is Jim Bull. He always planted a vegetable garden, and there was nothing better than going out and picking fresh corn, shucking, and boiling it a few minutes. One could not get any fresher corn than that. Bull's favorite corn was Silver Queen. Planting a vegetable garden was a normal routine for a lot of rural residents.

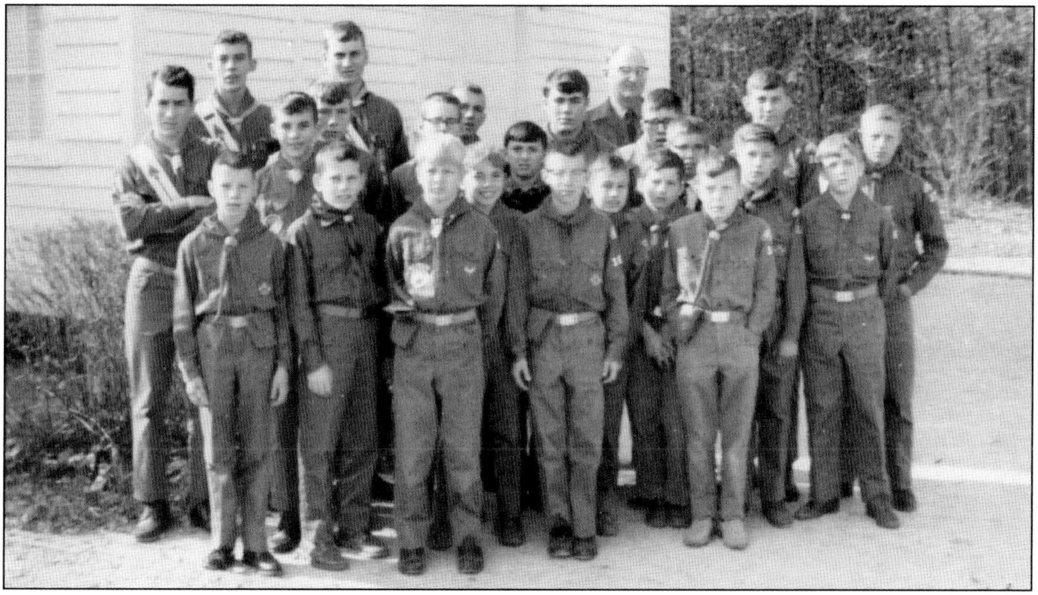

Boy Scout Troup 366 of White Rock in the early 1960s included, from left to right, (first row) Derald Edwards, Robert Tucker, Jamie Boozer, Mike Bull, Gerald Edwards, Randy Evans, Terry Bouknight, Vincent Cannarella, and Dick Watkins; (second row) Jimmy Springs, Max Sternenberg, Mendal Bouknight, John George, Danny Roof, Jimmy Bull, Lee Spradley, Steve Addy, and Harvey Amick; (third row) Jerry Derrick, Larry Troutman, Frank Bouknight, Buddy Troutman (Scoutmaster), and Harvey Amick. (Courtesy of Jim Bull.)

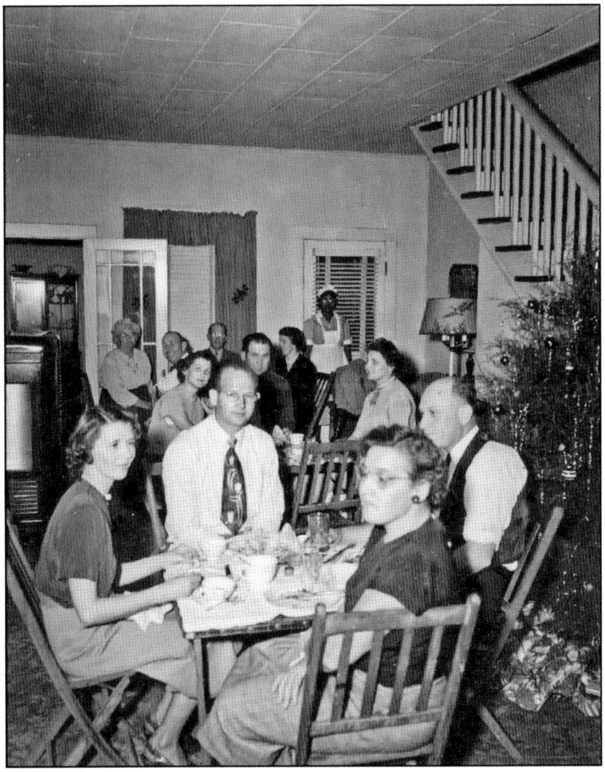

In the 1940s, the Ballentine family started a Christmas tradition that has continued through today. They have celebrated Christmas Eve with a family dinner every year (it has never been skipped). This photograph was taken in the 1950s. The family was joined by Pastor Paul McCullough (in the background at the last table) of Bethel Lutheran Church. Lillie Brazell (background) is also shown. She had worked for the family for years and was a valued employee.

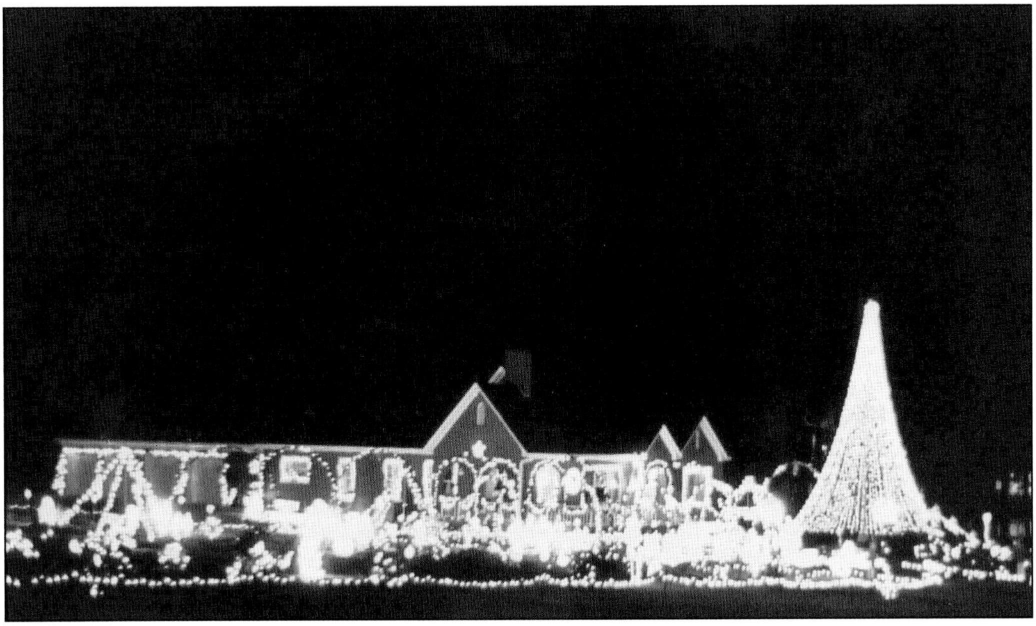

The Derrick family (Alvin, Pat, and Tracy) always decorated for Christmas and in later years for Halloween. Every year, hundreds of people came to see their lights, and every year, it seemed they added another display. Not shown in this picture is the pond beside the house that was also decorated in lights. It became a Christmas tradition for a lot of families to go and see the lights at the Derrick home. (Courtesy of Pat Derrick.)

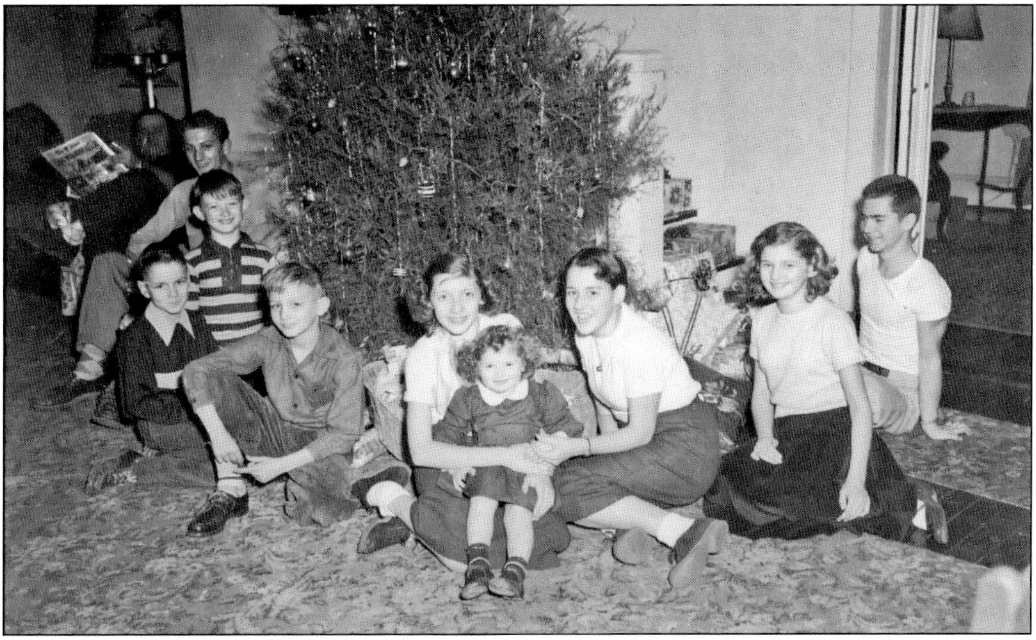

The Ballentine family celebrated every Christmas Eve with a Christmas Eve dinner. Usually it was just family but through the years friends have celebrated with them. Shown in the photograph above are, from left to right, John Willie Derrick, William Sheely, Rudy Ballentine, Edward McCullough (Reverend McCullough's son), Jerry Ballentine, Juanita McCullough (Reverend McCullough's daughter) holding Genie Sosnowski, Marilyn Shealy, Carol Black, and Johnny Derrick.

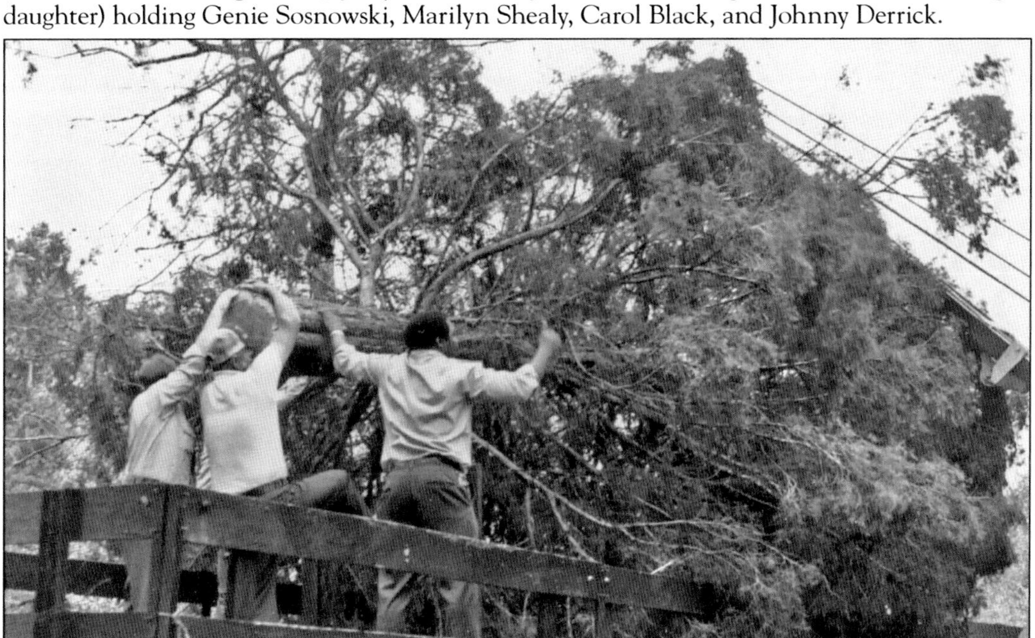

Joe Taylor, Trudy Taylor Smith, Joel and Dorothy Smith, and several state house workers loaded this 66-foot red cedar tree onto a truck for the 1984 South Carolina State House Christmas Tree Lighting. The tree came from the property of Ollie Mae Quick who had died the previous year, in September 1983. (Courtesy of Ann Cameron.)

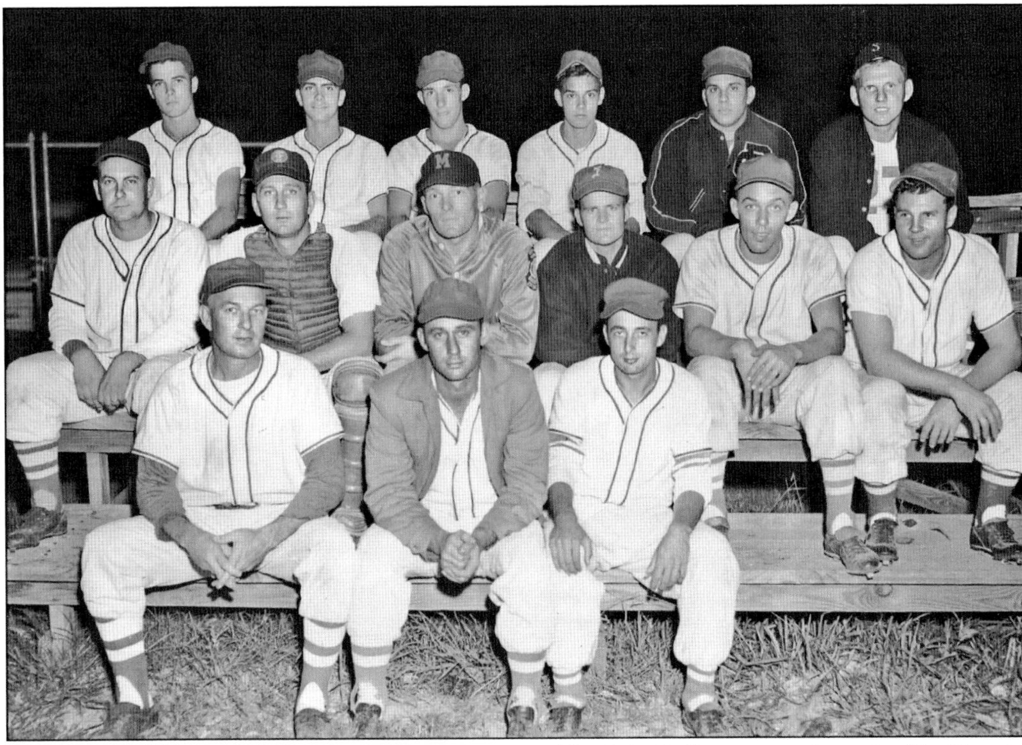

The Dutch Fork League of 1956–1957 was sponsored by Sebe Ballentine and coached by Brawley Meetze and Rudolph Ballentine. From left to right are (first row) Norm Sharpe, Billy Meetze, and Howard Meetze; (second row) Carl Rauch, Ward Fisher, "Buster" Rhame, "Cooter" Eargle, Odell Martin, and Ed Wilson; (third row) Dewey Clark, Mervin Derrick, Reynold Stoudemeyer, Marion Corley, Bobby Hall, and Dickie Anderson. "Buster" Rhame went on to play pro ball. (Courtesy of "Buster" Rhame.)

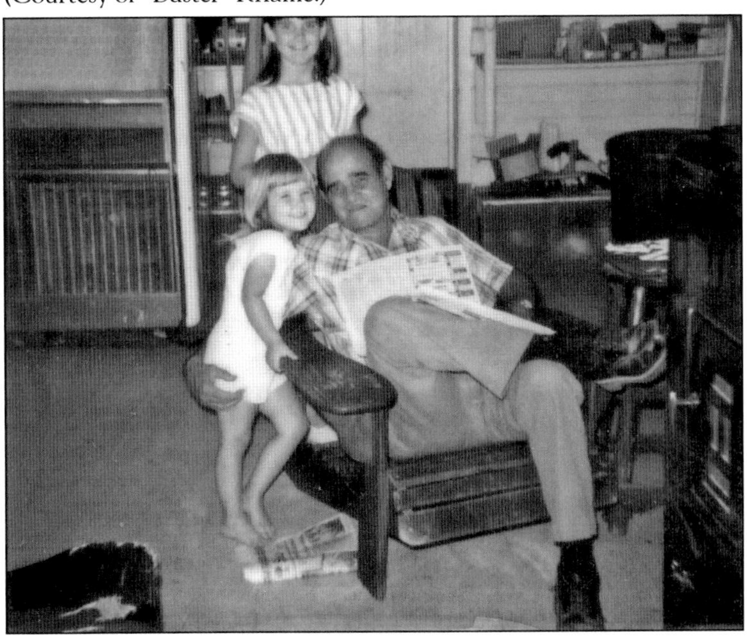

Jim Bull is shown relaxing in his favorite chair with two of his granddaughters, Jenny (standing behind the chair) and Melissa (leaning beside the chair) Bull, who called the chair "Pop's chair." Jim could usually be found in the E. A. Ballentine Store, which also housed the Bull Oil Company and the post office, sitting in his chair, when he was not delivering oil or working in his garden.

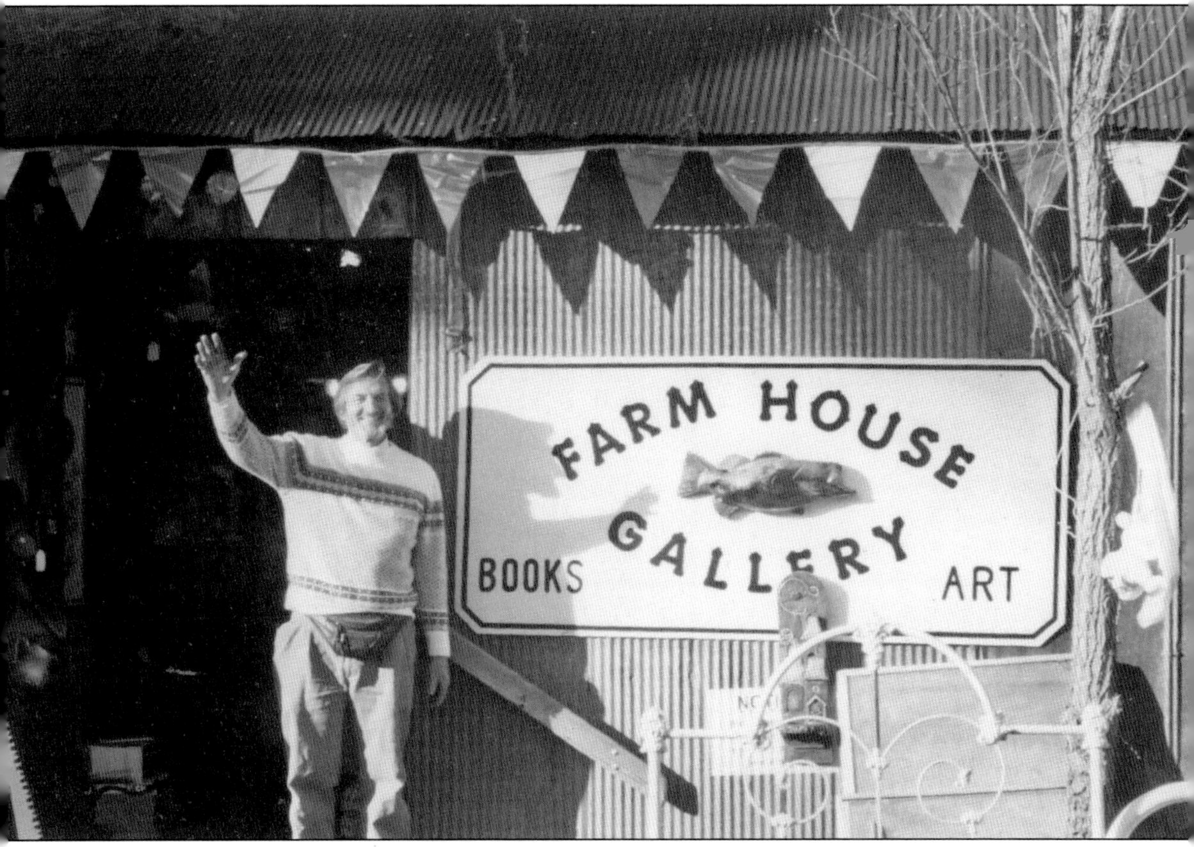

Dr. Carlos Gibbons was the proprietor of Farm House Antiques for more than 10 years. He was an educator, college professor, executive director of SCEA, and he started his antique business with his wife, Jean. Jean developed Alzheimer's disease shortly after starting the business, which led to Carlos and his family becoming involved with Alzheimer's treatment and education. Their daughter, Leeza, founded the Leeza Gibbons Memory Foundation, with its signature program Leeza's Place.

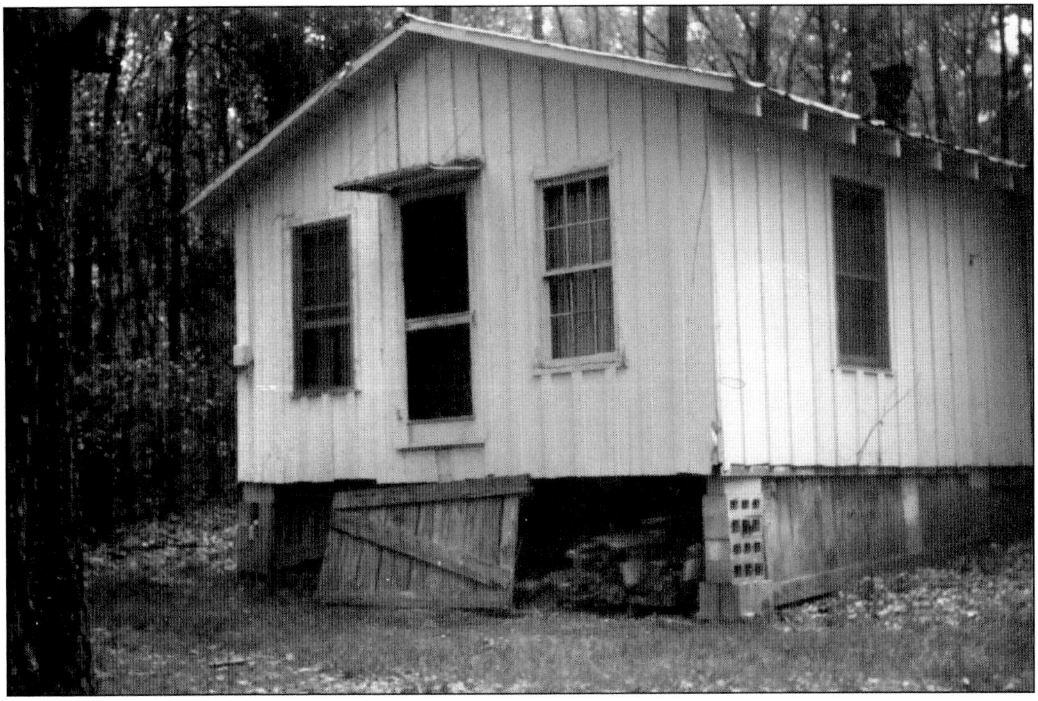

The building shown above is the same structure seen below. John Bouknight bought this building from the auction held at the chain gang camp in Ballentine. It was the mess hall, and he had the building moved to the lake, remodeled it, and has lived there since the late 1960s. (Courtesy of John Bouknight.)

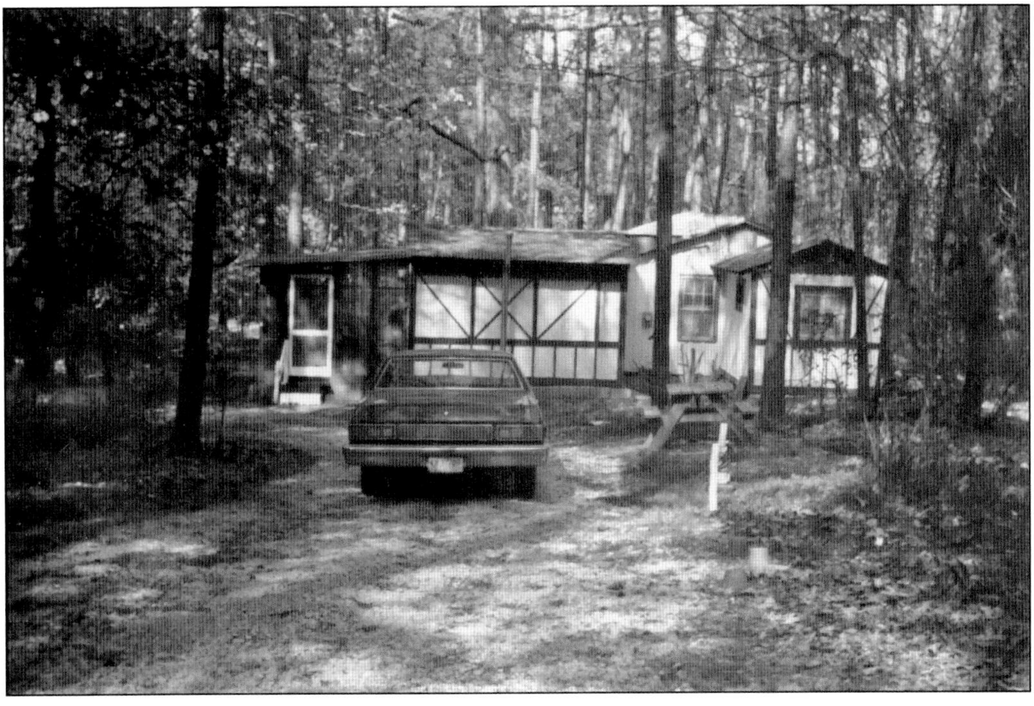

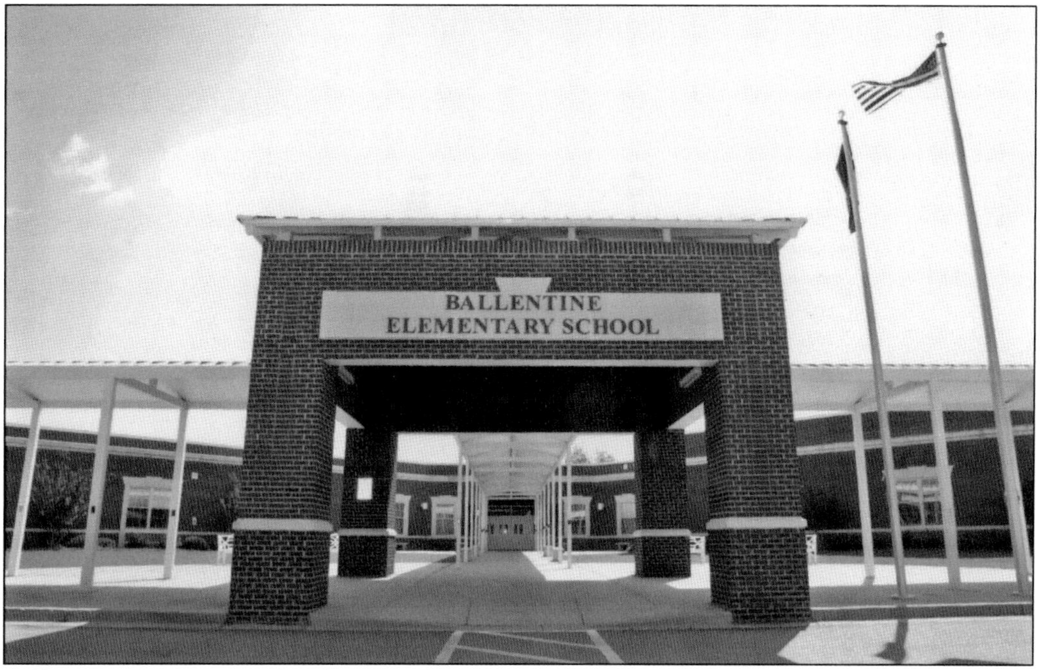

Ballentine Elementary School is one of the newest schools in the district and serves grades pre-kindergarten through five. There are a little over 800 students enrolled, and the teacher-student ratio is 1:16. The mascot for the school is the Ballentine Bears. (Courtesy of Jacob Dean.)

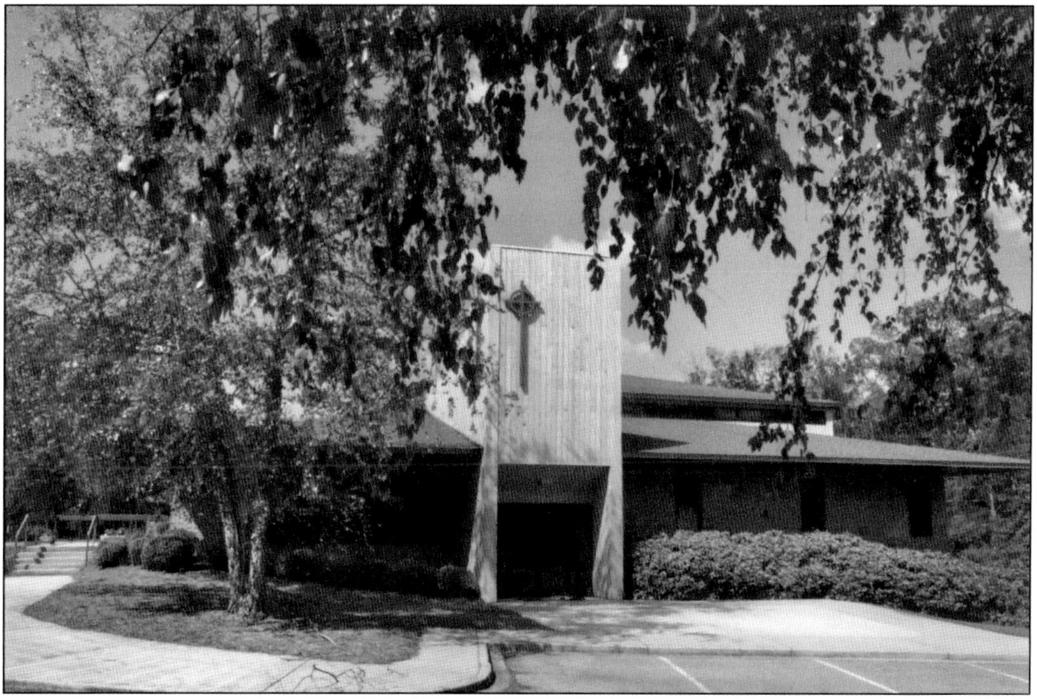

Lake Murray Presbyterian is located at 2721 Dutch Fork Road between Chapin and Ballentine. It has been in existence around 20 years and is a vibrant and growing church with more than 1,000 members of the Presbyterian Church (USA). (Courtesy of Jacob Dean.)

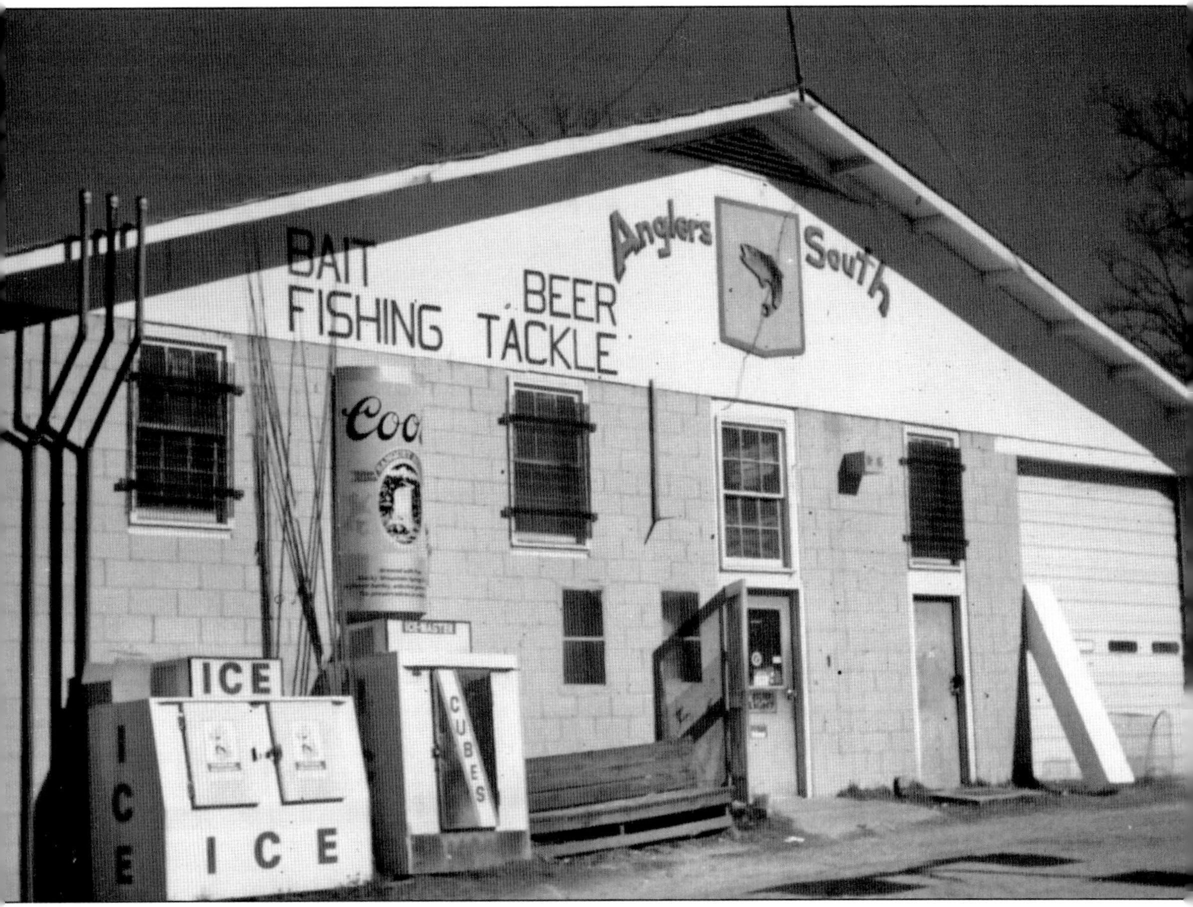

Angler's South was a well-known landmark. Many people bought their fishing license, fish bait, fishing supplies, and so on there. The business was owned by Smokie Goodwin, who was a retired marine. Angler's South no longer resides in this building but is now located less than half a mile away. (Courtesy of John Bouknight.)

The Dutch Fork Elementary School building caught fire in 1975, and fire trucks had to come from Lexington, Columbia, Irmo, Chapin, and South Congaree to fight the fire. Luckily, the building was no longer being used as a school and only six people were inside at the time. One of the secretaries stated it sounded like a big boom when the fire broke out. (Courtesy of Lucy Lindler.)

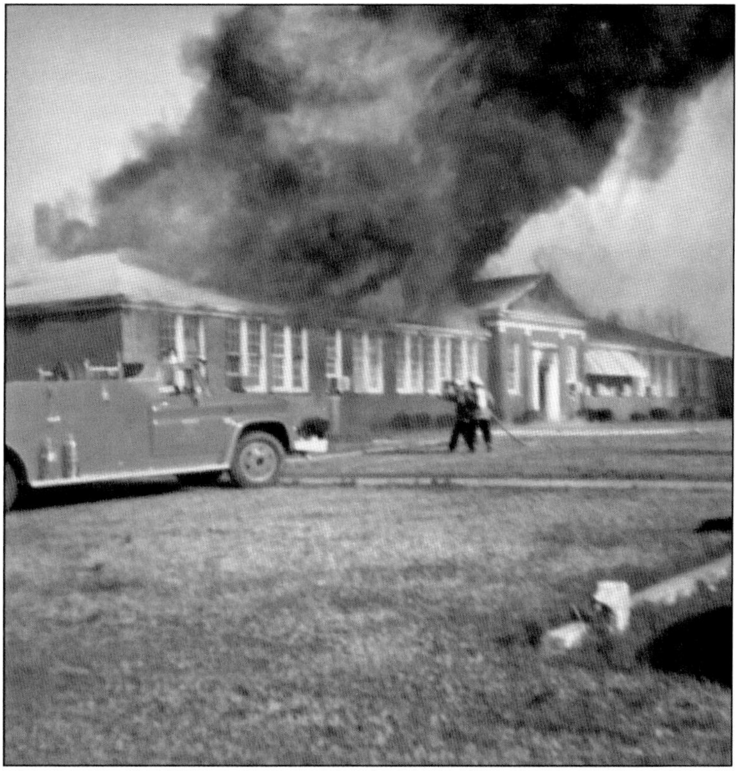

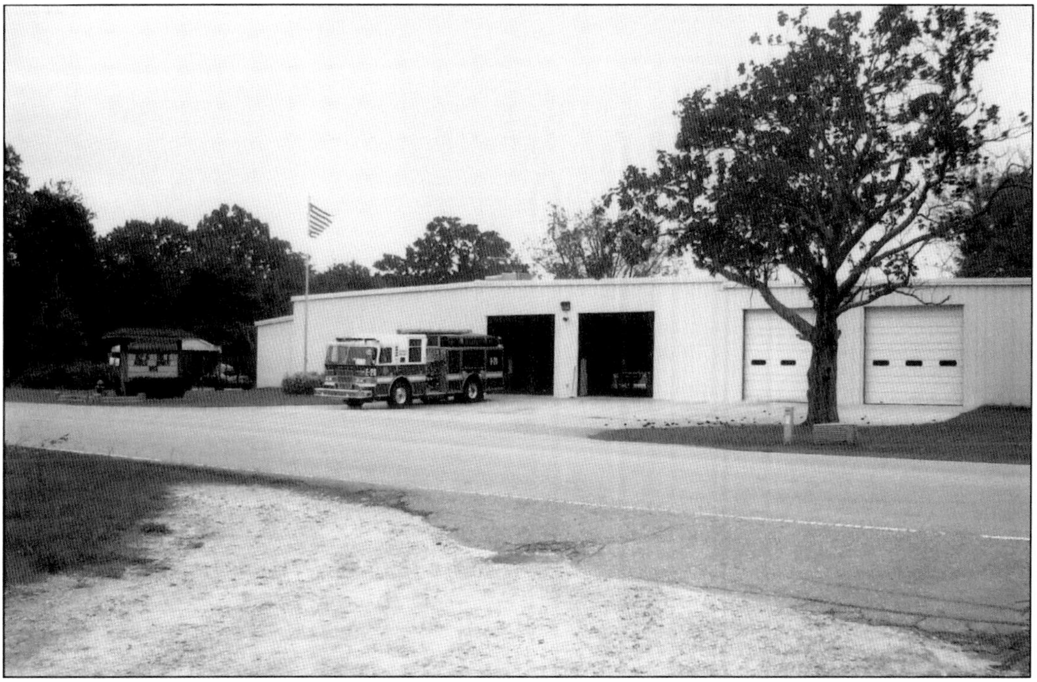

The Ballentine Fire Department started out as a volunteer fire department. Later it was staffed and was called the Ballentine Fire Department (Dutch Fork Fire and Rescue). (Courtesy of Marilyn Bull.)

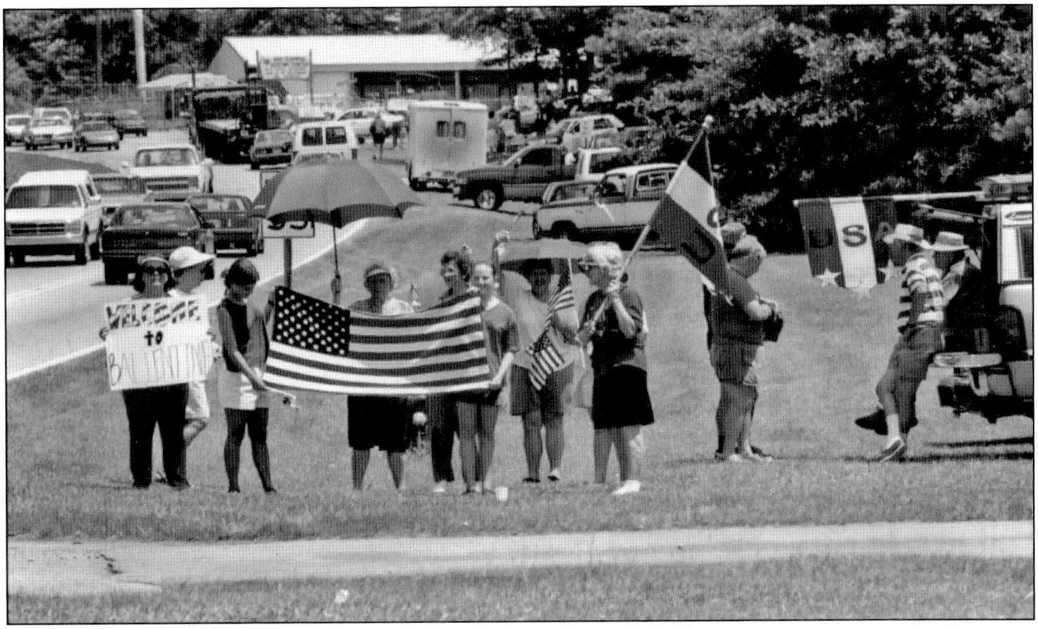

In 1996, the Olympic torch was carried close but not through Ballentine on its way to the Summer Olympics in Atlanta. This group gathered to watch the Olympic Torch Relay. The torch was lit in Greece and flown to Los Angeles. Over the next 112 days, the torch made its way to Atlanta, Georgia, as 29,016 kilometers were covered by 13,267 torch carriers. The cauldron that held the flame during the games in Atlanta was lit by Muhammad Ali. (Courtesy of Mike Bull.)

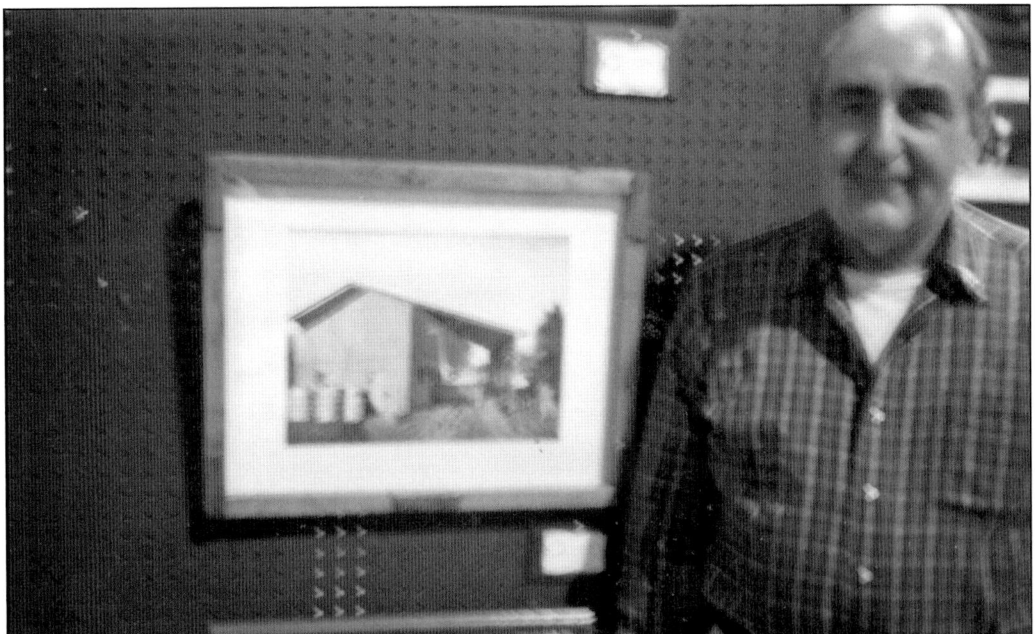

John Bouknight is shown with one of his many paintings. He did not begin painting until later in life after he had a heart attack. His physician recommended he take up a hobby that was not very strenuous, and he began painting watercolors. He likes to paint old barns and houses and has won some awards. (Courtesy of John Bouknight.)

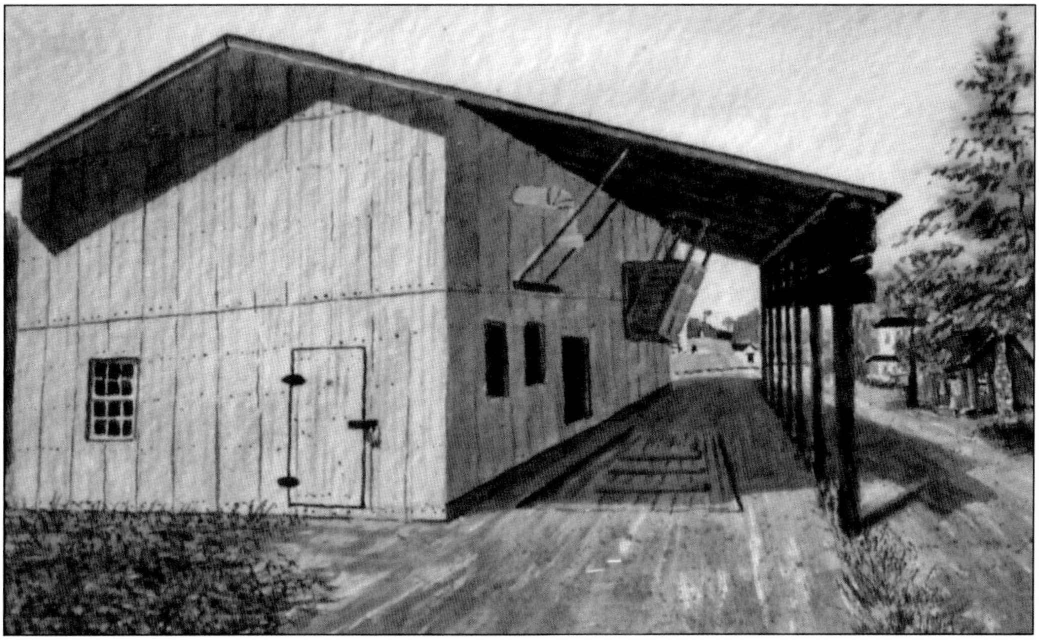

John Bouknight painted this picture from memory. It is a picture of the cotton gin in Ballentine. The cotton gin is still standing but does show aging and is hidden by trees and underbrush. John says he remembers going to the gin with his daddy when he was a little fellow and it was a lot of fun. The gin was built in 1926 or 1927 and continued to gin cotton through to the early 1950s.

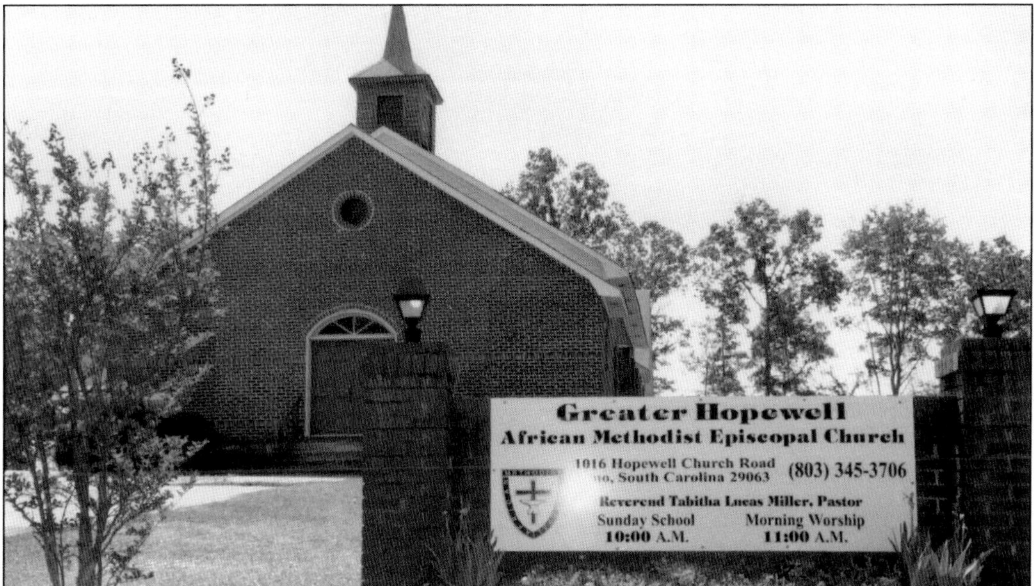

Greater Hopewell was established in 1863, when one acre of land was given to the founders to build their church. The person who donated the land told them, "I hope you do well," and that is how the church got its name. Greater Hopewell is one of the earlier, if not earliest, black churches established in the area. The original structure was wooden, then later was covered with cinder blocks, and is now brick. Two hundred very active members make up the congregation, which is led by its first black female pastor, Rev. Tabitha Miller. (Courtesy of Greater Hopewell.)

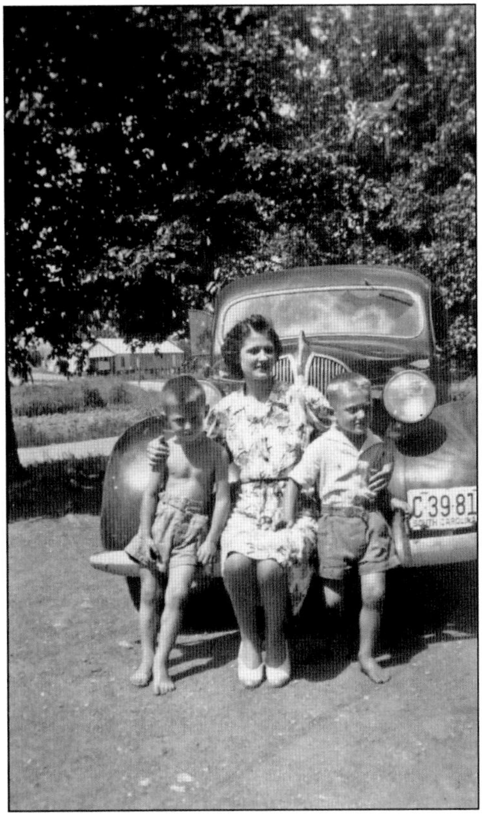

Bonnie Stevenson is sitting on the car with Johnny Derrick (left) and William Sheely. The tag on the car is a 1939 tag.

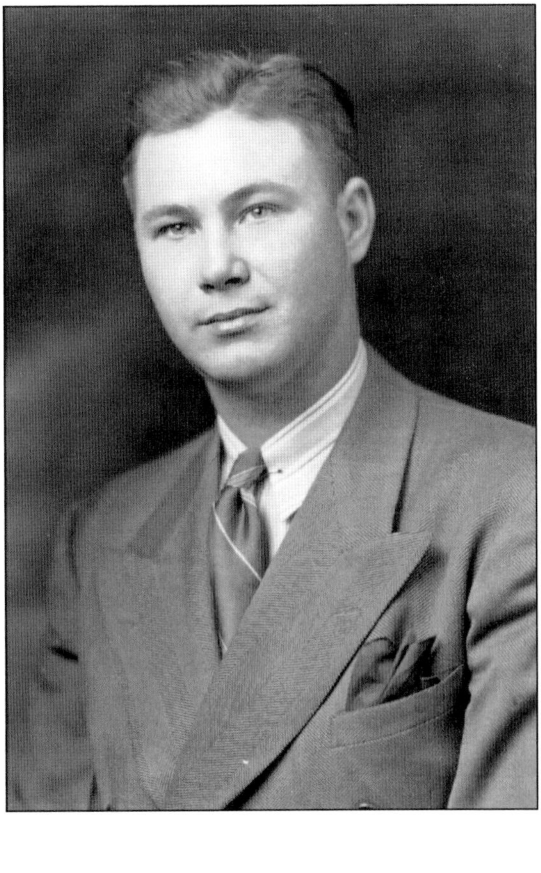

R. O. ("Buck") and Bonnie Stevenson were married in 1940. He was in the navy and was in underwater demolition (now known as Navy SEALS). Later he worked for the highway patrol, then for the Interstate Commerce Commission (later known as Department of Transportation or DOT) as a safety investigator. His younger half-brother was Floyd Spence, the late United States congressman and former South Carolina politician.

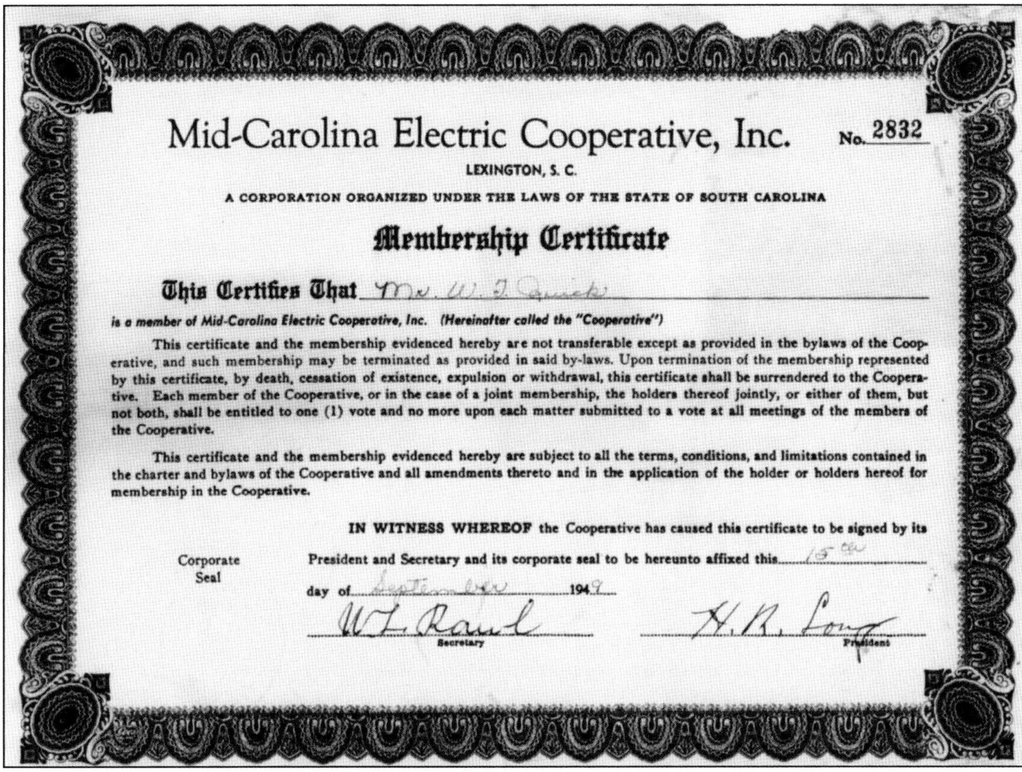
Mid-Carolina Electric Cooperative, Inc. No. 2832

LEXINGTON, S. C.

A CORPORATION ORGANIZED UNDER THE LAWS OF THE STATE OF SOUTH CAROLINA

Membership Certificate

This Certifies That Mr. W. T. Quick

is a member of Mid-Carolina Electric Cooperative, Inc. (Hereinafter called the "Cooperative")

This certificate and the membership evidenced hereby are not transferable except as provided in the bylaws of the Cooperative, and such membership may be terminated as provided in said by-laws. Upon termination of the membership represented by this certificate, by death, cessation of existence, expulsion or withdrawal, this certificate shall be surrendered to the Cooperative. Each member of the Cooperative, or in the case of a joint membership, the holders thereof jointly, or either of them, but not both, shall be entitled to one (1) vote and no more upon each matter submitted to a vote at all meetings of the members of the Cooperative.

This certificate and the membership evidenced hereby are subject to all the terms, conditions, and limitations contained in the charter and bylaws of the Cooperative and all amendments thereto and in the application of the holder or holders hereof for membership in the Cooperative.

IN WITNESS WHEREOF the Cooperative has caused this certificate to be signed by its President and Secretary and its corporate seal to be hereunto affixed this 15th day of September 1949

Corporate Seal

W. L. Rawl, Secretary

H. R. Long, President

Mid-Carolina Electric Cooperative issued certificates of membership to their customers. This certificate was issued in September 1949. (Courtesy of Ann Cameron.)

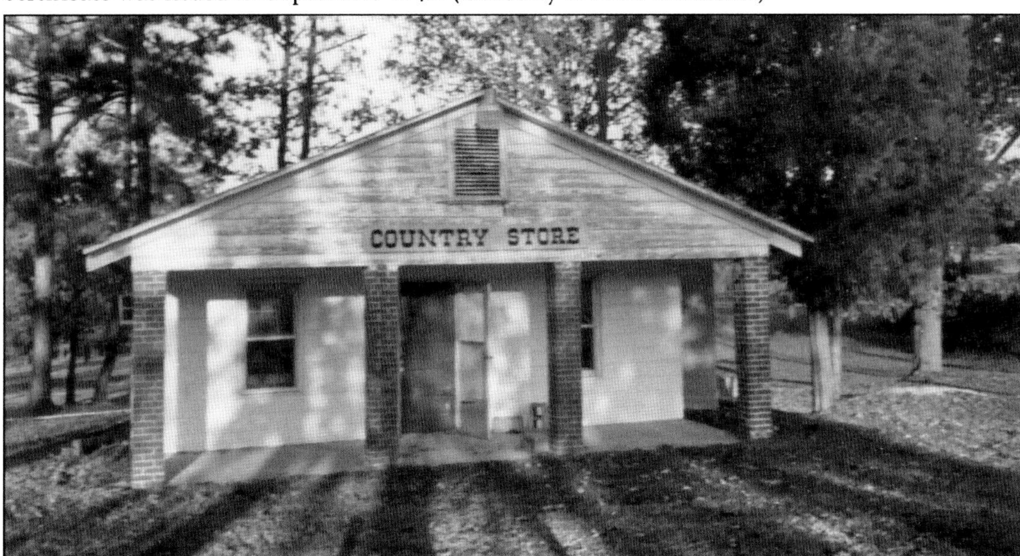

The Ballentine Civic Association began meeting at the Ballentine Park, which was comprised at the time of two remodeled cinder-block buildings (originally part of the chain gang prison once located there), a playground, and a ball field. The larger building was used mainly for meetings, but sometimes the above structure was used. (Courtesy of the Ballentine–Dutch Fork Civic Association.)

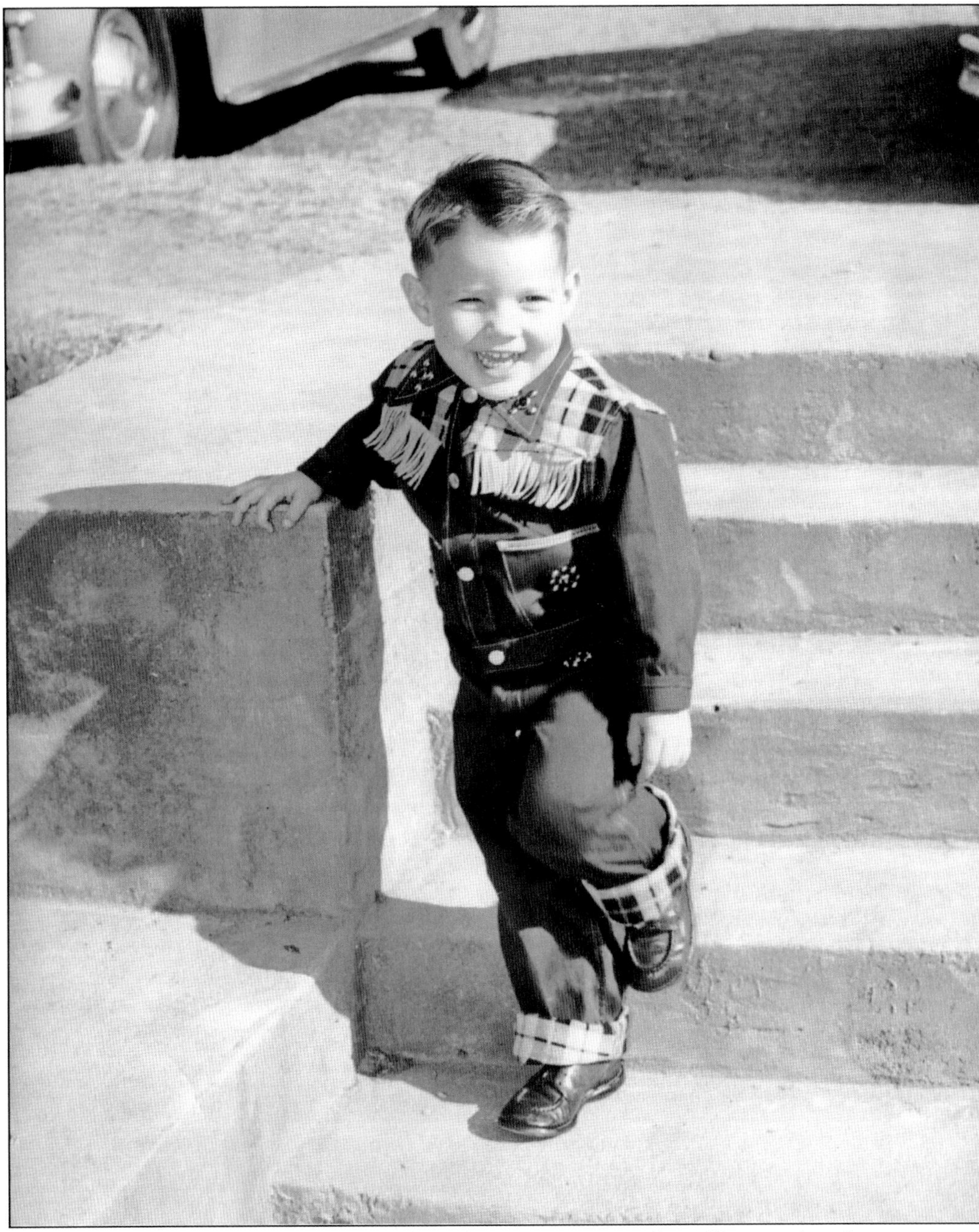

Jimmy Bull was only three years old when this picture was taken. He was the class mascot of 1953–1954 for Irmo High School, along with a little girl by the name of Marcie Parker. Bull graduated from Irmo in 1969, from Clemson University with two degrees in 1974, and then went to work for Lexington Five School District as the guidance director at the Irmo-Chapin Career Education Center. Later he became assistant director and then director of the Irmo-Chapin Career Education Center. He retired as the director of career and adult education.

Mama Jennie and her youngest grandson, Mike Bull, are sitting in the shade and enjoying the afternoon. The bridge in the background is the bridge going into Ballentine from Irmo on Highway 76.

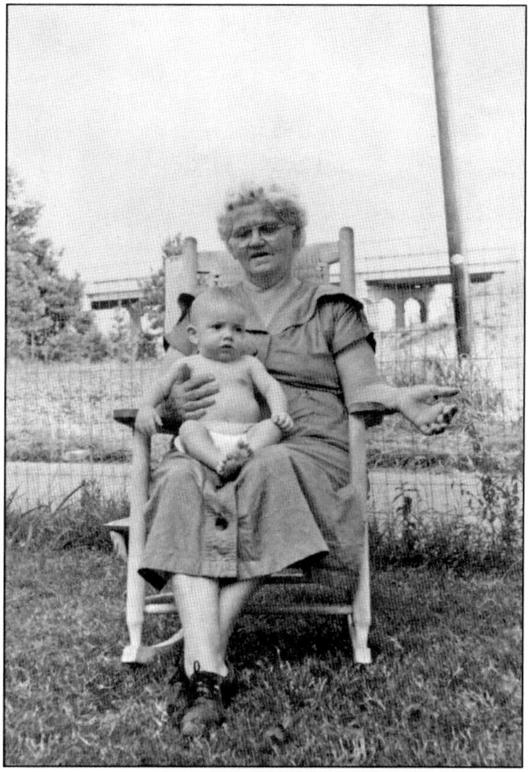

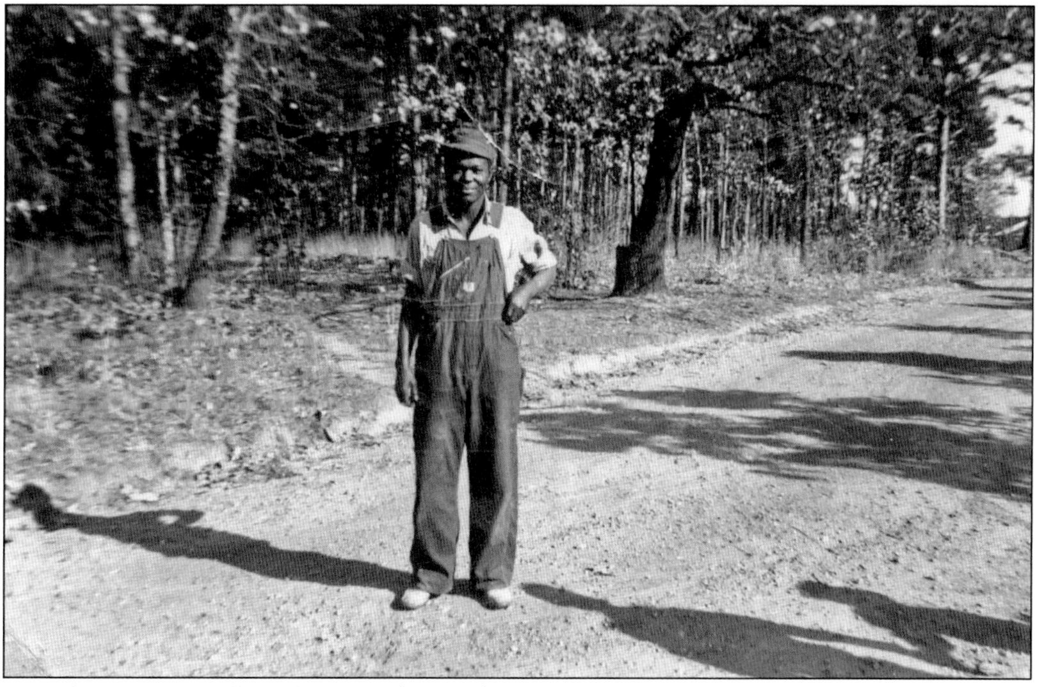

J. E. Thompson is walking from Eusebius and Jennie Ballentine's house to their store, which was less than a quarter mile away. Thompson's sister, Lillie Brazell, worked for the Ballentines and later the Bulls, and he would often visit her.

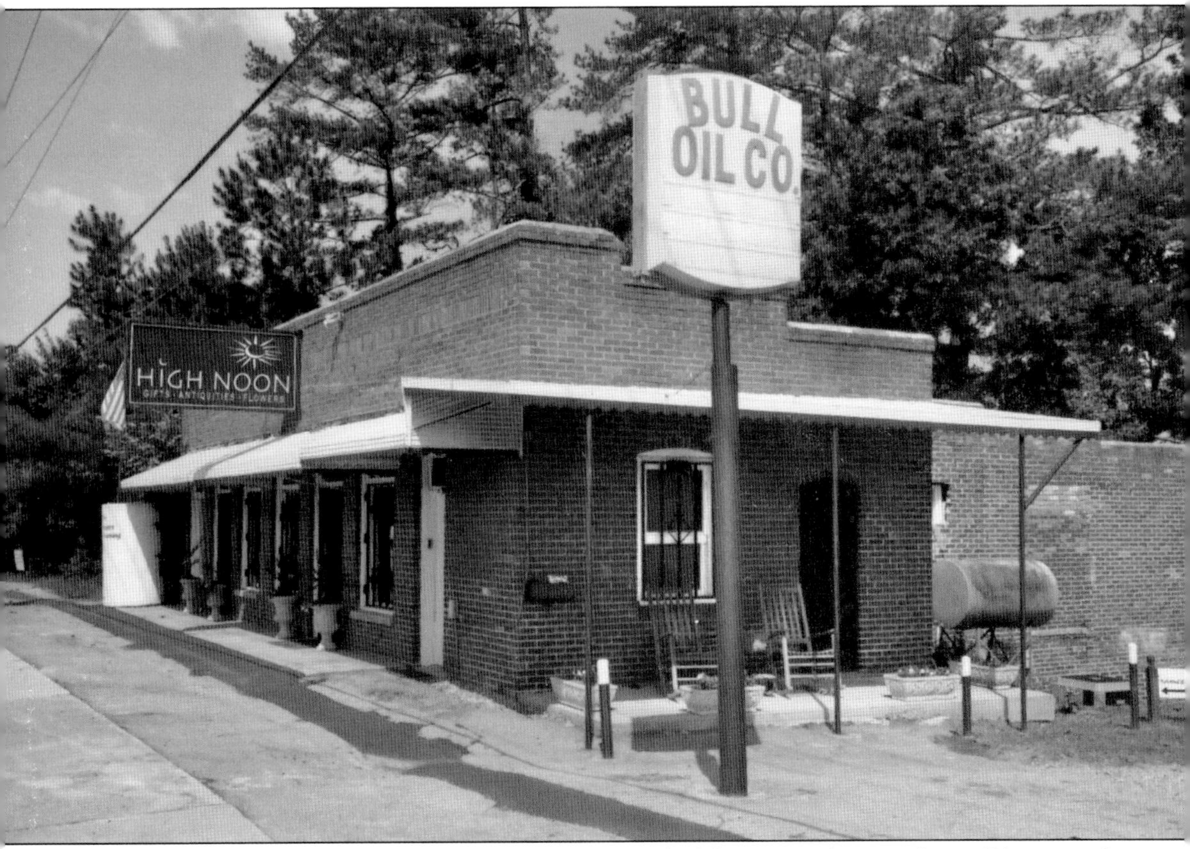

High Noon is a unique gift shop that carries a wonderful variety of items. Angie Rhame is the proprietor. She also operates a frame shop in the back room of the building. The original building was constructed in 1929 and remodeled in 1938 by E. A. Ballentine. It was originally a general store. The old oak wooden counter that is being used by Angie now was the original store counter. (Courtesy of Jacob Dean.)

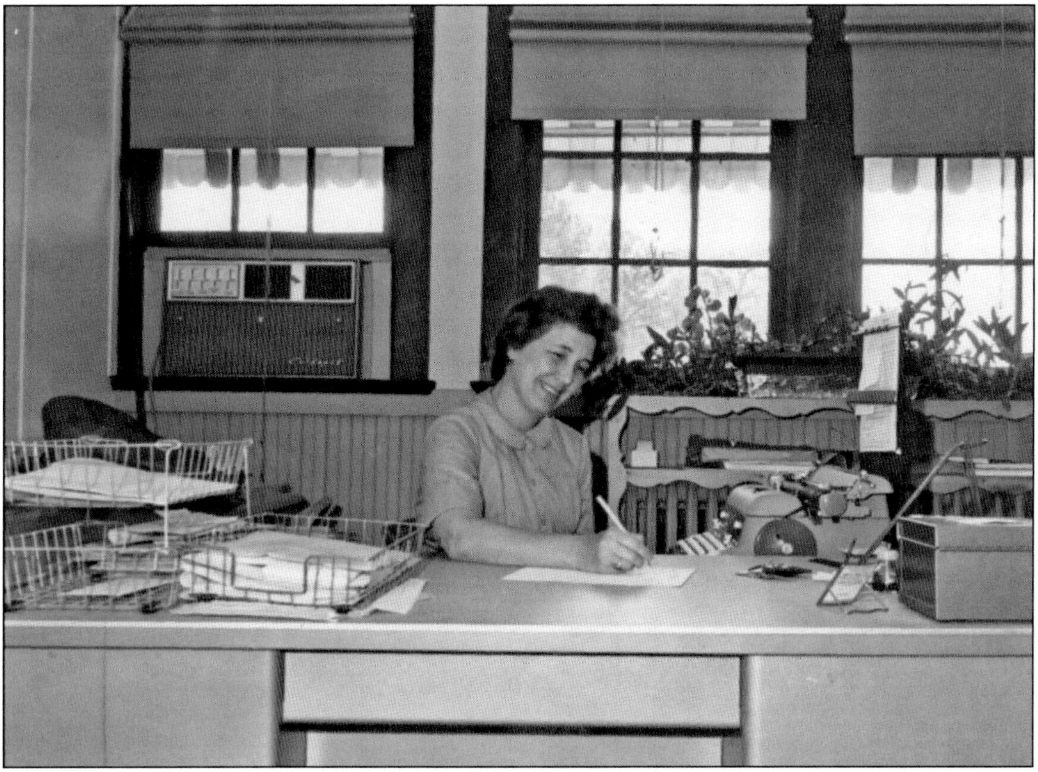

Lucy Lindler was the first secretary for the Lexington Five School District superintendent in the 1950s. This picture from the mid-1960s shows her working at her desk. The window air-conditioning unit was a fairly new addition, and "Mrs. Lucy" typed everything on an electric typewriter. (Courtesy of Lucy Lindler.)

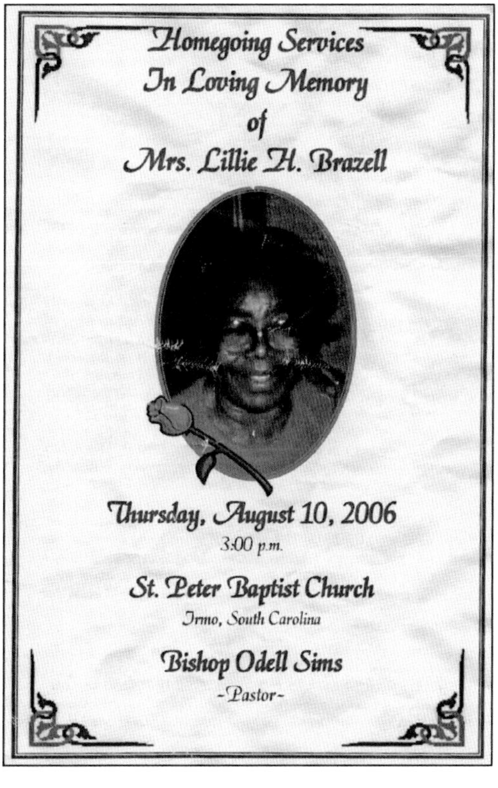

Homegoing Services
In Loving Memory
of
Mrs. Lillie H. Brazell

Thursday, August 10, 2006
3:00 p.m.

St. Peter Baptist Church
Irmo, South Carolina

Bishop Odell Sims
-Pastor-

Lillie Brazell was born October 28, 1912, in Chapin, South Carolina, and passed away on August 6, 2006. She was married to Johnny Brazell and was described as a loving, caring person and an excellent cook. She was employed for over 50 years by the family of James and Myrtle Bull. They were her extended family.

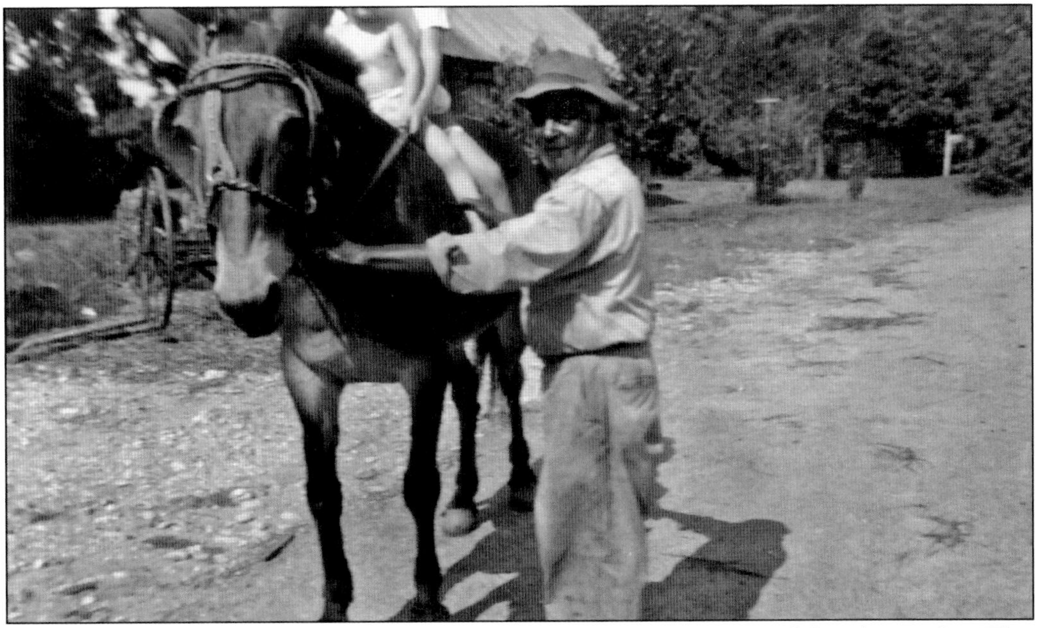

Raymond Geiger is giving a ride to two unidentified children on one of the plow mules. This picture was taken in 1945, the same year World War II ended. Geiger farmed and did a lot of odd jobs around the area. Bryson Lowman states that he and Clay Geiger, Raymond's son, were playmates and good friends. They would eat at each other's house, and he recalls they had two old tire rims from autos and would push them around the yard, pretending they were trucks.

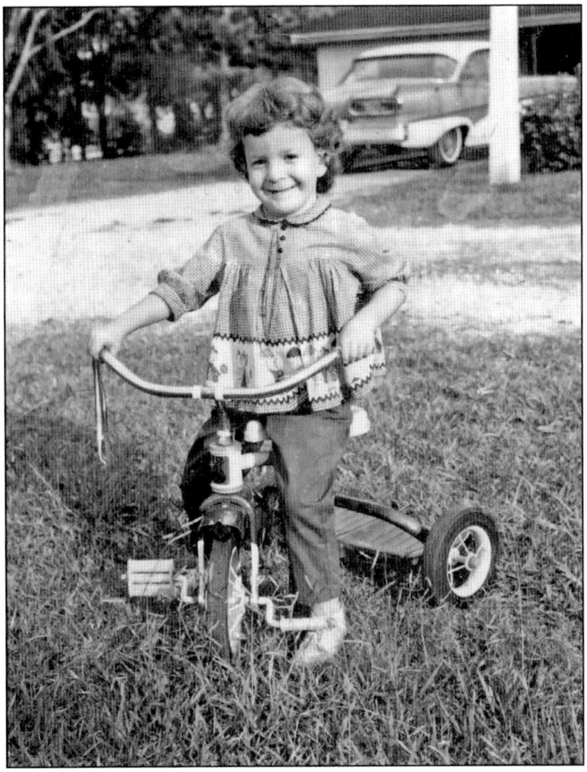

Laura Sites Bull is riding her tricycle in the front yard of her home. Laura's family (on both sides) has lived in the Dutch Fork area for generations. She and her family now reside in the old home place on several acres of land, which still houses the family cemetery. Family cemeteries were common years ago. (Courtesy of Laura Bull.)

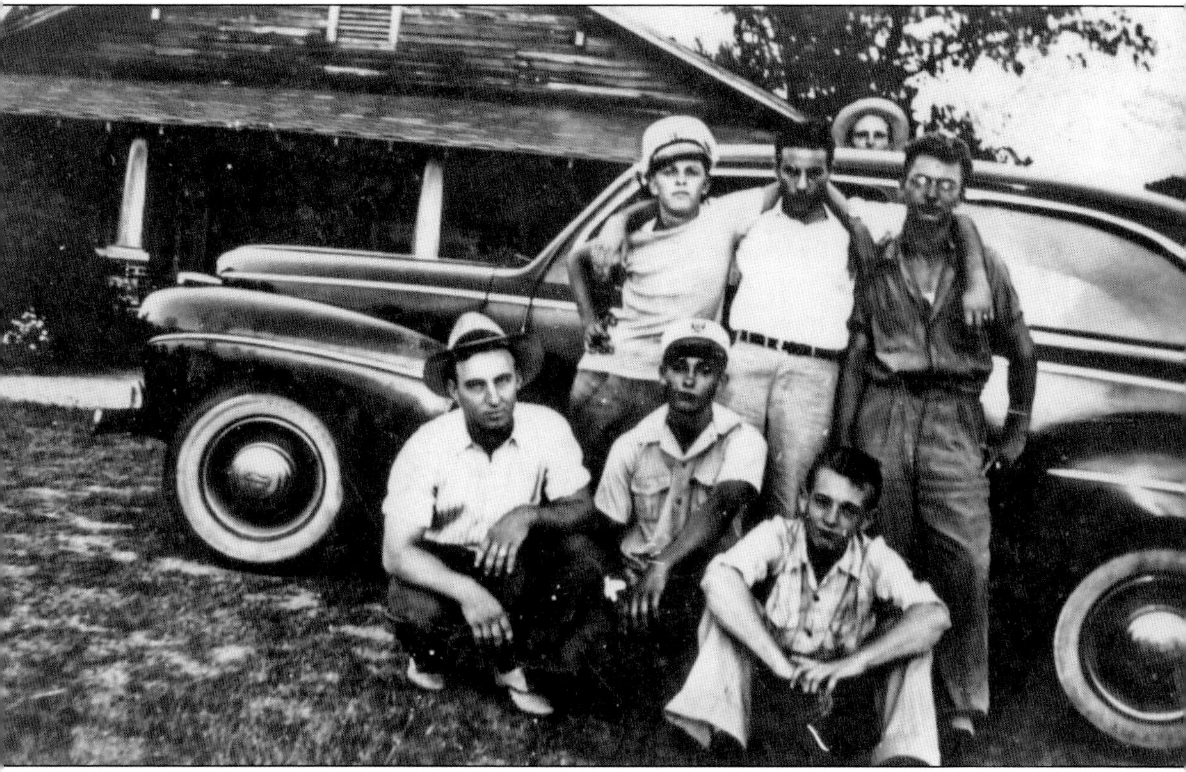

Lila Schuler, a schoolteacher, had just bought herself a new 1941 car and had gone to show Lila and Dan Drafts. All the guys gathered around the car to admire and check it out. From left to right are (first row) Kirby Bickley, J. D. Drafts, and Henry Peebos; (second row) Fred Steepe, Edwin Schuler, and Claude Weed. Peeping over the top of the car is Herman Koon. (Courtesy of Lucy Lindler.)

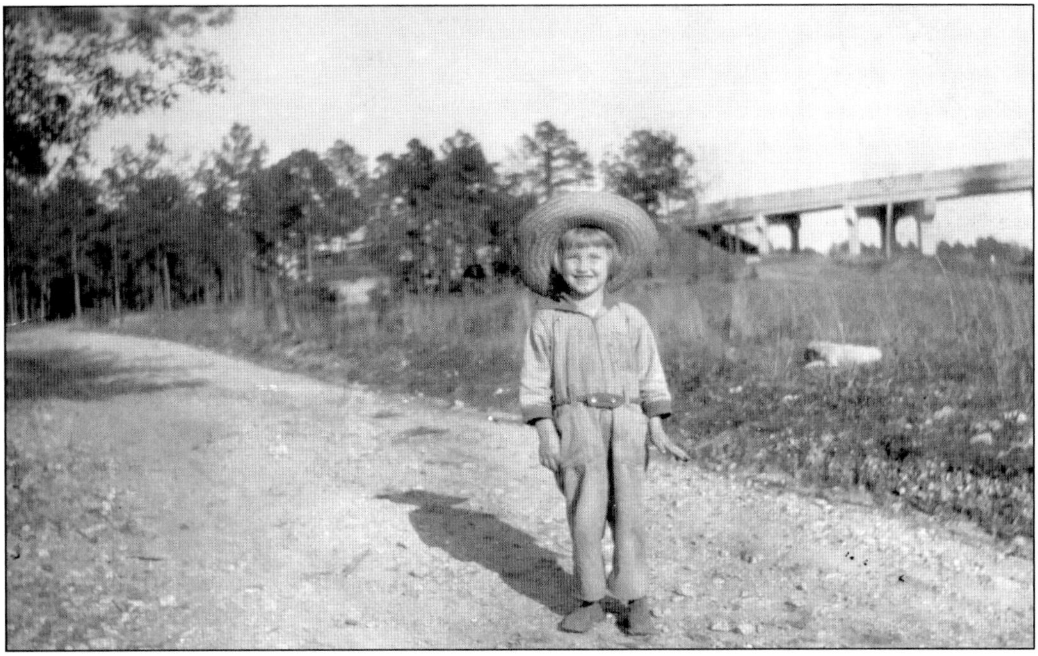

The little tomboy shown in the foreground is Myrtle Bull. In the background to the right is the original bridge that ran through Ballentine, and to the left is the cotton gin. Myrtle stated that, as they built the new bridge, they were dynamiting and a piece of rock flew off, hit her in the head, and knocked her out.

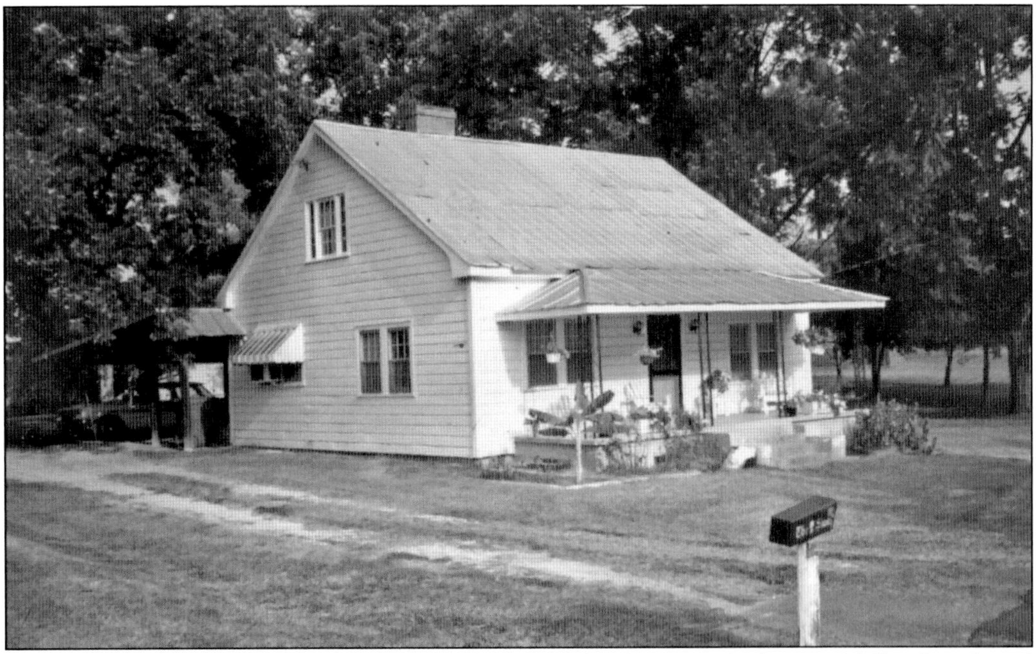

This house was originally the home of the Edgar Wise family. Later Herbert and Ollie Amick and their children lived there for many years. The land was sold and now there are storage buildings on the site. This home was one of the original homes in the area, according to some residents. (Courtesy of John Bouknight.)

Five

Lake Murray

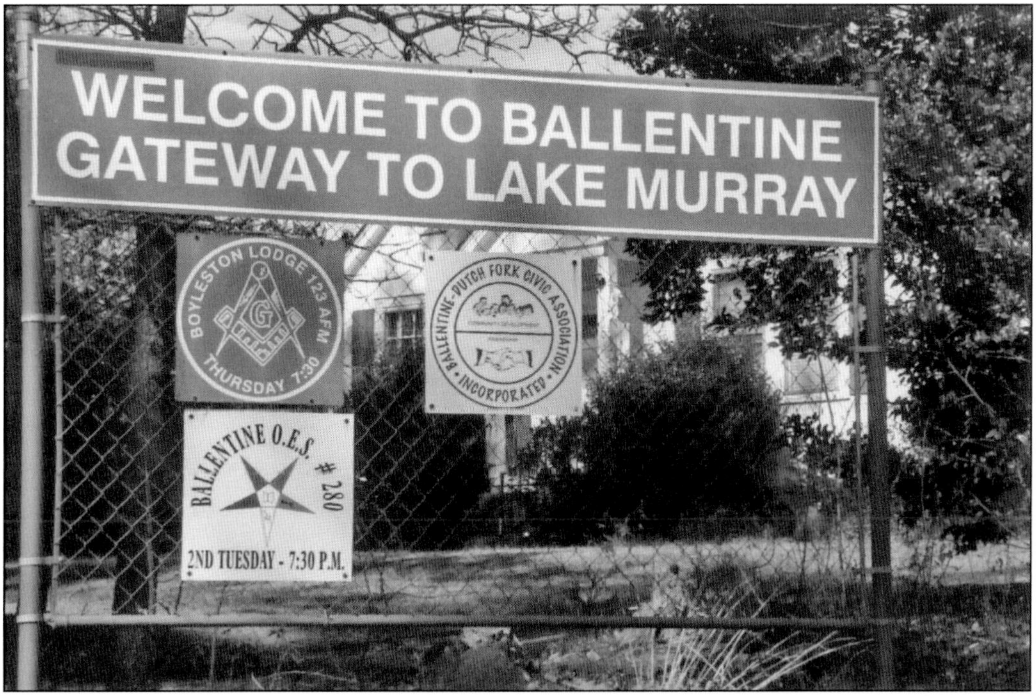

"Welcome to Ballentine! Gateway to Lake Murray!" This sign was erected in the 1970s by the Ballentine–Dutch Fork Civic Association, the Boyleston Lodge, and the Ballentine Order of the Eastern Star. This describes the area perfectly because, as travelers enter Ballentine from Highway 76 and take any left after passing Highway 6, they will find themselves at the shores of Lake Murray. (Courtesy of Jacob Dean.)

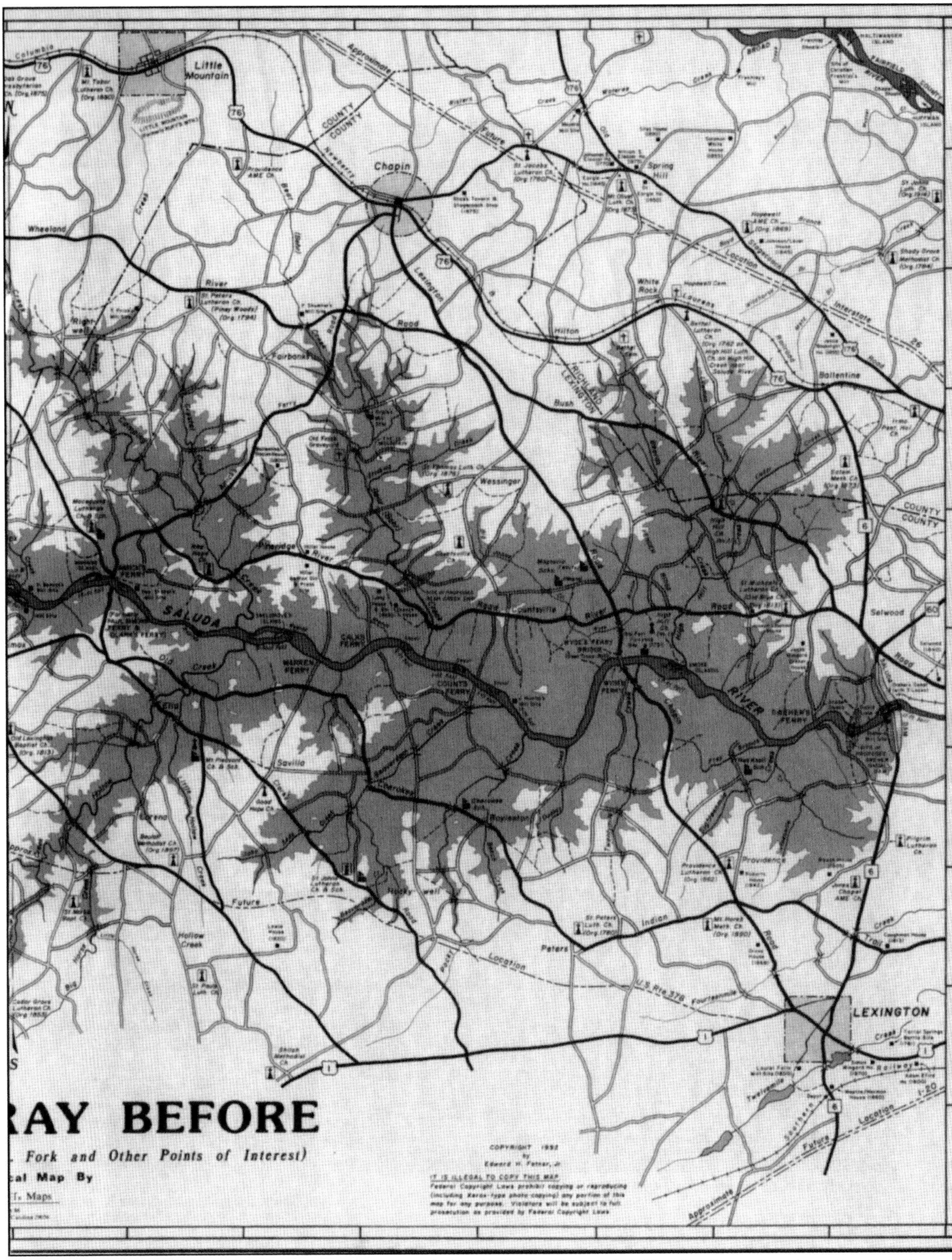

"Lake Murray Before" is a historical map of the Saluda River Valley before the dam by Ed Fetner. Fetner conceived the idea of drafting a map of the lake after becoming lost at Santee. His first map was of Lake Marion. In 1952, the Lake Murray Map was created and has helped many fishermen in navigating the lake. Later he created the "Lake Murray Before" map as he is interested in the local history of the area. (Courtesy of Fishunt Maps; copyright Edward H. Fetner Jr.)

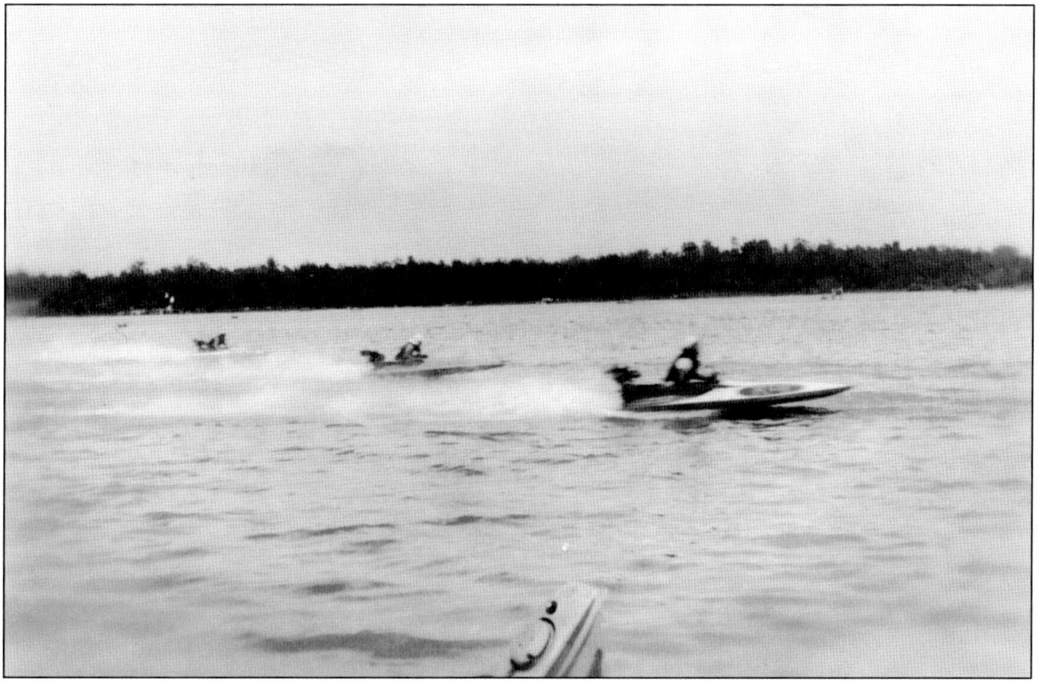

Boating is a favorite pastime on Lake Murray; years ago, there were speed racing competitions on Lake Murray. The lake was not as developed or as crowded as it is today, as one can see from the shoreline. This race occurred in the 1930s.

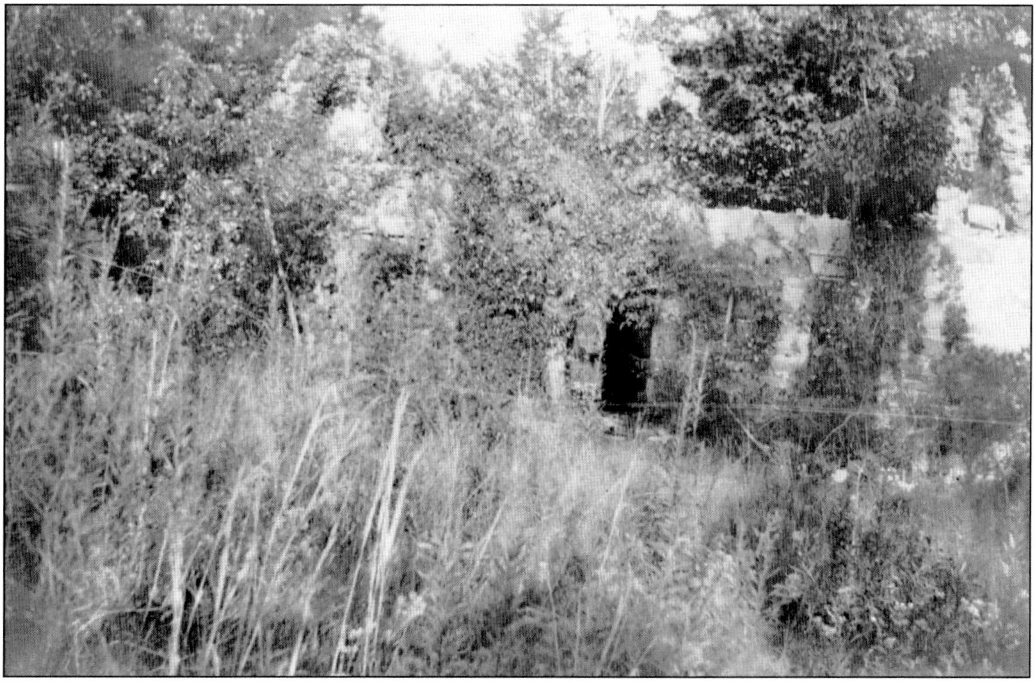

It cannot be seen very well, but this is a picture of the old Rock House. It is now under the waters of Lake Murray near the dam. It was used as a residence for lockkeepers.

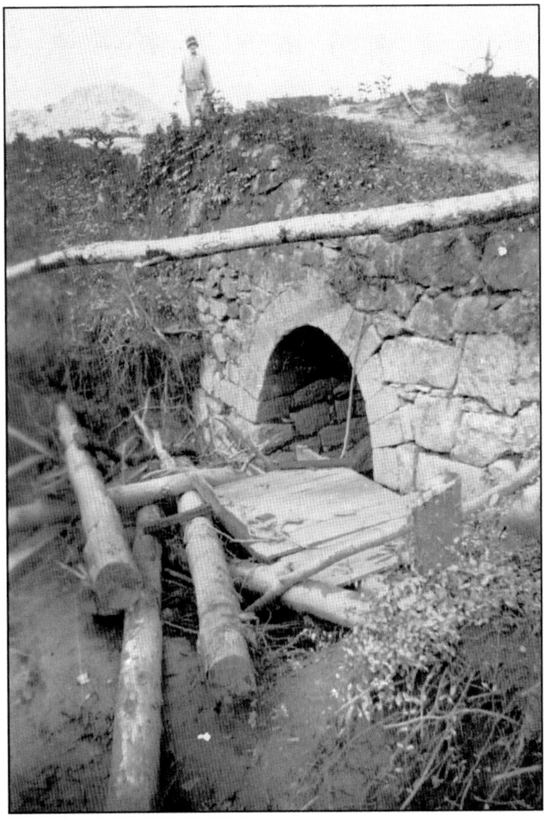

An unidentified woman is standing on top of a bridge. The caption on the back of the picture states, "A scene of the land before the dam was built." Construction on the dam began in 1927, so this picture must have been taken shortly before then.

The dam was built to provide hydroelectric power to the area. The Saluda River Dam, also known as the Lake Murray Dam, was an engineering feat at the time of its construction. It was built using native red clay soil and bedrock and was the largest earthen dam in the world when it was completed in 1930. The lake was named after the chief project engineer, William S. Murray.

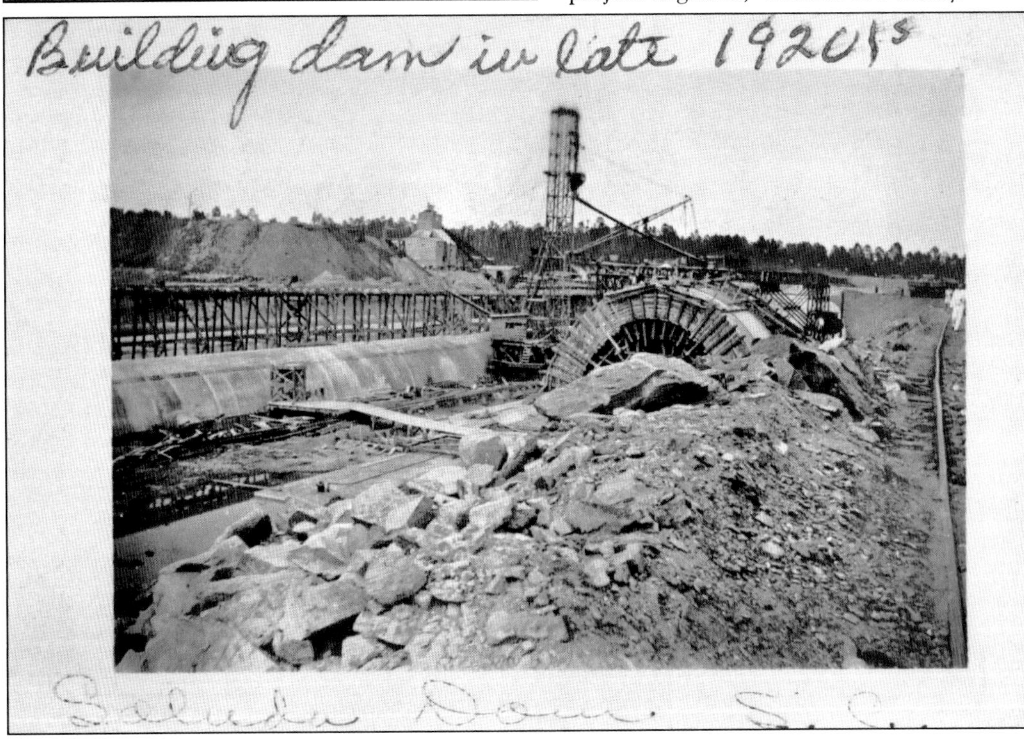

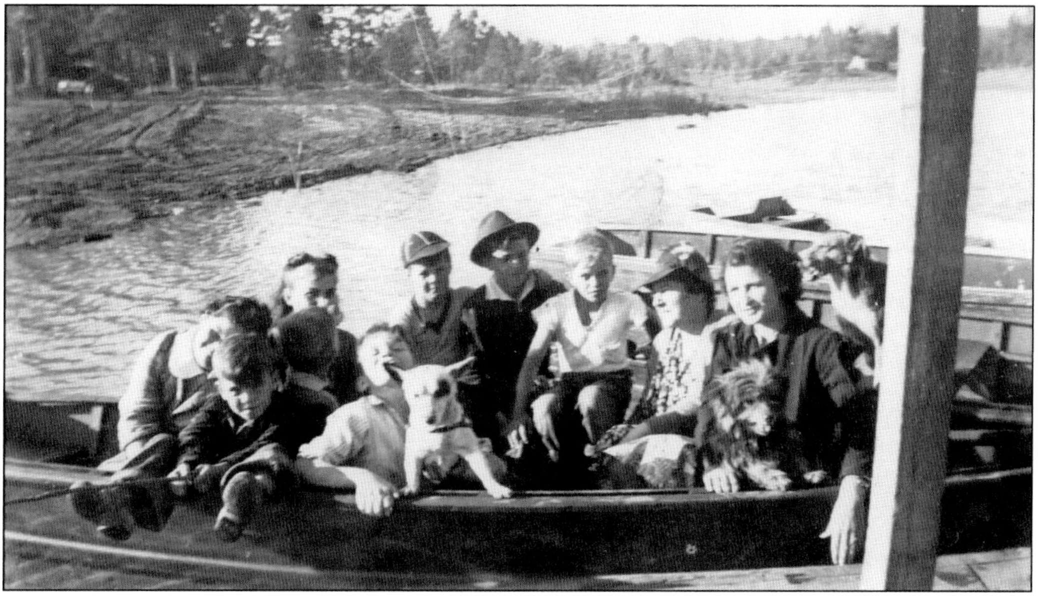

This boat was loaded down with people and dogs. There was a boat landing at the end of what is now Sunset Point, off Marina Road, where people could rent boats or take a boat ride. The lake was fairly new, and there were several small boat landings popping up on the lake. Lake traffic was light, and the regulations of today were not in existence. The position of chief game warden was established in 1910.

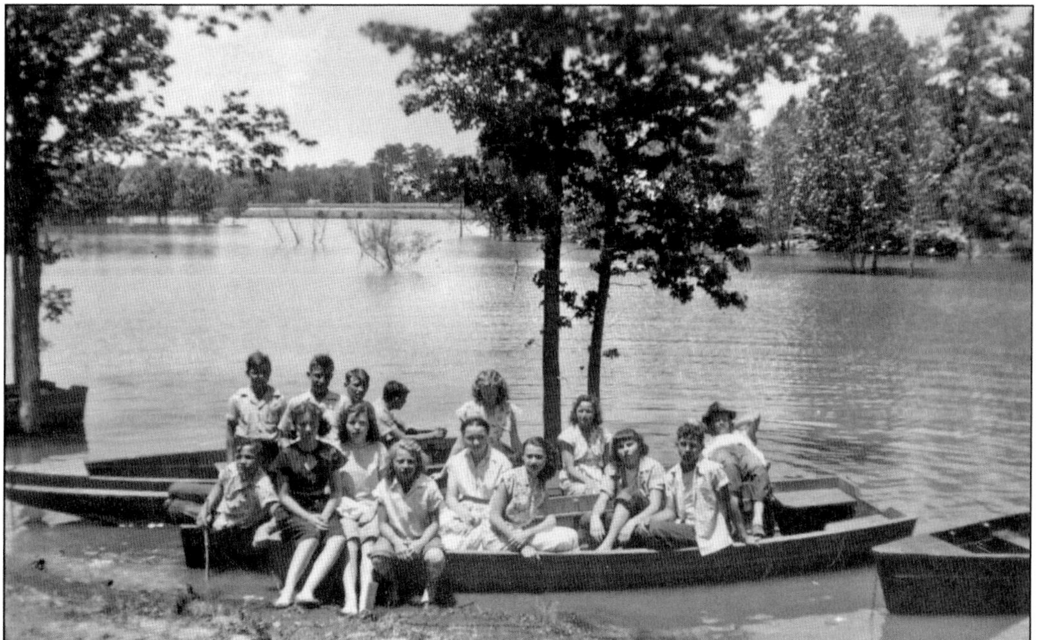

The Sheely family always held a family reunion down at the lake. They were descended from George Robert and Laura-Ann Derrick Sheely. This one was held in the early 1940s. A barbeque pit had been built on the lake property, so the family always barbequed instead of having covered dishes. They usually barbequed chicken. (Courtesy of Kay Sheely.)

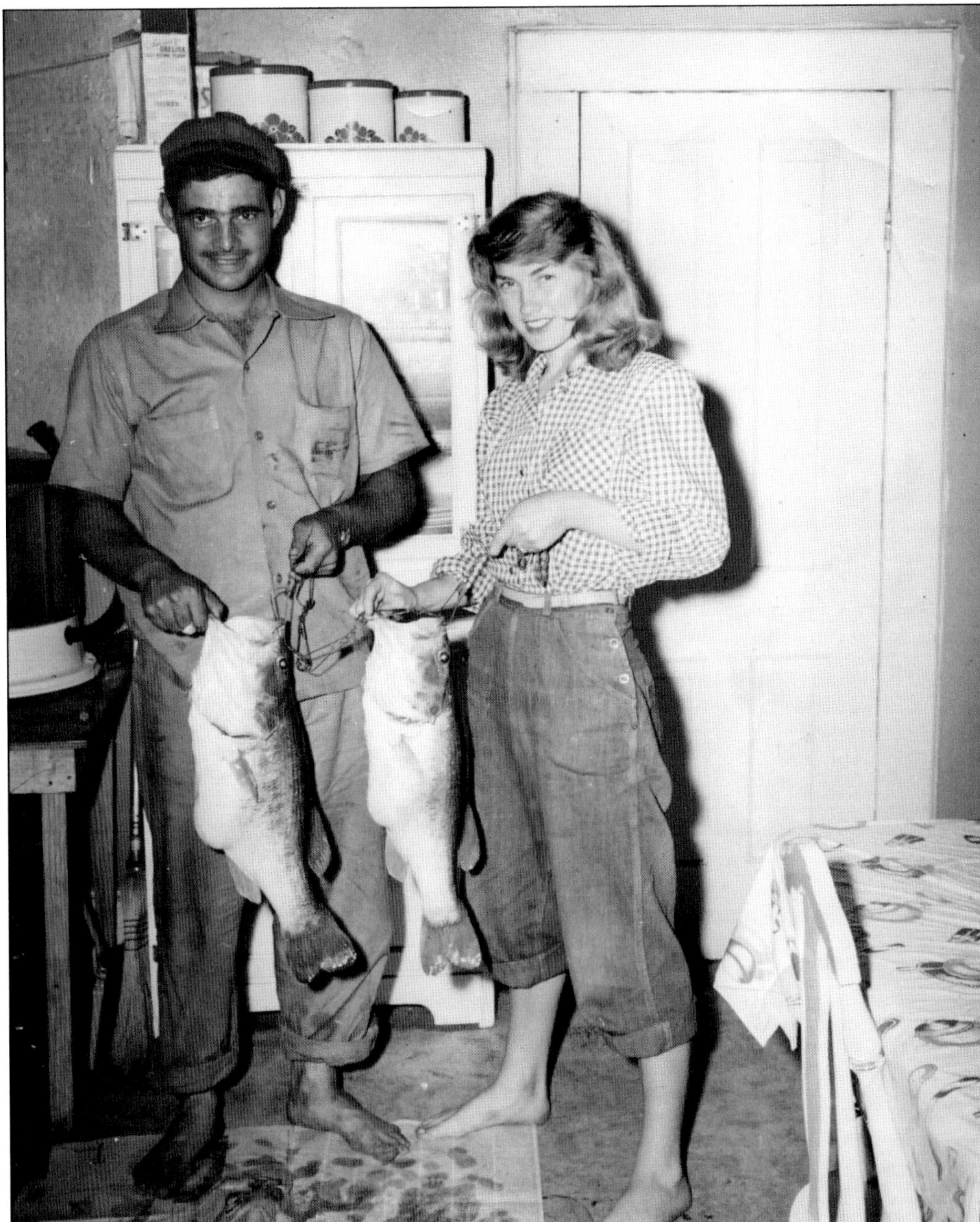

Fishing on Lake Murray was a favorite pastime of Myrtle and Jim Bull, along with swimming, diving, and boating. They were still newlyweds when this picture was taken in 1947.

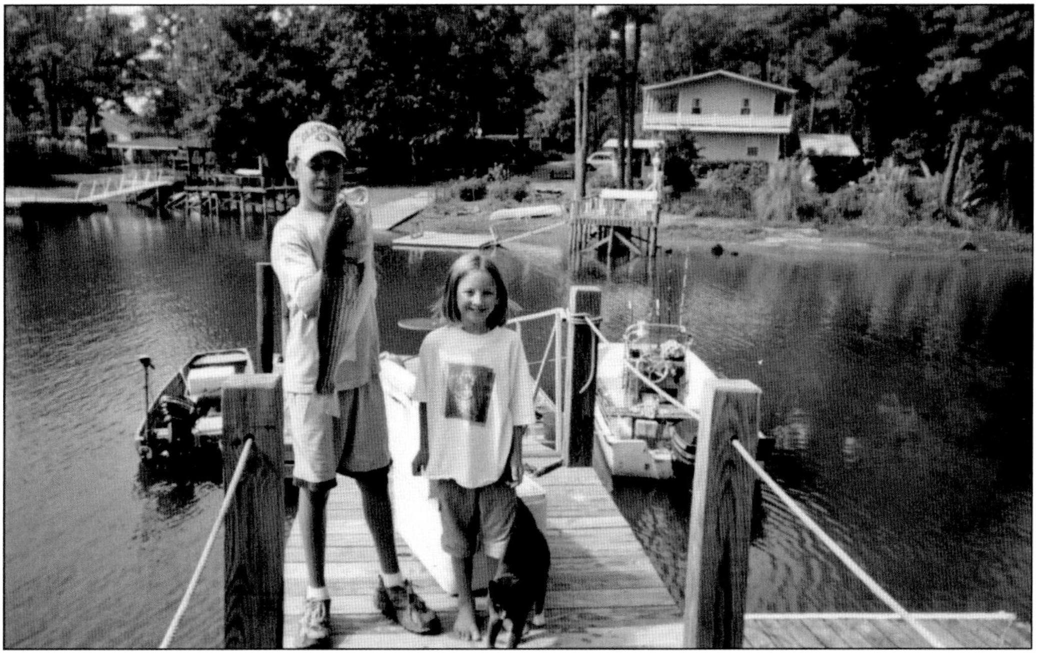

Their dad, Mike Bull, took them fishing a lot when they were younger and Bonnie and Brendan Bull always seemed to catch some nice fish. Fishing is a nice, relaxing pastime for many families living on the lake but is big business for some of the professional fisherman. There have been several big fishing tournaments on Lake Murray. (Courtesy of Mike Bull.)

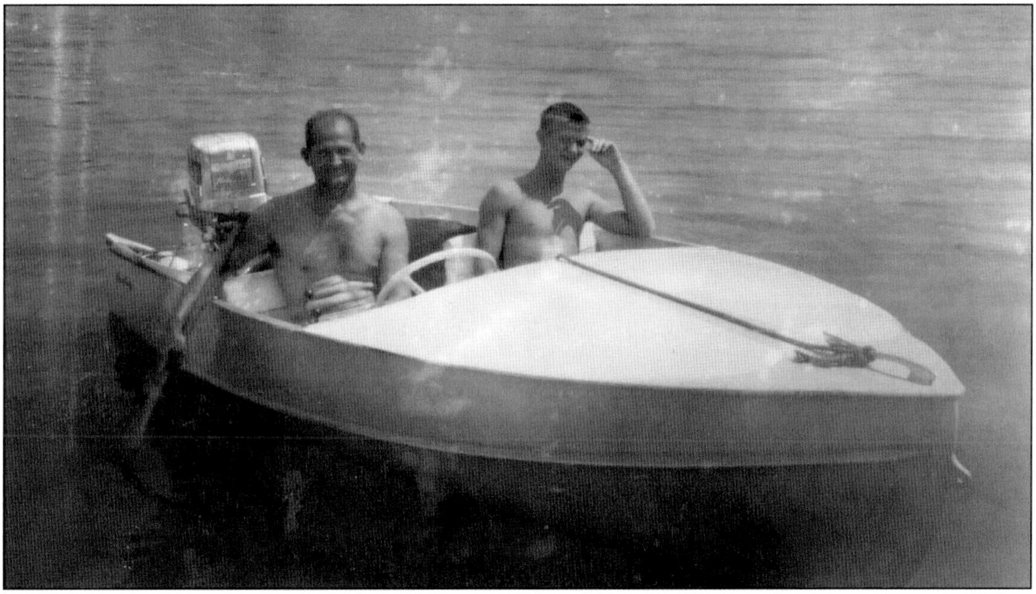

Rudolph Ballentine and his son Rudy are cruising around the lake in their boat at about the time Rudy was attending Duke University. Rudolph was a teacher and later the director of the South Carolina Public Service Commission. Rudy graduated from Duke University and Duke University Medical School. Dr. Ballentine was a pioneer in holistic medicine, combining his knowledge of modern science with his studies of various healing traditions, and is recognized internationally as an expert in the integration of various schools of holistic medicine. (Courtesy of Pat Derrick.)

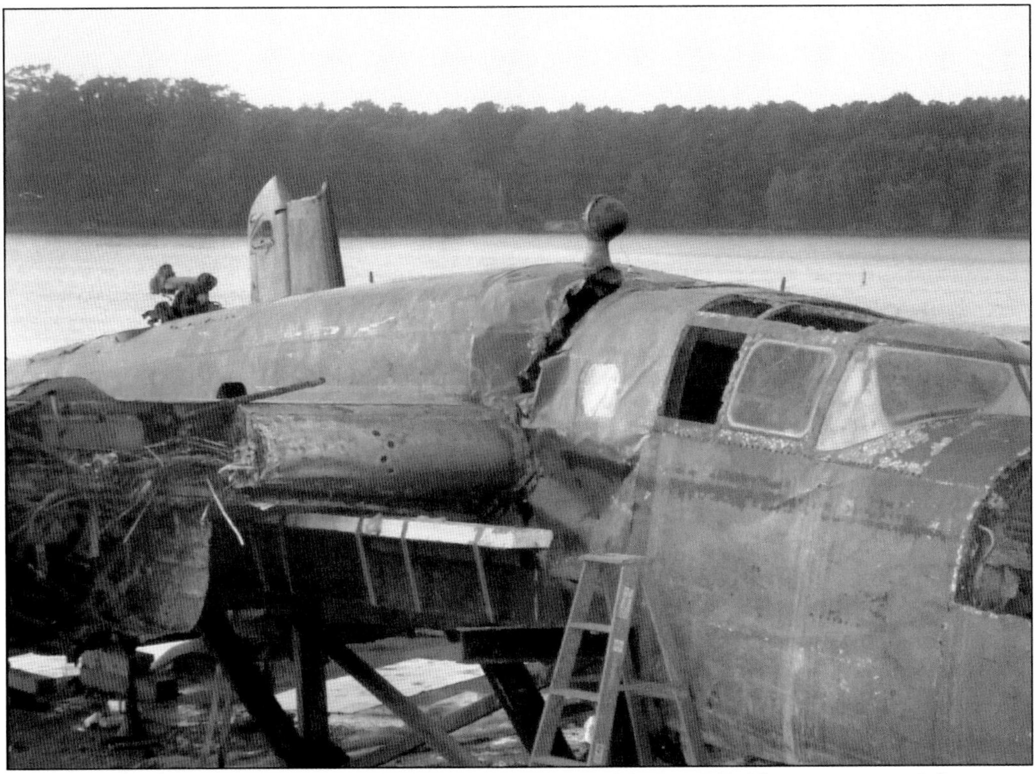

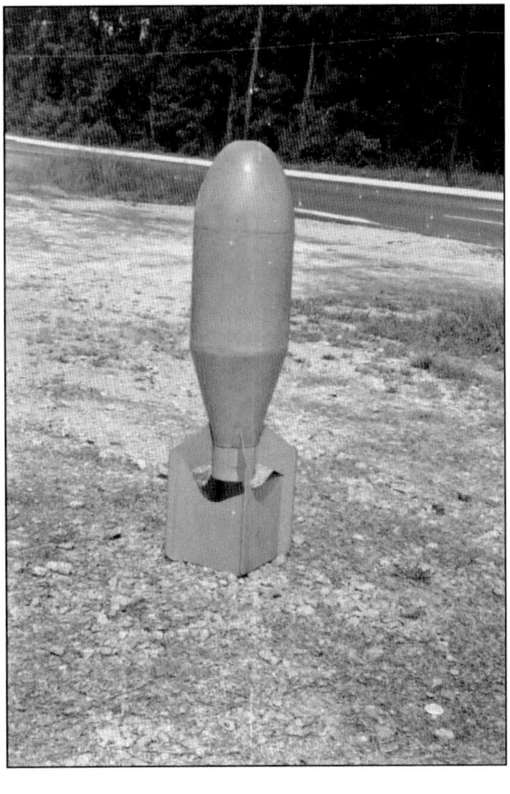

A World War II B-25 was recovered from Lake Murray after 60-plus years of being underwater. The recovery team was led by Gary Larkins, an internationally known aviator salver. The aircraft went down on April 4, 1943, during a training mission after losing power. The crew escaped and was rescued, but the aircraft was unable to be salvaged because of the water depth. (Courtesy of Marilyn Bull.)

Bomb Island is an island in the middle of Lake Murray. It acquired the name because it was used by the military during World War II as a training site for pilots and their crew. This is one of the training bombs used at that time. Louise Riley, known as "The Peach Lady," permitted John Bouknight to photograph the bomb. (Courtesy of John Bouknight.)

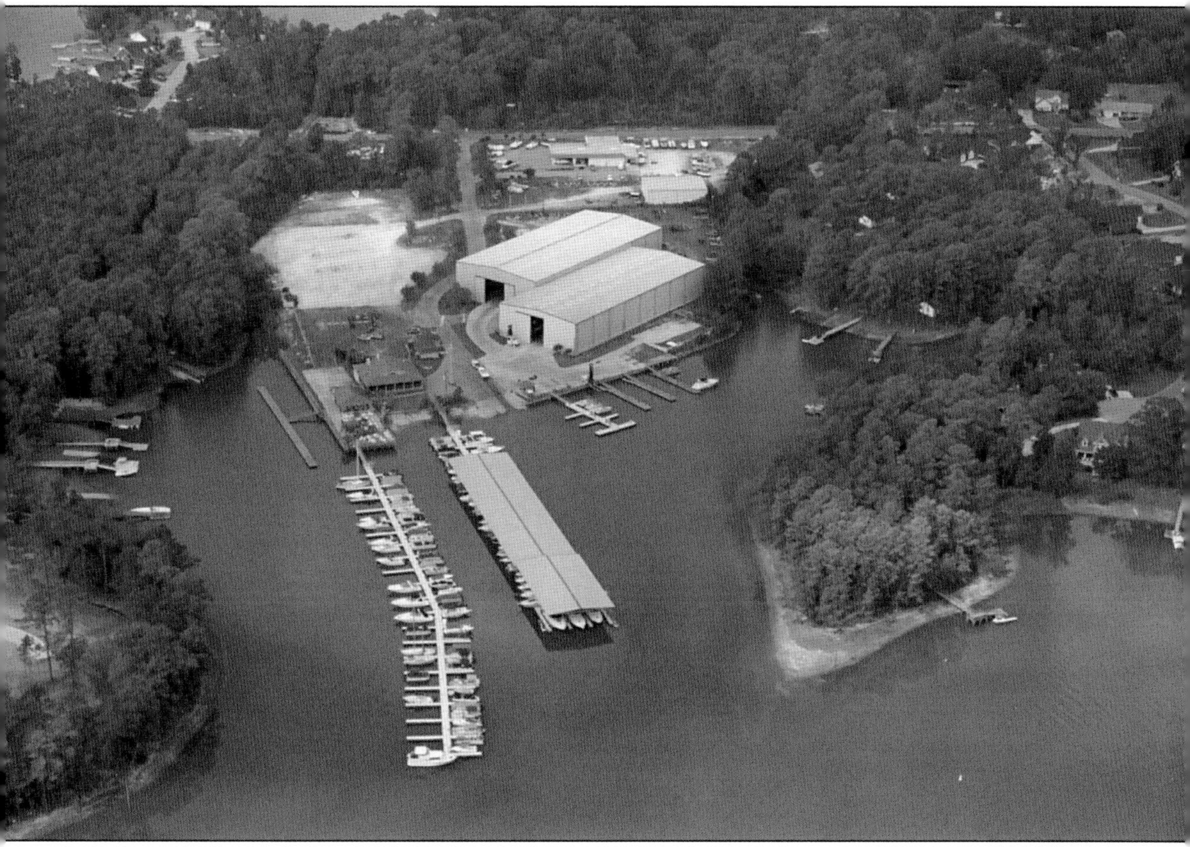

Lighthouse Marina, located off of Johnson's Marina, is a full-service marina at one time called Johnson's Marina. Services they offer are gas and courtesy docks, gated covered and uncovered wet slips, dry storage, and rental boats. Also on the premises is the Rusty Anchor Restaurant, which offers a picturesque unique dining experience and specializes in seafood. Adjacent to the Rusty Anchor is the Quarterdeck, which offers a light menu, cool drinks, and live entertainment for afternoon boaters. (Courtesy of Lighthouse Marina.)

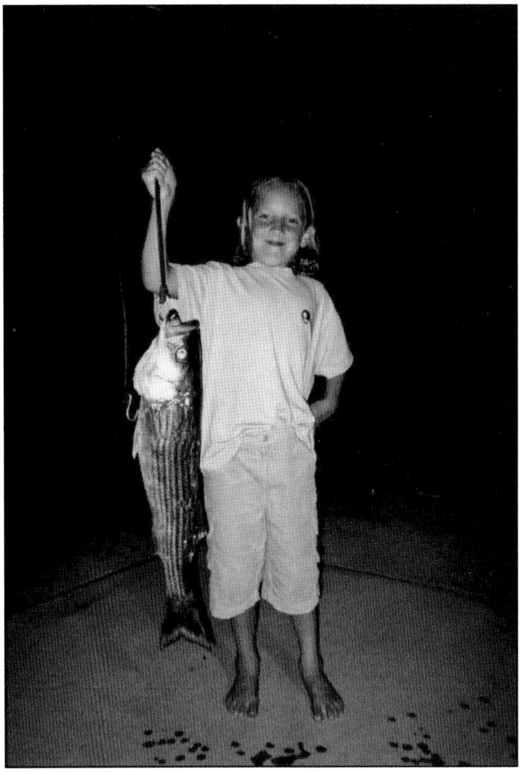

Bonnie Bull was very proud of her catch. She worked hard to catch it. Bonnie has grown up on Lake Murray and loves to fish and swim, but she especially likes to ride around with her friends on her Sea-doo. (Courtesy of Laura Bull.)

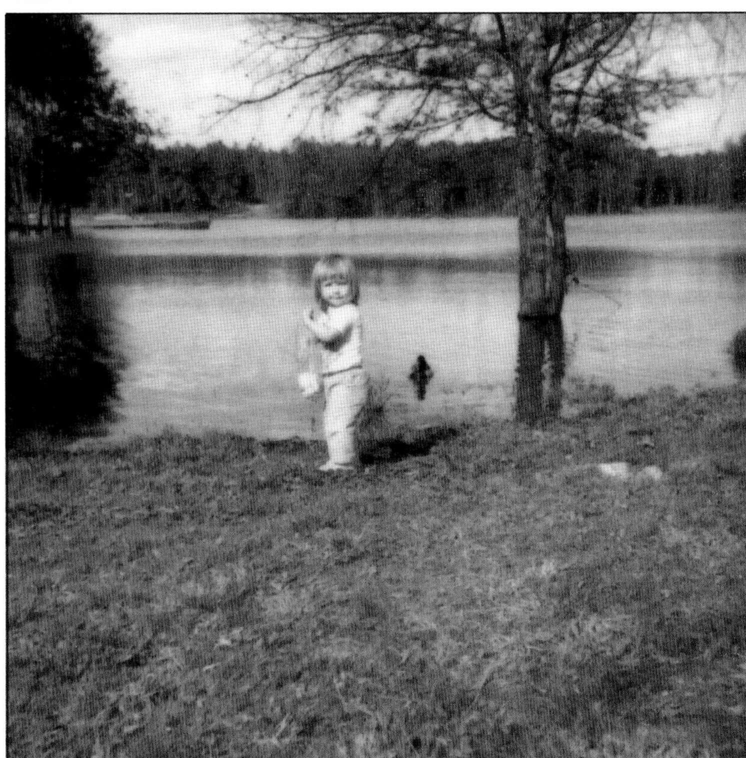

Melissa Bull is feeding the ducks in her backyard. She was around two years old when this picture was taken. (Courtesy of Marilyn Bull.)

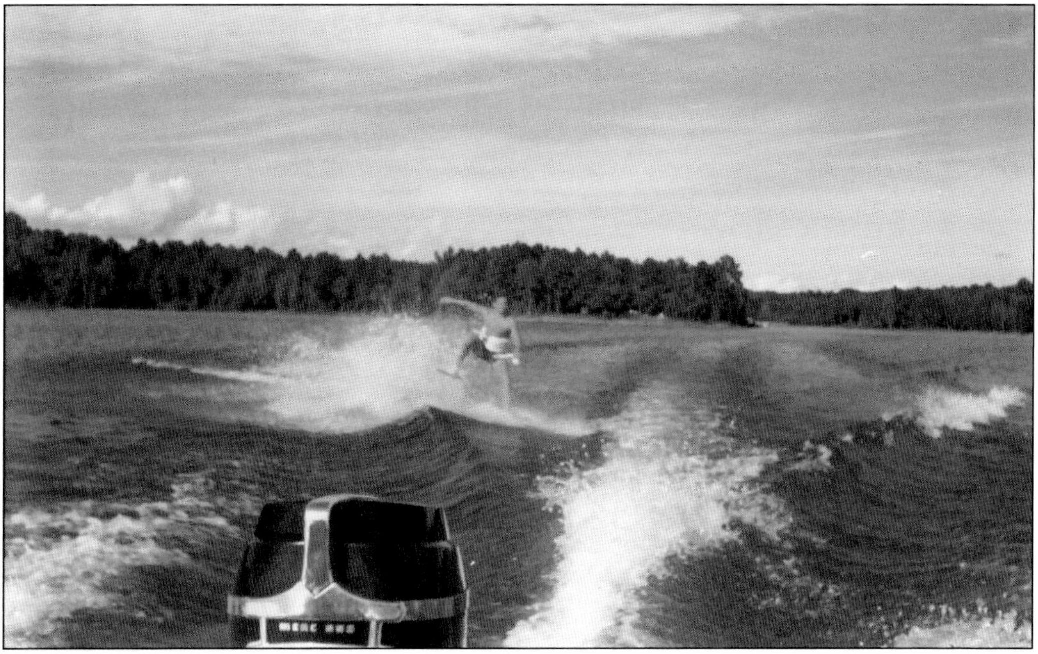

Water-skiing is so much fun, but it can hurt when one falls. This water skier is attempting barefoot skiing, which is skiing without skis. One can start off without any skis or with only one ski (slalom) and drop that ski after being pulled up. The boat has to be going at a faster speed for barefoot skiing than skiing with two skis.

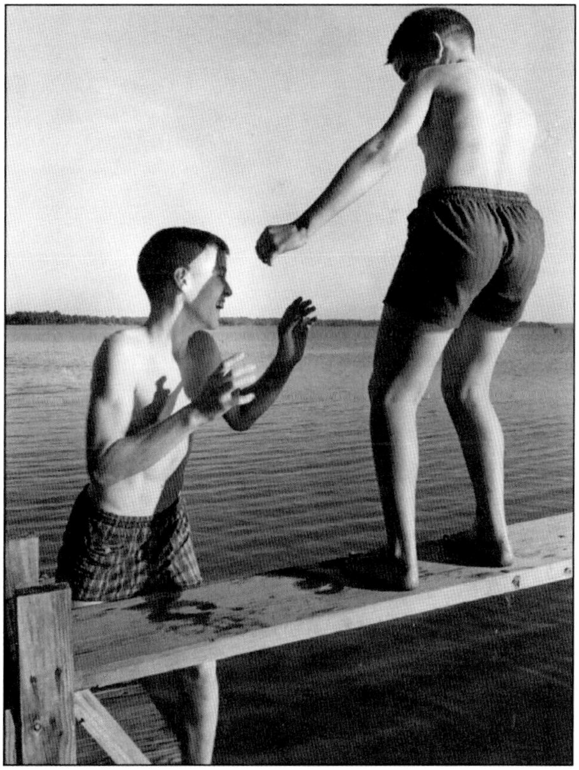

There are a lot of fun activities around the lake: swimming, boating, skiing, fishing. It looks like these two young boys have come up with another sport, the combination of diving and wrestling.

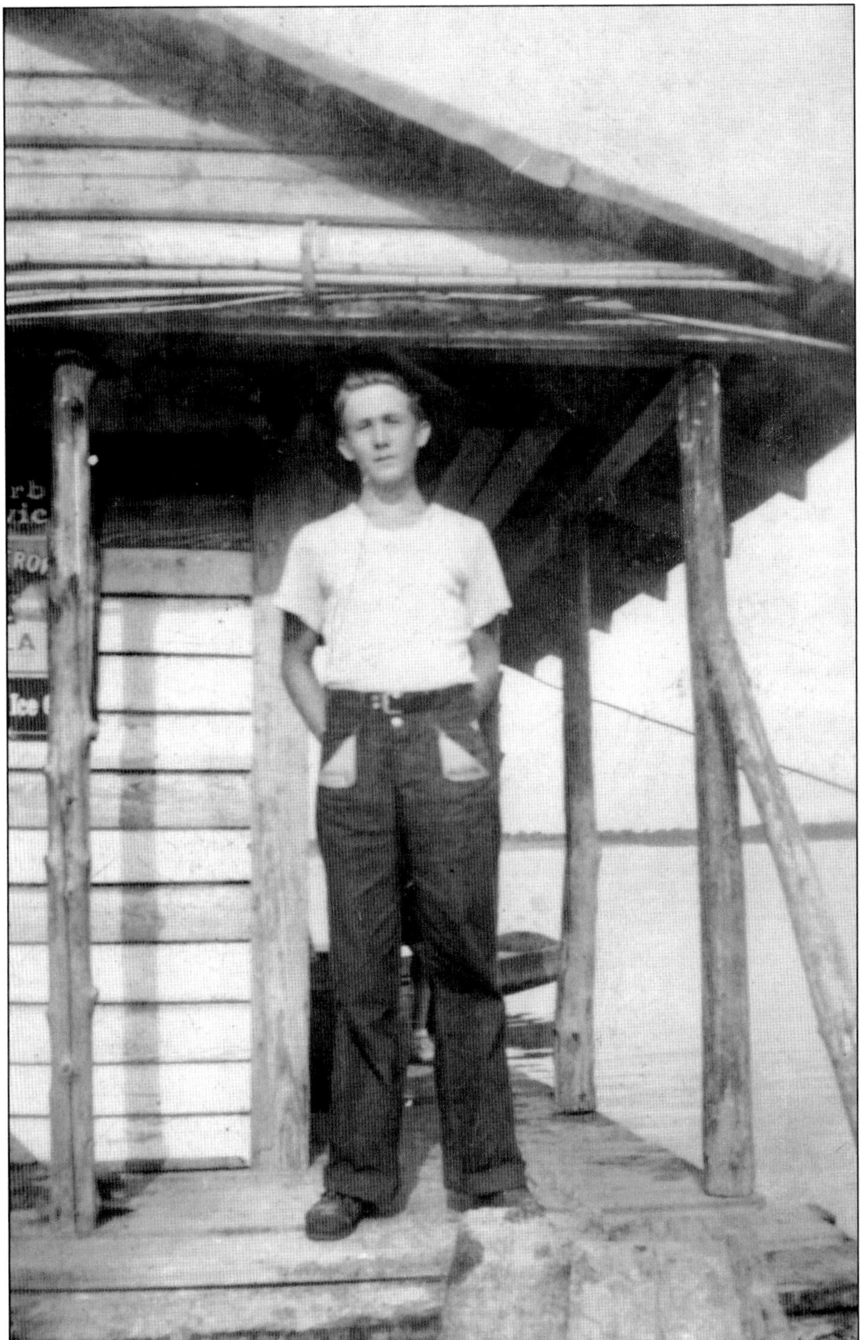

Tom Bailey is standing on Riddle's boat dock, located out of White Rock at the end of Johnson's Marina Road. When he was in high school, Tom was always up to some prank. One day, the teacher left the room and Tom was out of his seat playing around. The teacher saw him through the glass pane in the door, went back to the office, and said over the loudspeaker, "Tom, get back in your seat." When he returned, Tom said, "I knew you could talk through that thing but I didn't know you could see through it, too." (Courtesy of Lucy Lindler.)

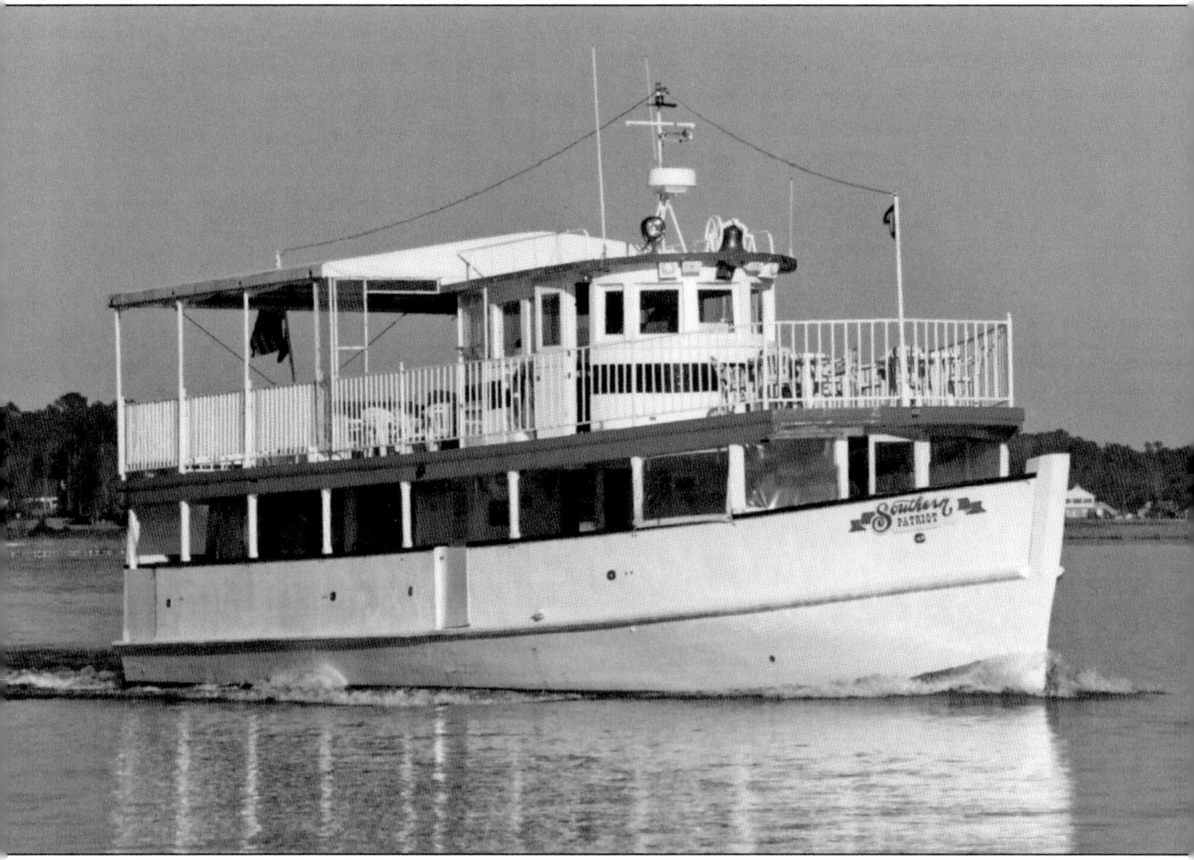

The *Southern Patriot* is a huge tour boat on Lake Murray. Joe Agnew bought the boat, which was built in 1949, from a museum in Maryland. He had to bring the boat down the intercoastal waterway, up through the locks as far as Low Falls Landing, and from there, it traveled via trailer over land. The Agnews owned and operated the boat from 1989 to 1999, when they sold it to J. Downs. The Agnews still operate Agnew Lake Service, and Downs operates the tour boat out of Lake Murray Marina. (Courtesy of Norman Agnew.)

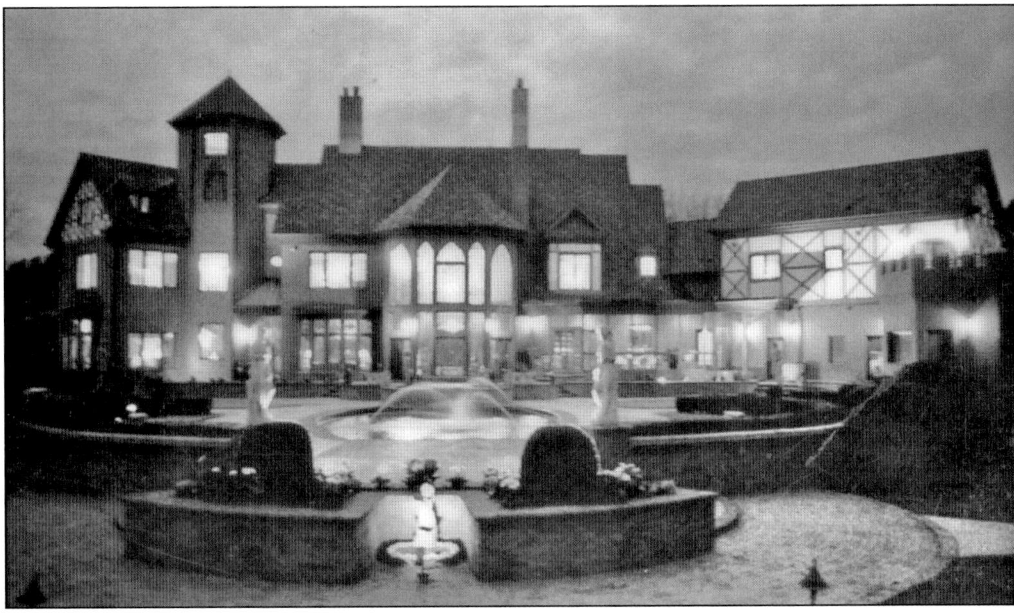

Several years ago, Eugene Brantley built what is now known as the Brantley Manor on Lake Murray. In the home's 13,000 square feet, there are 4 kitchens, 2 swimming pools, a library, game room, butler's quarters, 7 bedrooms, 11 baths, and an observatory. There is also a 3,000-square-foot guesthouse, a pool house, and a three-car garage. A 16th-century pulpit is suspended from a balcony in the main receiving room. A paved motor court at the entrance to the Brantley Manor features a marble fountain that was originally the baptismal font at the Sanderman Estate Church in Lanchashire, England. The home was built in the Tudor architectural style using the finest materials. This house was designed for grand-scale entertaining, with an incredible great hall featuring an intricate floor patterned with a Greek key border of three woods, an inner border of green marble, and a walnut center. The exterior brickwork was designed and made by Brantley, exclusively for this home. The home overlooks 12,500 waterfront feet and has two sandy beaches surrounded by manicured lawns and sculptured gardens. (Courtesy of Eugene Brantley.)

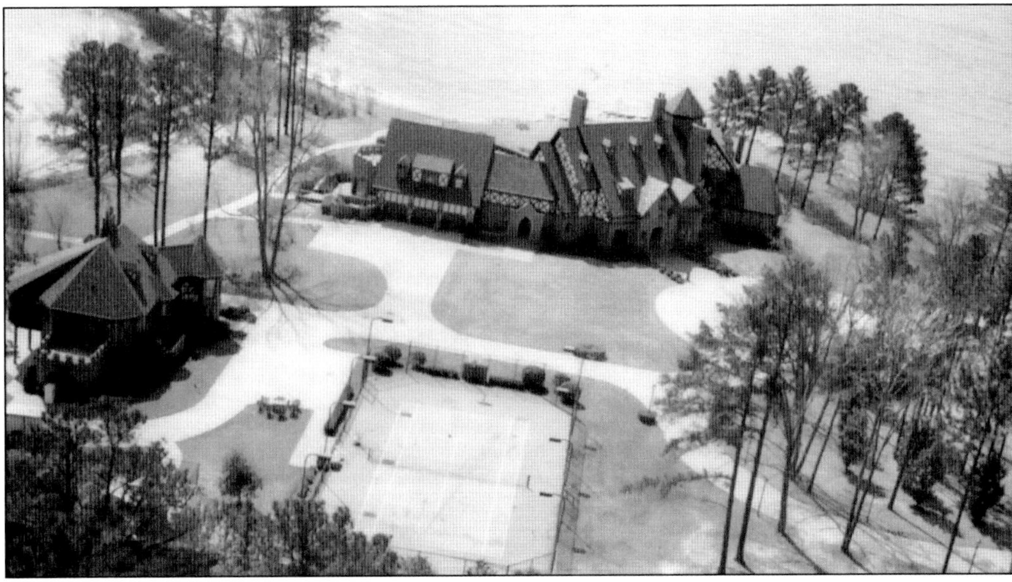

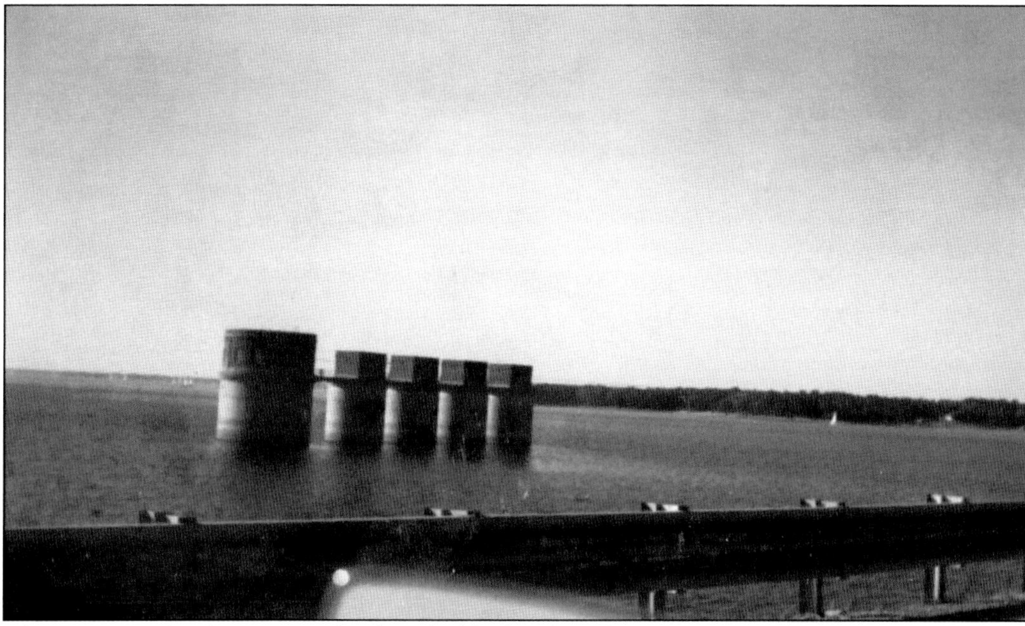

The towers at the dam are easily identified by local residents. These are large intakes rising 223 feet high. The four smaller towers provide water from the bottom of the lake into the 986-foot-long penstocks with a 16-foot diameter. The largest tower feeds water to the massive arch conduit, which diverted the river during construction and afterward served as the course for an additional penstock to supply a future turbine. (Courtesy of John Bouknight.)

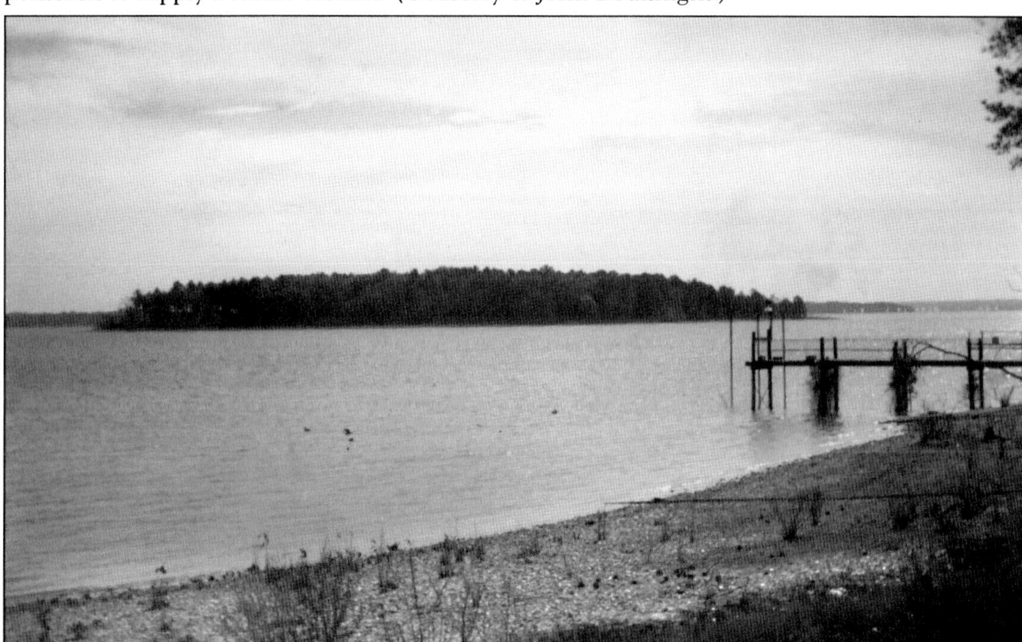

Lake Murray is a beautiful lake and has many islands for boaters to stop and picnic on. Susie Ebert Island, named after Susie Ebert, is a favorite island of many because of its location near two marinas. Some boaters will camp on this island or other islands for the weekend. (Courtesy of John Bouknight.)

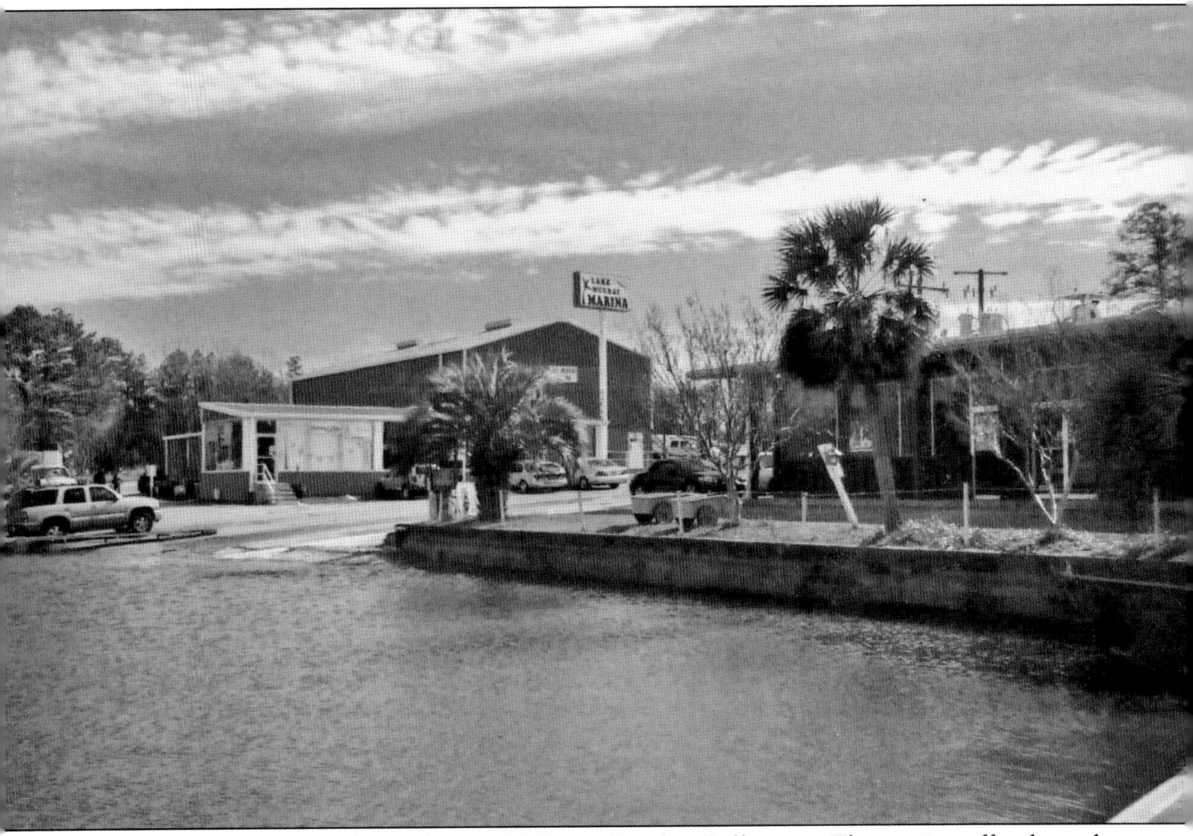

Lake Murray Marina is located at 1600 Marina Road in Ballentine. The marina offers boat slips for rent, boat rental, boat storage, and a fuel dock. There is also a restaurant on the premises. The marina has been in existence for over 60 years and had changed names and owners. At one time, it was known as Wells Marina.

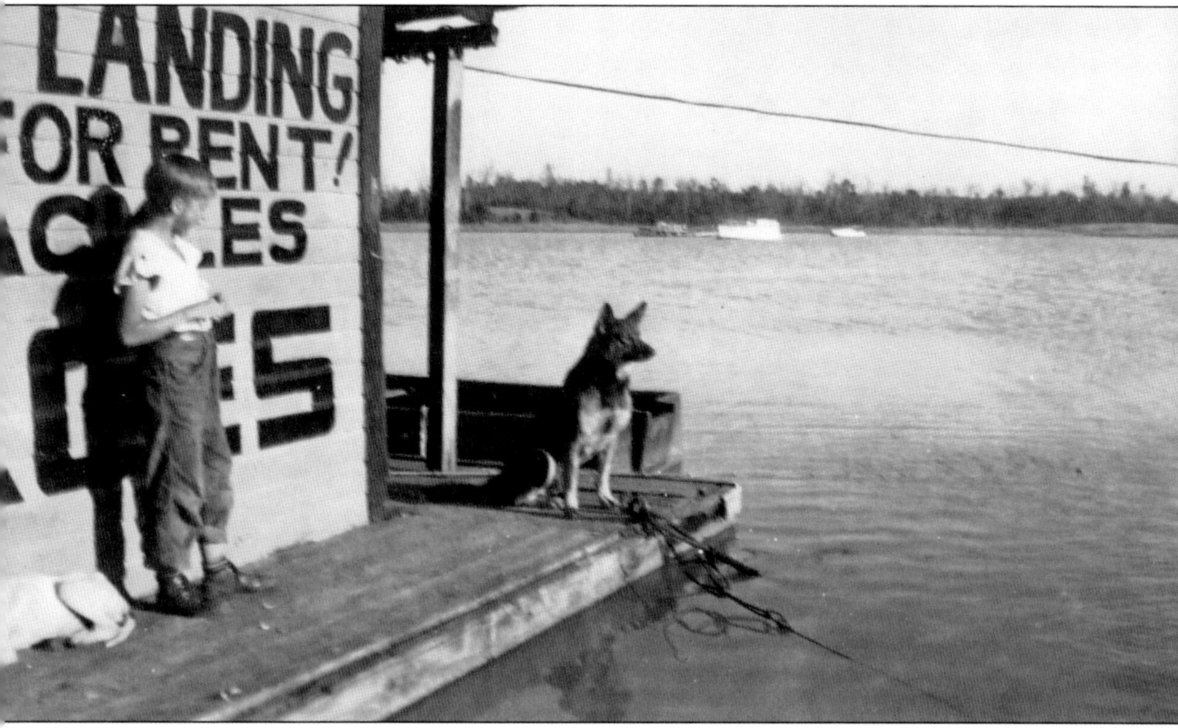

A young boy is relaxing at the boat landing near Ballentine with his two dogs. The landing was located at the end of what is now called Sunset Point, off Marina Road. People could rent boats or canoes and buy snacks and fish bait at the landing. Some of the local residents remember diving off of the top of the boathouse.

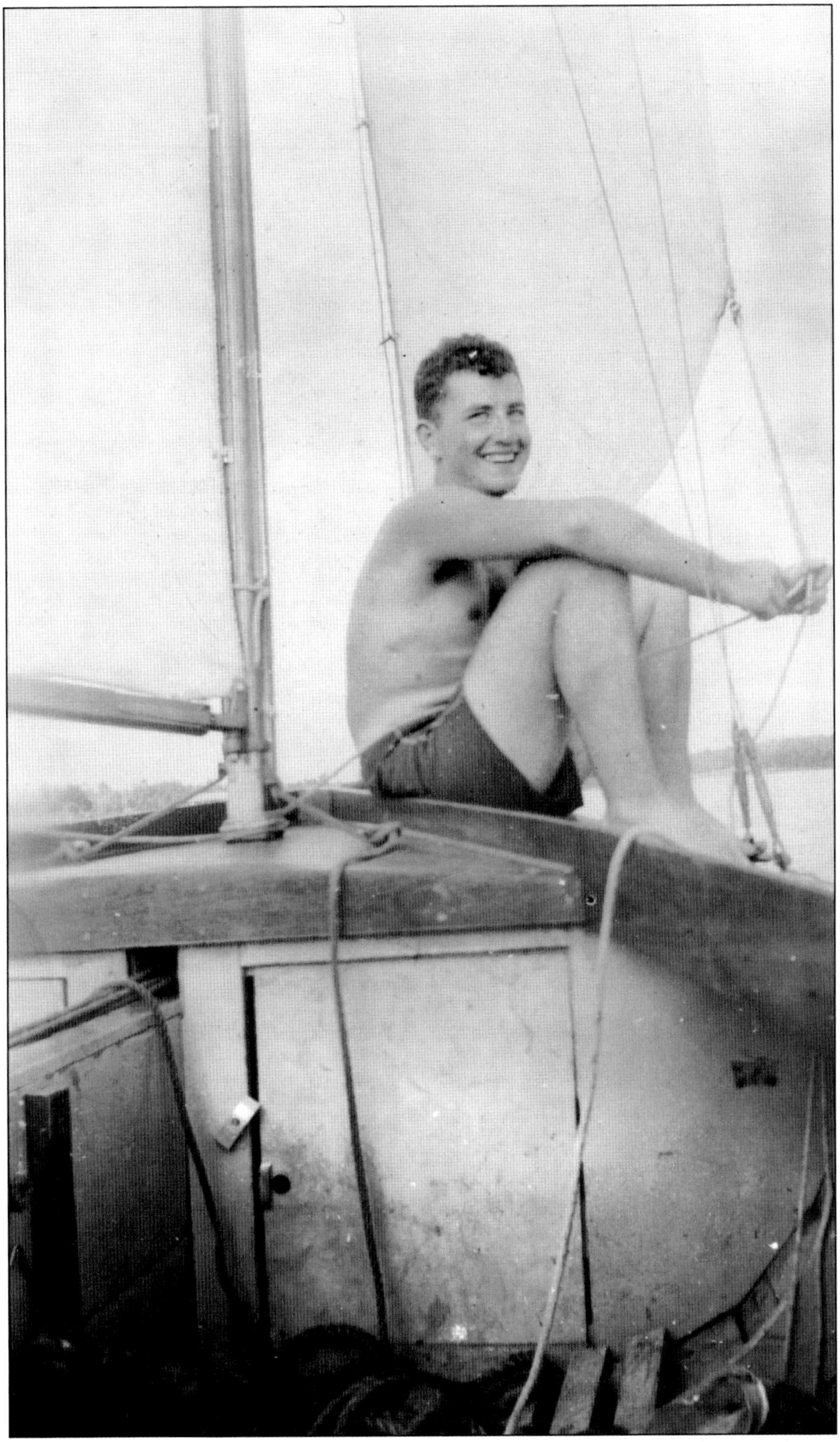

Sailing on Lake Murray is a sport enjoyed by many. Max Gergle was a student at the University of South Carolina when this picture was taken in the 1940s. He and his friends spent a lot of time on his sailboat.

Six

White Rock

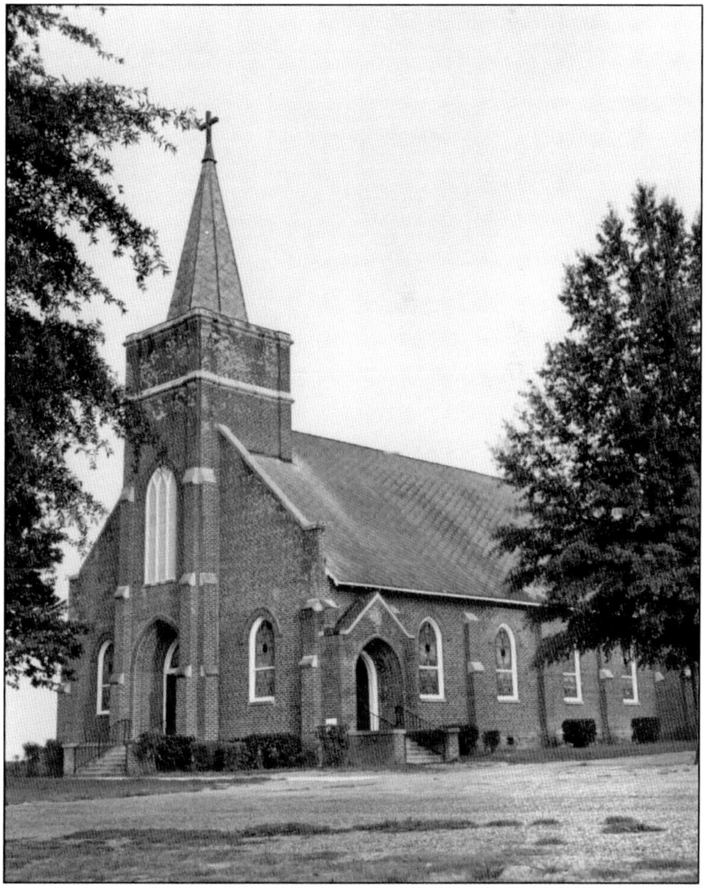

Bethel Lutheran Church in White Rock was incorporated December 17, 1929. Bethel was formed from the merger of Mount Vernon and Bethel High Hill. Bethel High Hill would soon be covered by water because of the building of the dam on the Saluda River, and Bethel members were considering a new location, perhaps near Ballentine, but at the suggestion of the Reverend Walton H. Greever of the Southern Seminary faculty and the Lowman Home Board, the two congregations decided to merge.

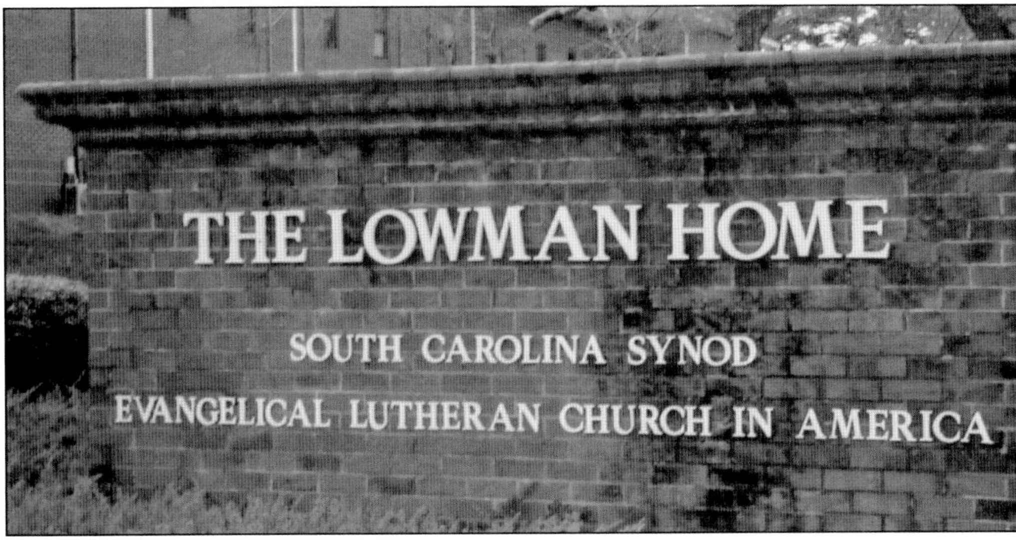

The Lowman Home, located in White Rock, South Carolina, was founded in 1911 as a home for the care of the "aging and infirm." Melissa Rauch Lowman, widow of Paul Enoch Lowman, offered her entire estate of 951 acres of land and some money for the assurance that she and her invalid children would be cared for. The South Carolina Synod of the Lutheran Church accepted her offer, designated a board of directors, specified the aims of the institution, and today owns and operates the home. Currently the Lowman Home serves approximately 450 residents in various types of living arrangements and levels of care.

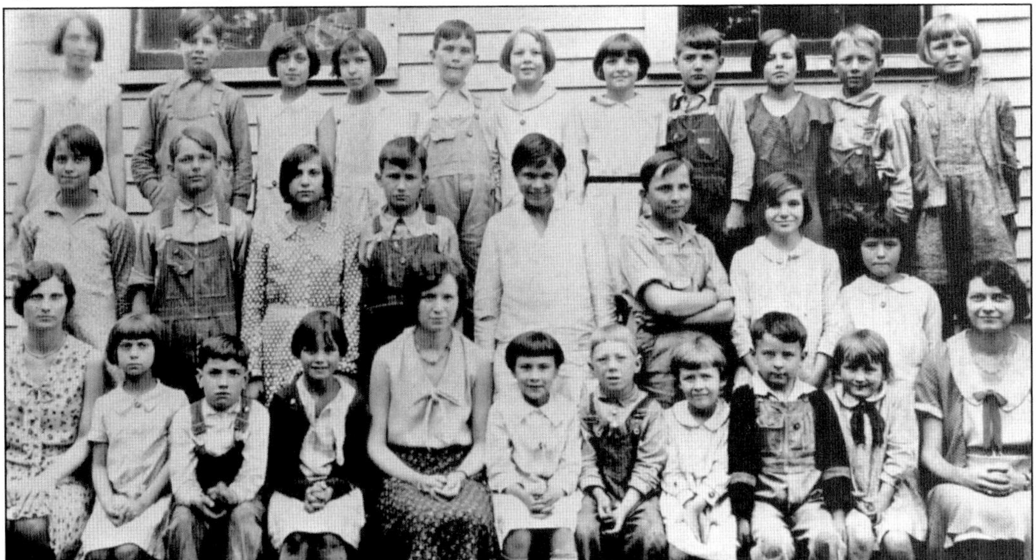

The White Rock School in the 1930s included, from left to right, (first row) Ruby Willis (teacher), Madeline Shealy, F. C. Shealy, Etheleen Meetze, Edna Coogler (teacher), Fay Warner, Glenest Killian, Jonnie Hiller Sites, N. Ray Sites, Doris Bickley, and Elizabeth Heite (teacher); (second row) Evelyn McCartha, Willie Derrick, Nell Rose Shealy, Grover Sandel, Katie Bell Bickley, Bunyan Slice, Evelyn Guise, and Lorraine McCartha; (third row) Lillian Shealy, Ellis Boknight, Anita Shealy, Lou Ella Sites, Cecil Riddle, Estelle Killian, Irene Guise, Sephus Sandel, Mildred Bouknight, James Killian, and Martha Slice. (Courtesy of Jonnie Mae Sites.)

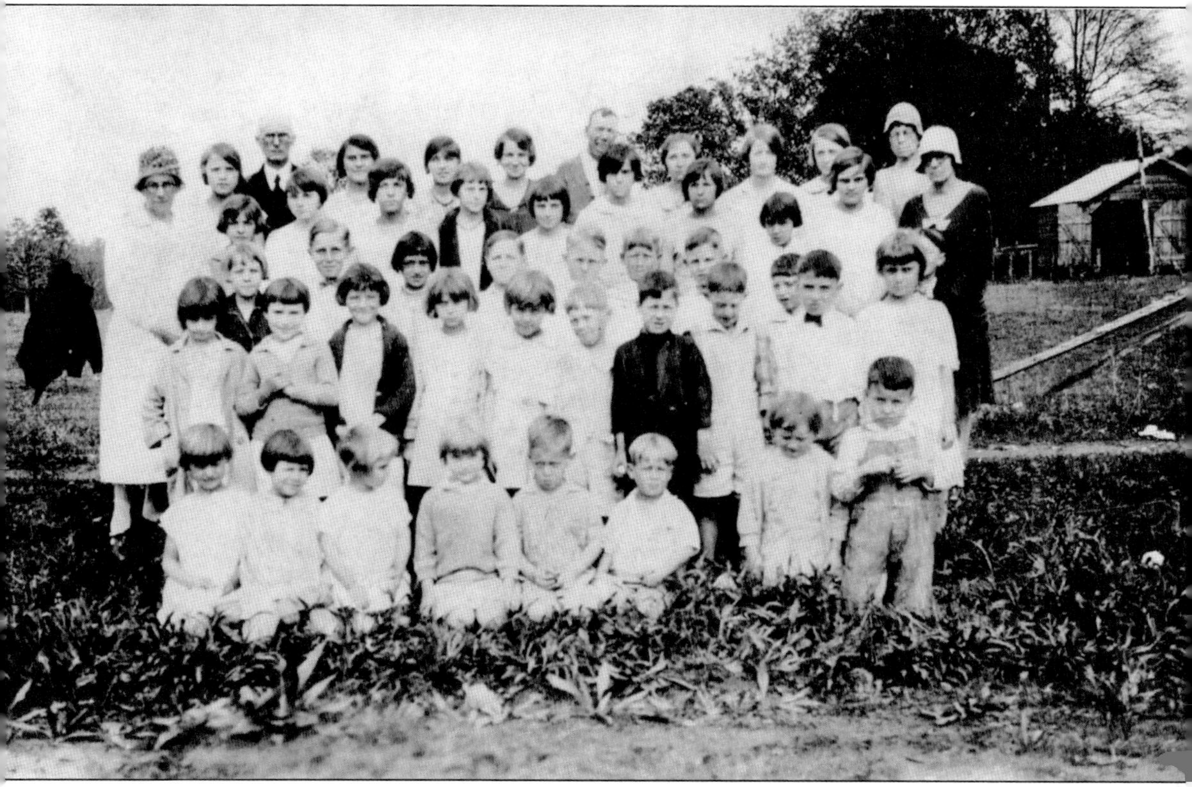

This is the Light Brigade Children of Bethel Lutheran Church in 1930. From left to right are (first row) unidentified, Florine Bickley, Dorothy Bouknight, Majorie Derrick Troutman, unidentified, Watson Hatinger, J. B. Killina, Doris Bickley Waldrop, and Nathan Ray Sites; (second row) unidentified, Fay Warner Clina, Lorraine McCartha Mitchell, Madeline Shealy Ballentine, unidentified, Glenest Killian, Robert Lee Eleazer, Murphy Wessinger, Elon Epting, F. C. Shealy, and Floyce Derrick Brown; (third row) Estelle Killian Boland, Homer Derrick, Anita Shealy Monts, Oneal Derrick, Joe Eleazer, James Killian, Otis Wessinger, Lou Ella Sites Thompson, unidentified, Elsie Shealy, Margaret Derrick Corley, Mary Corley Shealy Boland, Elberta Wessinger, Lillian Shealy Sites, Evelyn McCartha, Neel Rosa Shealy Nichols, Corrine White Bickley, and Ernestine Warner; (fourth row) Emma Haigler, Bernice Sites Graham Kyzer, Rev. J. B. Haigler, Gurnelle Shealy Coker, Caro Bouknight Frick, Minnie Reel Derrick Eargle, Daniel Huffard, Sarah Epting Comalander, Hattie Mae Derrick Demay, Elizabeth Eleazer, and ? Huffard. (Courtesy of Jonnie Mae Sites.)

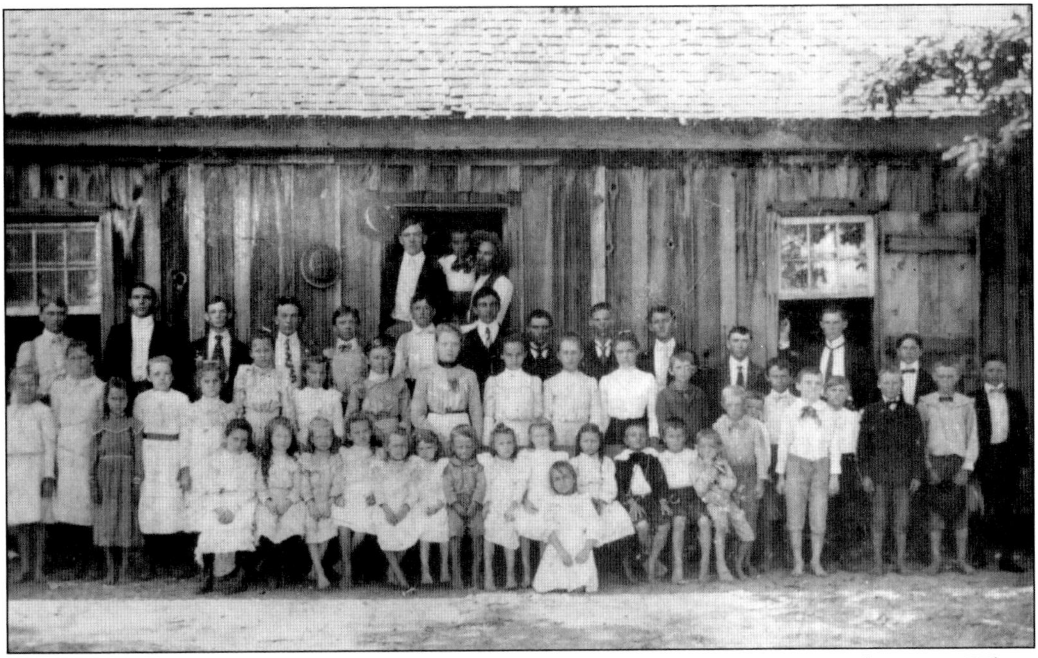

The Springhill Academy was located in the Springhill area on Highway 176 between White Rock and Peak. This is a very early photograph, and as can be seen, very few of the children are wearing shoes. (Courtesy of Jonnie Mae Sites.)

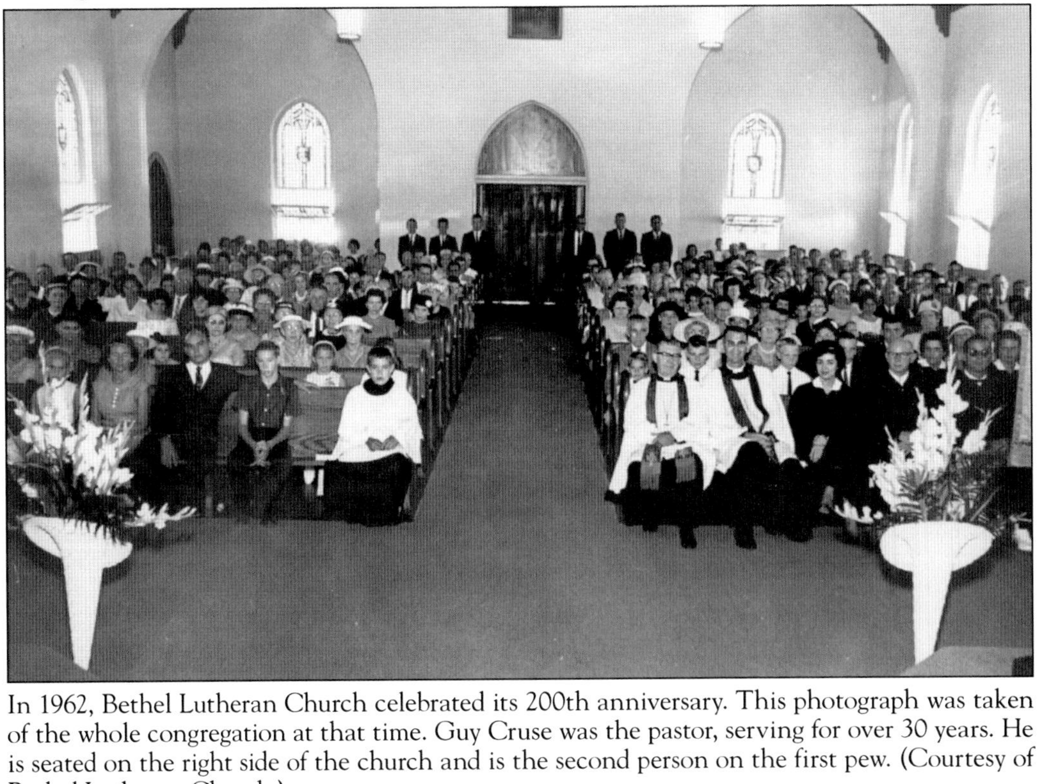

In 1962, Bethel Lutheran Church celebrated its 200th anniversary. This photograph was taken of the whole congregation at that time. Guy Cruse was the pastor, serving for over 30 years. He is seated on the right side of the church and is the second person on the first pew. (Courtesy of Bethel Lutheran Church.)

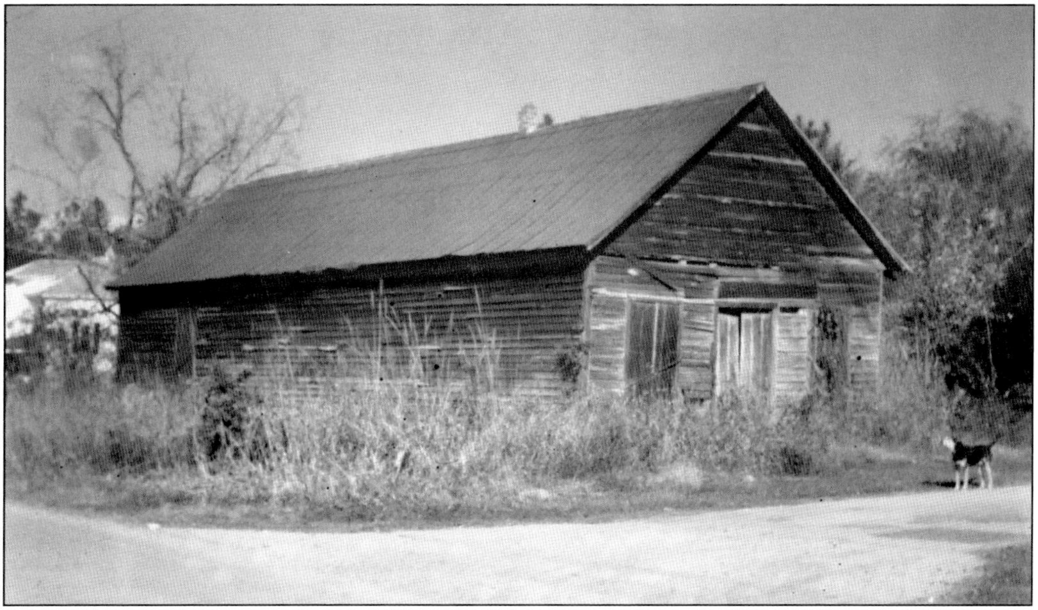

This was once a country store owned and built by father and son J. David Richardson and John P. Richardson in the early 1900s. The store also housed the first post office of White Rock. A painting by John Bouknight of this building now hangs in the current post office. (Courtesy of John Bouknight.)

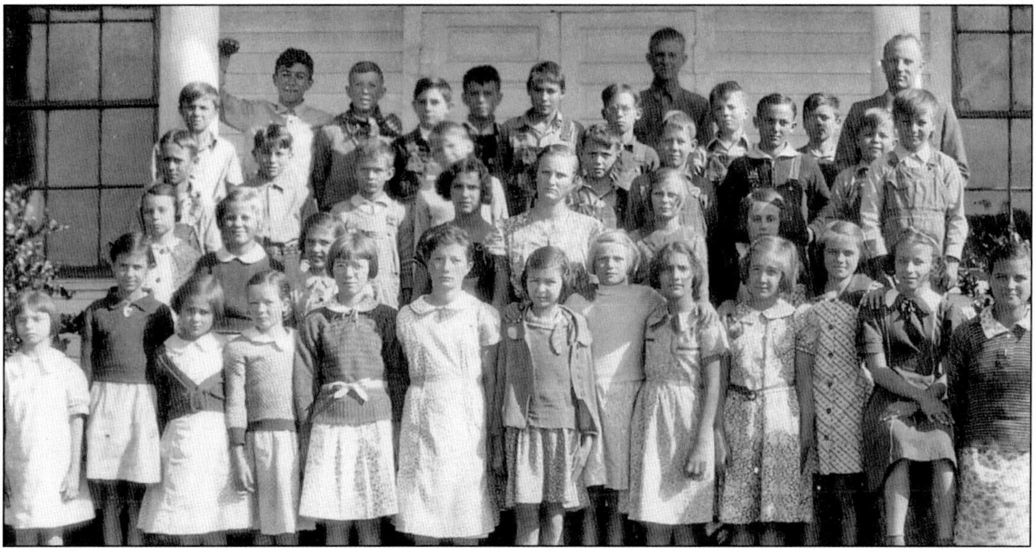

The White Rock students shown here in 1937 are, from left to right, (first row) Doris Rowe, Madge Eargle, Ruby Stoudemayer, Irene Slice, Dorothy Clark, Sarah Slice, Betty Kennedy, Alma Shealy, Amanda Bundrick, Lucy Bailey, Marjie Derrick, Helen Swygert, and Ethelene Meetze; (second row) Frances Eleazer, Cecil Sites, Joyce Shealy, Edna Mae Bundrick, Gertrude Derrick, Carola Richardson, Thema Meetze, and John Adam Ellisor; (third row) Billy Meetze, David Shealy, John Morgan Kennedy, Jack Derrick, Joe Joyner, J. B. Killian, Charlie Smith, and B. L. Eargle; (fourth row) Fred Shealy, Ollie Eargle, Glenest Killian, James May, Ray Sites, J. Q. Swygert, J. P. Richardson, Johnnie Sites, John Adam Ellisor, Cecil Bowers (principal and teacher), and James Killian. (Courtesy of Lucy Lindler.)

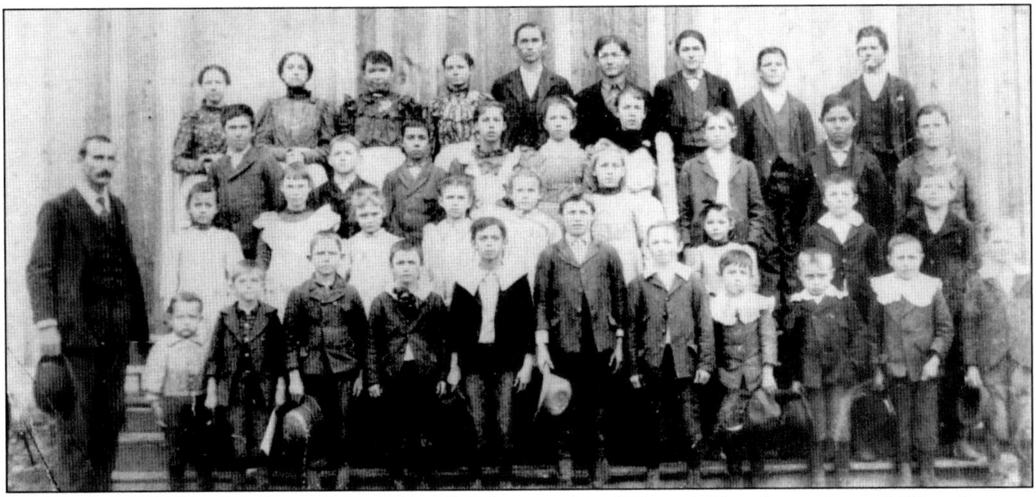

The White Rock School was located on land owned by Edward Shealy in the middle of town. This picture was taken around 1902. From left to right are (first row) Jake Rauch (teacher), Lonnie Richardson, Collie Guise, Leroy Derrick, Heber Meetze, Forest Shealy, Willie Oscar Addy, Lonnie Meetze, Verne Fulmer, Hollie Meetze, Willie Meetze, and James Ernest Addy; (second row) Eva Kleckley McCartha, Hary Lowman, Irene Lowman, Annie Guise Meetze, Anna Richardson Sites, Claudia Amick Sites, Narcissus Amick Eargle, John Meetze, and Berley Richardson; (third row) John Joseph Lowman, Harless Shealy, Sebe Swygert, Mary Shealy, Collie Shealy, Carrie Hiller Eargle, Elmer Derrick, Jake Swygert, and Julius Richardson; (fourth row) Orrie Mae Shealy (Hiller), Alma Shealy Eleazer, Bessie Leona Lowman (Addy), Lillie Derrick, Edd Derrick, Roland Fulmer, Pierce Bickley, Jonas Pickens Addy, and George Lever. (Courtesy of Jonnie Mae Sites.)

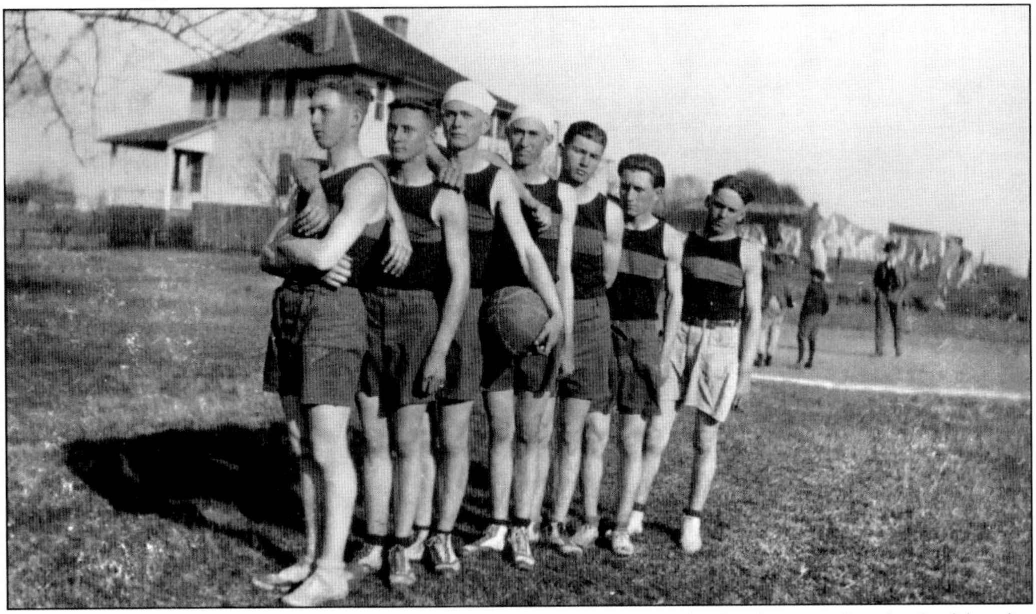

The White Rock basketball team is shown posing outside. In the background, it looks like the original Lowman family home place. This team from the 1920s consisted of Malcolm Lowman (coach), Deal ("Buddy") Sandel, Marle ("Buck") Meetze, Frank Haltiwanger, Charles Shealy, Orin ("Bone") Sandel, Clifford Meetze, and Karl Lowman. (Courtesy of Virginia Haltiwanger and Jonnie Mae Sites.)

This is the White Rock School. According to local resident Jonnie Mae Sites, the classrooms were upstairs and the bathroom was an outhouse a fair distance away from the main building. (Courtesy of Jonnie Mae Sites.)

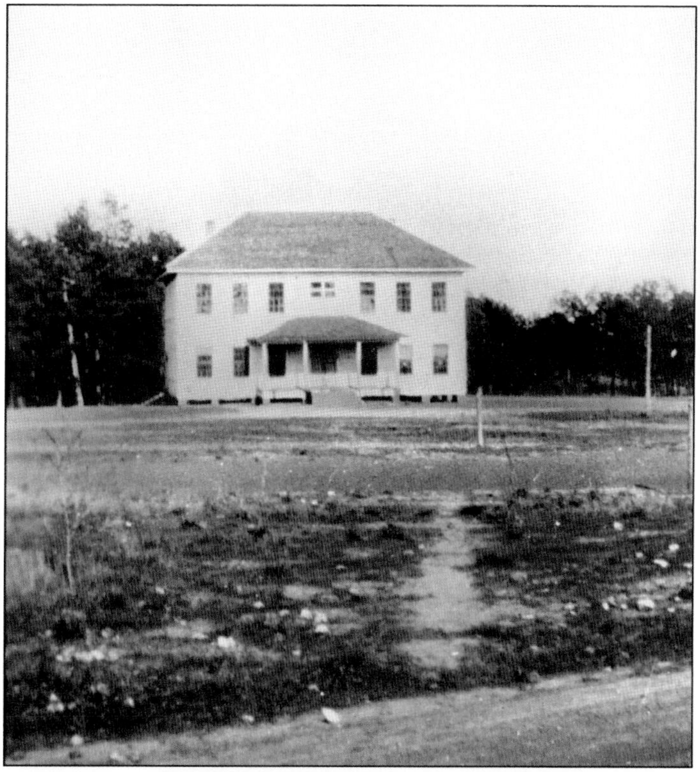

Bethel Lutheran Church celebrated its 225th anniversary in 1987 with an anniversary pageant. More than 60 members and the choir took part in the pageant, which told Bethel's history highlights. Some of the participants were Lisa Koon Rector, Renee' McCartha Doyle, Jenny Bull Dean, Melissa Bull, Nina Crowder, and Matthew Derrick. (Courtesy of Marilyn Bull.)

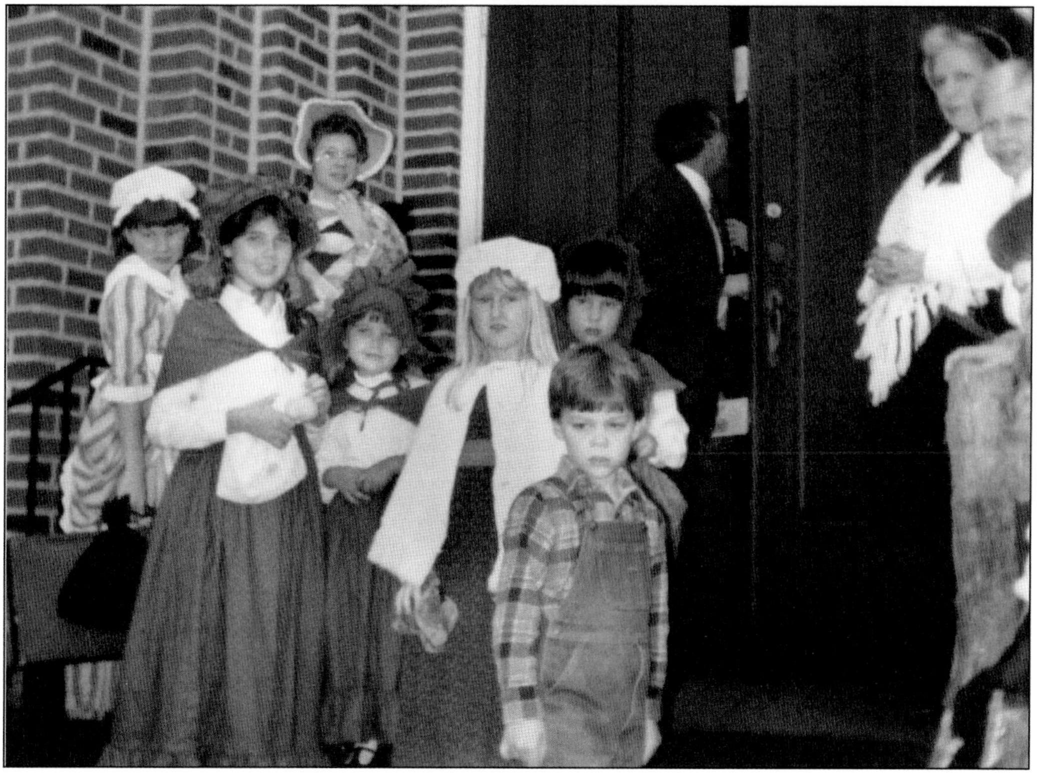